Roos Keja
Political Silence of Youth in Togo

Connectivity and Society in Africa

Edited by
Mirjam de Bruijn and Jonna Both

Volume 1

Roos Keja

Political Silence of Youth in Togo

Mobile Phones, Information and
Civic (dis)Engagement

DE GRUYTER
OLDENBOURG

ISBN 978-3-11-135331-9
e-ISBN (PDF) 978-3-11-067530-6
e-ISBN (EPUB) 978-3-11-067533-7
ISSN 2628-6564

Library of Congress Control Number: 2021948904

Bibliographic information published by the Deutsche Nationalbibliothek
The Deutsche Nationalbibliothek lists this publication in the Deutsche Nationalbibliografie;
detailed bibliographic data are available on the Internet at http://dnb.dnb.de.

© 2023 Walter de Gruyter GmbH, Berlin/Boston
This volume is text- and page-identical with the hardback published in 2022.
Cover image: Roos Keja
Printing and binding: CPI books GmbH, Leck

www.degruyter.com

For you, Eva Luna, for the stillborn babies in Sokodé,
and to all the people who manage to find hope in their hardship

Acknowledgements

This monograph could never have materialised without the support, involvement and input of many people, though any errors in this work are my responsibility. Firstly, Adamou, thank you for pointing me at the opportunity of a PhD project supervised by Hans Peter Hahn in a joint research project about digital civic engagement in Togo. Hans, I have very much appreciated our collaboration in Frankfurt, Lomé, Kara, Sokodé and on the phone. You encouraged me to write, to continue writing and to finish without hesitation, and I am grateful for your support and patience. I also want to thank Mirjam de Bruijn for inspiring me, sharing yet another adventure, and for the opportunity to publish my book in this series. The team of De Gruyter has been amazing, with a special thanks to Verena, Sridevi and Rabea.

Without the relentless support of Kathrin Knödel in almost every conceivable way from the very first moment we met, I would have abandoned this project ages ago. Kathrin, you are the best. The Institute of Ethnography of Goethe Universität Frankfurt, especially the people who supported me with administrative challenges deserve to be mentioned; Isabel Völker, Julia Malaika, Julie Cordell and Sabine Barth. Mareike Spät, thanks for your hospitality and sharing a room during the ECAS conference. Silvia Gerlinger, thank you so much for your research assistance, your patience and your ability to adapt. Kathrin Heitz Topka, thank you for sharing your valuable theoretical ideas about trust with me. To various degrees, I shared ethnographic research 'challenges' with Adamou Amadou, Eef Gilbert, Eva Quansah, Inge Ligtvoet, Kassim Assouma, Karin van Bemmel, Loes Oudenhuijzen, Melina Kalfelis and Martina Cavicchioli. I thank Voice4Thought and MOWAD for the good vibes, and my teachers and colleagues at the African Studies Centre Leiden and Utrecht University, especially Geert Mommersteeg and Gerdien Steenbeek.

The collaboration with the University of Lomé was valuable, and a special thanks goes to LaDySir, Professor Hetcheli and his research team for their help at crucial junctures of my research – *grand merci* Edem Gnamatchi, Ifa Adanto, Koffi Adaba and Georgette Kronvi – and for offering me the opportunity to present my findings at the University of Lomé in a seminar. I also want to thank DIE for our collaboration, especially Anita Breuer, and the GFA team – Mrs. Wegener, Mrs. Brenner, Mrs. Zillich – and the German embassy represented by Mr. Tech, for all our exchanges and support at several stages of my research. I am grateful to KfW, especially Mrs. Bott and Mr. Jahn, for making this research financially possible, and for our insightful exchanges.

This long trajectory was facilitated by my precious friends who believe in me, especially our anthro++ group, Heather, Dineke, Kirsten, Elina, Miek, Betsie, Mustapha, Yooku and family Mbaye. I am deeply grateful to my father, for planting the seeds for my desire to get to know people's dreams and search for deeper connections, and my mother, who has shown me that no combination of tasks is ever impossible – it 'only' requires managing inevitable practical obstacles such as running a household, as well as an awful lot of hard work, dedication and love. I thank my sisters for being the mirrors that are closest to my skin, for our continuous reflections on our paths that take us somewhere, somehow. Margo, I did it. Linde, our mind-blowing discussions have really taken this 'thing' somewhere.

In Senegal, after I had been given the name Mame Diarra, I was often told the story of her unconditional love and support for her husband. One night, in a thunderstorm, her husband asked Mame Diarra to go outside and hold on to a pole of their hut so he could fortify it. Accidentally he forgot her, so she stood outside until dawn, when her husband came out and saw her. The feminist in me always interpreted this story as another example of the injustice of gender inequality. Lately however, I have begun to understand that support has many faces. It takes courage to go through thunderstorms, with heavy rain pouring down, and continue to keep the faith. Roel, thank you for standing by me in all kinds of weather, and in my stormy undertaking of doing research and raising our children. Midas and Dorian, no book compares to you. Without you, this project would not have been fun; it would not even have been worth it. You bring bright light.

The relentless efforts of Kossi Essodézime Dao N'Dja, the best consultant of West Africa, have taken this book to another level. Dao, I thank God for having you in my life. *Grand merci* to Bataka, Dao, la Douce, le Général, Monsieur Bio, Désiré and Moussa, Freddy and Johnny, for being the persons you are. Words are a poor representation of what you mean to me. The heart is not easily understood; part of it remains unknown, even to ourselves. Amadou and Moussa, the crossing of our paths in Cameroon, Niger and Togo has changed not only your lives, but also mine. *Mi yeti.* I am also deeply grateful to Aicha, Afissou, Allahbura, Alassani, Antoine, Brice, Elom 20ce, Emile, Faras, Jef, Kader, Léa, Omar, Prince, Patrick, Pauline, Stéphanie, my late grandmother in Sokodé, and all others in Sokodé and Lomé for sharing parts of their lives with me.

Desperate and hopeless as some situations may appear, I found something in the Togolese spirit that is always fizzing and alive; some inexplicable, stubborn hope for the best, against all odds. Without this energetic love for life, my research would have been unbearable. I share the hope that tomorrow will be a better day for all the people in Togo whom I hold so dear.

Contents

Figures —— XI

Abbreviations —— XIII

1 Introduction —— 1
   1.1 The silence of young people in Togo —— 1
   1.2 A contextualised understanding of new media —— 4
   1.3 Doing research with young local development leaders —— 12
   1.4 Overview of the book —— 17

2 Keeping the faith in enduring economic and political hardship —— 20
   2.1 Introduction —— 20
   2.2 "With our politicians, things cannot work" —— 21
   2.3 Subsidiarity and the weight of social inequalities —— 29
   2.4 The city of Sokodé and its media landscape —— 36
   2.5 Making a living in the telecommunication business —— 45
   2.6 Concluding remarks —— 54

3 Private and public information and communication —— 56
   3.1 Introduction —— 56
   3.2 The intimacy of information flows —— 57
   3.3 Phones in the public-private continuum —— 66
   3.4 Mobile communication: Private information in public —— 70
   3.5 The intimacy of information —— 76
   3.6 Concluding remarks —— 83

4 Economic and techno-social basis of mobile phone use —— 85
   4.1 Introduction —— 85
   4.2 Techno-social relations between phones and people —— 86
   4.3 Material basis of mobile phones in Sokodé —— 91
   4.4 Everyday mobile phone use —— 98
   4.5 Maintaining relationships over the phone —— 104
   4.6 What phones reflect: Desires, realities, identities —— 110
   4.7 Concluding remarks —— 116

5 Sociality and the mobile phone as connector and liar — 118
5.1 Introduction — 118
5.2 Locality, mobility and phones in the public space — 119
5.3 "The phone turns all of us into liars" — 124
5.4 Freedom and control in intimate relations — 129
5.5 'Endangered' morality in social relations? — 135
5.6 Concluding remarks — 138

6 Civic (dis)engagement and protest — 140
6.1 Introduction — 140
6.2 Civic-ness or civil society in Togo — 141
6.3 Towards a Togolese civil society? — 144
6.4 Public spheres and civic (dis)engagement in Sokodé — 148
6.5 Civic (dis)engagement in Sokodé: Protest and voice — 154
6.6 Concluding remarks — 163

7 The imaginary of ICT4D and civic (dis)engagement — 165
7.1 Introduction — 165
7.2 The ICT4D project in Sokodé — 166
7.3 Power relations in the ICT4D project — 169
7.4 Phones and civic engagement from within the community — 177
7.5 Young people's quest for community development — 183
7.6 Concluding remarks — 186

8 Conclusions: Political silence and new ICTs in a repressive state — 188
8.1 Introduction — 188
8.2 Silence and civic (dis)engagement in a repressive state — 189
8.3 Civic-ness and ICT4D — 194
8.4 Towards a political anthropology of communication — 197
8.5 Concluding remarks — 198

References — 200

Appendix 1: Graphs mobile communication logs — 216

Appendix 2: Questionnaire mobile communication logs — 217

Index — 218

Figures

Figure 1: Johnny and Freddy interviewing each —— 15
Figure 2: Map of Sokodé —— 37
Figure 3: Streetview with Togocel and Moov sales point —— 38
Figure 4: 'Togocel' and his motorbike —— 50
Figure 5: Participatory budget of the municipality of Sokodé —— 60
Figure 6: WhatsApp conversation about Moussa's illness —— 78
Figure 7: Mistaken WhatsApp exchange —— 81
Figure 8: Phone shop 'Super boys' —— 96
Figure 9: Daily calling frequencies —— 98
Figure 10: Who is researching whom? —— 112
Figure 11: Désiré with his new phone —— 122
Figure 12: Stéphanie's reasons for calling —— 137
Figure 13: Protest in Sokodé on 19 August 2017 —— 157
Figure 14: The burning sugar truck on the bridge —— 160
Figure 15: Flow chart of SMS citizen monitoring and evaluation system —— 167
Figure 16: Mobilisation meeting for SMS survey —— 174

Pictures in all figures were taken by me, except for figure 13 and 14, which were sent to me by different people through WhatsApp, and figure 16, which was taken by Dao.

Abbreviations

AfDB	African Development Bank
ANT	Actor Network Theory
CDQ	Comité de Développement du Quartier
CNDS	Concertation Nationale de la Société Civile
DIE	Deutsches Institut für Entwicklungspolitik
GU	Goethe Universität
ICT	Information and Communication Technologies
ICT4D	ICT-for-Development
KfW	Kreditanstalt für Wiederaufbau
LaDySir	Laboratoire Dynamique Spatiale et Intégration Régionale
NGO	Non-Governmental Organisation
PASEORSC	Programme d'Appui et de Soutien aux Enfants Orphelins pour leur Réinsertion Socio-Culturelle
PDC	Plan de Développement Communal
PDV	Point de Vente
PNP	Parti National Panafricaniste
RESODERC	Réseau des Organisations de Développement de la Région Centrale
SMS	Short Message Service
UNIR	Union pour la République

1 Introduction

1.1 The silence of young people in Togo

Friendship and treason in an unstable political environment

> I have found out who was the one who tried to poison me. It was David. After all that I have done for him... I will know what to do, don't worry. You are the only one who knows. (WhatsApp call with Felix, 14 May 2018)

During this WhatsApp call with Felix, I was on my way home in Utrecht, the Netherlands. While it was spring in Utrecht, I imagined him sipping a beer at one of his favourite bars in Sokodé, sitting alone at a table on a sultry evening, surrounded by the scent of diesel and exhaust fumes from the traffic nearby. Two months before this, during my field trip to Central Togo in March 2018, I had learned about the poisoning that had contributed to the disintegration of a group of friends, on whom this book is partly based. Felix had apparently taken a sip of water from a glass on his veranda, immediately felt that something was wrong and had started vomiting. He was sure that someone had tried to poison him, and he suspected the people closest to him. The final piece of 'evidence' had been provided by one of his recent ex-girlfriends who had suddenly broken up with him. Apparently, David had been sending her images of Felix and another girl through WhatsApp, until she could take it no longer and told Felix it was over. For Felix, her confession made clear that David had betrayed him. In a WhatsApp call two months later, Felix told me that he was no longer in contact with David, and explained that: "In our environment, trust is essential; it is dangerous to assume that one is among friends while they are actually driven by envy".

In 2015, I had set out to study the role of mobile phones in everyday political participation of people in urban Togo. Felix's poisoning took place in the city of Sokodé, the capital of Togo's Central Region, against the backdrop of increasing political tension. Not only had the social relationships of the people I knew undergone important changes between my visits in 2017 and 2018, but the entire atmosphere of the town was different. Burnt official buildings were reminders of the street protests that took place in late 2017, as were the extra troops of soldiers in town. People referred to these protests as 'the troubles' or 'the events'.

The 'troubles' began after 19 August 2017, when thousands of people gathered on the streets of several Togolese cities, responding to a widely circulated call on social media by the political opposition party *Parti Nationaliste Panafricaine* (PNP), demanding constitutional reforms. The social unrest and spontaneous street protests that followed in Sokodé, were brutally silenced by the security forces towards the end of October 2017. In February 2020, Faure Gnassingbé started his fourth term as President of Togo, continuing the Gnassignbé 'dynasty' founded by his father in 1967. As security forces were still present in Sokodé in 2020, the reinforcement of troops in the city seemed to be a long-term strategy of oppression. People resorted to subtle jokes or remarks to air their discontentment, though the soldiers did not take any action – at least not for the moment. Friends and acquaintances sought discreet places to meet me, such as their own house or a quiet bar, though maybe the bars had simply become quieter.

In his book *Africa: The Politics of Smiling and Suffering*, Chabal (2009) describes how people strive to improve their livelihoods amidst their daily struggles to make a living. In the introduction, he argues that if one wants to understand politics in African states, it is imperative to examine what politics means to those living in these states, and how they understand their relationship to the state and the plethora of non-state actors. This calls for a meticulous analysis of mundane conflicts on the micro-level. The poisoning of Felix could be regarded as a mundane conflict, just as it could be the start of a stunning novel about friendship, romance and treason in an unstable political environment. However, this book portrays a sociality in duress and delves into matters of trust and mistrust, against the backdrop of new information and communication technologies (ICTs) and their impact on society. In the field of ICT-for-Development (ICT4D), ICTs are mostly approached one-sidedly as vessels of progress. The current study describes the manner in which the realities of new ICT usage translate to possible changes in political engagement and civic-ness.

The link between new ICTs and civic engagement has been made often, as Dwyer (2015) shows, but often through quantitative studies with the conclusions being volatile. Empirical research in this field is needed, as it contributes to a more holistic image of the social impact of new ICTs. This ethnographic study demonstrates that there is a connection between new ICTs and social change. Through their phones, the most ubiquitous new ICT in Sokodé, people inform themselves in new ways, and they also react to social or political changes differently. As a result, their perspectives on politics are also altered, even though this might seem minimal. This book demonstrates that the mobile phone has an impact on the political movement of sociality, and contributes to this nascent field of research.

Digital lives and civic (dis)engagement of young people

In the aftermath of the French colonial rule, the first president after independence, Sylvanus Olympio, was overthrown in a coup d'état in 1967. He was replaced by the general who assassinated him, Eyadéma Gnassignbé. When Gnassignbé died after 36 years of often repressive rule, his son Faure was put into power and 'won' the elections of 2005 under troubling circumstances. Street protests flare up from time to time, usually 'silenced' by the heavy deployment of security forces. The political impasse in the late 2010s, in which the regime undermined efforts to limit the term of mandates of the president, is indicative of the 'thorny path' of democratic change (Kohnert 2008). Therefore, the street protests and ensuing violence that occurred in late 2017 are not isolated incidents but part of a larger narrative of popular discontent in the context of continuing political repression. While these street protests were not a new phenomenon, there was something new in the manner in which they were organised as well as perceived.

The potential of new media as a channel for popular discontent was also demonstrated in the early 2010s, when large groups of people gathered at Tahrir Square in Egypt for the anti-government protests, responding to widely shared messages on Facebook. Not unique to Egypt, this wave of anti-government protests began in Tunisia and spread to Libya, Yemen and Syria, and became known as the Arab Spring. Optimistic evaluations of these 'Facebook Revolutions' or 'Revolutions 2.0' soon faded away, as they did not necessarily translate to democratic leaders coming into power in these countries (Alozie, Akpan-Obong & Foster 2011; Comunello & Anzera 2012; Lowrance 2016). This indicates that the outcomes of such events are highly ambivalent, and, as Mutsvairo (2016a) also indicated, 'revolution takes more than a mobile phone'. Setting aside this aspect for the moment, an interesting phenomenon that comes to the fore in the above cited literature about the Arab Spring is the image of youth who employ new technological tools to engage with the world. Through their mobile phones and internet connections, these youth inform themselves, form an opinion and voice it, and then get out on the streets to claim their rights – for instance, the right to participate in democracy.

Similarly, protests regularly flare up in Togo. However, the youth do not take to the streets with the same tenacity and perseverance, even though they appear to have every reason to do so. The question 'Why do they not revolt' is not as interesting to explore as the question of what they do instead and why they do it. How can the circumstances and social processes that are leading to this 'political silence' be understood, and how do frustration and anger find an outlet?

Togo is an interesting place in this regard, as the country has been ruled by the same family for over half a century now. Every child that was born after 1967, has only known the Gnassignbé family as rulers of their country. For decades, society has been under pressure from a dictatorship that has been very repressive, and often violent. Political repression and the reactions to it differ from place to place, and examples from the sub-region shall illustrate this. In Burkina Faso, youth have managed to gain political influence in the movement 'Balai citoyen' – a reggae and hip-hop-driven youth movement to 'sweep the streets'. Youth expressed their anger and, in certain ways, managed to bring positive change (Touré 2017). The political system in Togo does not seem to be as repressive as in Chad, where the harsh political and economic situation has become normalised (de Bruijn & Both 2018). The deep distrust regarding the nation's leaders and security forces share some similarities with Togo, although the mistrust seems to be relatively more deeply engrained in Chad (see Seli 2012).

It was when I shared a meal with my host family in Thiès, Senegal, in December 2019 that I realised to what extent I had gotten used to what I call the political silence in Togo. Casually, the brothers entered into a loud discussion about the position of Macky Sall in the upcoming elections. It shocked me somehow that my immediate internal comment was: 'As if they have nothing to hide!' Indeed, even though Senegalese politics is more complicated than what I highlight here, the openness of the debate indicates the space available for expression. The brothers did not fear revealing their political opinions to one another, or being overheard by the neighbours.

In Togo, this sort of open debate is rare, even in the seemingly intimate sphere of a family meal. The choice of Sokodé, the capital of Togo's Central Region, is not a coincidence; it is widely seen as a place where political opposition is fierce (Miraftab 2012). Hence, political oppression is also fierce in Sokodé, and tensions simmer just below the surface. In this sense, this urban setting is appropriate to better understand the forms that civic engagement can take and the roles that new ICTs can play in such a setting.

1.2 A contextualised understanding of new media

The newness of new media

It is imperative to develop a deep understanding of the role of social media and mobile phones regarding political participation in different contexts. This book contributes to ethnographic studies dealing with questions of civic engagement, digital activism and political reform in African countries (Mudhai 2013; Mudhai,

Tettey & Banda 2009; Mutsvairo 2016a; Pype 2016). There is a rapidly growing body of literature on the use of ICT in relation to democratisation and political engagement in African societies (Adeiza 2014; Best & Meng 2015; Ekine 2010; Kareem, Olaewe & Odeniyi 2008; Mutsvairo 2016a; Pommerolle & Heungoup 2017; Seli 2012; Smyth & Best 2013). Smyth and Best (2013) have studied the role of new ICTs in election campaigns in Liberia and Nigeria and assert that a new networked public sphere contributes to overcoming information scarcity, by enabling a culture of citizen monitoring, which in turn contributes to the perception of increased transparency, which then helps defuse tensions around the credibility of election results. However, the limitation of their study is that it mainly targeted elites, insiders and early adopters, and they find it likely that "the average Nigerian or Liberian knows little to nothing about Facebook or Twitter" (Smyth & Best 2013: 140).

Miller et al. (2016) call for a contextual understanding of new media, in which the meaning of the same social media platform can differ from place to place. Several authors indicate the need for more research on new media practices in African contexts (Etzo & Collender 2010; Mutsvairo & Harris 2016; Sey 2011: 397). While Bratton (2013: 305) speaks of the mobile phone as a 'neutral tool' for civic engagement in Africa, anthropologists such de Bruijn and van Dijk (2012) and Hahn (2008) have demonstrated otherwise. According to these authors, it is far from being a neutral object; instead, the mobile phone imparts a sense of ambivalence in its users. In a recent book chapter in Bell and Kuipers (2018), Keane (2018) argues that every claim about mobile phones is akin to a coin with two sides, not necessarily contradictory but mutually reinforcing. In order to highlight the various forms of everyday mobile phone usage, it is useful to employ notions such as 'appropriation' (Horst & Miller 2006), 'domestication' (Hahn & Kibora 2008), 'provincializing' (Coleman 2011) and 'de-Westernising' (Nyamnjoh 2011). The importance of contextualising mobile phone use is outlined by de Bruijn and van Dijk (2012a: 8):

> People have reasons for connecting and disconnecting and do so in meaningful ways that are informed by the cultural and social repertoires in the specific societies that are relevant to the connections. These processes of change cannot be understood without analysing people's agency, which focuses on individual and collective decisions, interpretations, reactions to and reflections on changes in their environment, or without understanding the ways in which these interactions shape their social world.

While many of the authors mentioned above describe the transformation of social relations through the use of new information technologies, they also outline continuities and are wary of the risk of technological determinism (Archambault 2009; Kenaw 2016). Before the spread of social media, Stephens (1998) suggested that 'video' or 'moving images' introduced by the television had a far more revolutionary impact than the use of computers and the Internet. Though this can be contested, his insight remains important: the change in the social fabric of society due to the introduction of new media is real, but the scope of the change cannot be fully grasped until decades or even centuries after their introduction.

This research was conducted during the period when the mobile phone was introduced and gained widespread use in Togo, with a special focus on young users who are at the heart of this study. During the fieldwork between 2015 and 2019, the situation rapidly changed: in the beginning of 2015, the networks were highly unstable, and most people owned what they described as 'simple phones'; the ones without an internet connection and without a touchscreen, like the popular Nokia 3310. Three to four years later, all my informants had switched to smartphones. In the evening in the roadside bars, these phones lit up circles of people sitting on plastic chairs and drinking. In this regard, this study illustrates the changes brought about by the introduction of smartphones in society through the lives of these young people. This study contributes to a better understanding of social relations in which duress constrains people's lives, and impacts people's civic engagement. This period is significant and it is worth examining the possible effects of mobile phones and social media during this time.

Disclosing information, social change and digital publics

In her article *'[Not] talking like a Motorola'*, Pype (2016) discusses the information that can and cannot be shared through the mobile phone in the context of Kinshasa's political landscape. Similarly, in Sokodé, the mobile phone unlocks new ways of concealing and revealing information, and in certain ways reconfigures people's relationship with the state. As several authors have indicated, the mobile phone contributes to both increased possibilities of disclosing information and controlling others, and increased possibilities of evading or contesting the control of others, whether this is in the political realm (Pype 2016), within transnational family configurations (Nyamnjoh 2005a; Tazanu 2012) or in romantic relationships (Archambault 2009, 2017; Kenaw 2012). The mobile phone seems to have altered the ways in which people are discreet and keep up appearances, which according to Archambault (2017), are directly linked to issues of morality. This book establishes links between the influence and role of the mobile phone on relationality at the household level and at the civic and political level. In this way, this study contributes to the anthropology of communication by merging the fields of research as scrutinized by Pype (2016) and

Archambault (2017), where the first departs from vertical political sociality and the latter from sociality between peers.

In media studies, especially in audience and internet studies, various authors call for an approach in which the everyday usage and perceptions of media users occupy centre stage; Willems and Mano (2016) emphasise the value of ethnographic approaches in understanding audiences and publics in Africa, 'de-Westernising' and 'provincialising' hegemonic histories (see also Nyamnjoh 2011; Willems 2014). Their work responds to the call to move away from a media-centric focus in media studies to a society-centred (Couldry 2006) and more materialist focus (Morley 2009). In a similar vein, Willems and Mano (2016), Srinivasan et al. (2019: 2–4) call for a decolonisation of media studies in Africa, leaving behind Western-based perspectives on the 'not yet' and on what Africa's digital transformation should or could be or what it is not, but instead on what it is. The current book belongs to this line of empirically grounded analyses of digital transformation in and of public spheres and networks of communication.

The studies of the digital transformations that followed the introduction of the mobile phone have paved the way for a debate beyond Habermasian views on civil society and public spheres in the vein of the influential work by Comaroff and Comaroff (1999). One such example is the study carried out by Willems (2012) and Srinivasan et al. (2019). The concept of 'digital publics' is interesting here, though it blurs the convergence of media use as Srinivasan et al. note (2019: 5). The communication ecologies that people inhabit entails a mixture of physical spaces, older media and mobile technologies. In this dynamic and relatively new field of studies, a new set of concepts is yet to be established, and this study contributes to this emerging field. Existing conceptualisations of citizenship and civil society serve as a point of departure for the current analysis of communication ecologies in Sokodé, to enable a connection with the rationale of the ICT4D-project that is part of the empirical grounding. This forms the basis of a further exploration of digital sociality and political subjectivities.

Civic-ness and ICT4D

The political branch of ICT4D – which includes development practitioners and researchers alike – is firmly of the opinion that civic engagement increases with the spread of ICTs and as a result, numerous changes in the political domain are inevitable (Bratton 2013; Jagun et al. 2008; Southwood 2009). This study was partly conducted within the framework of a research project that 'accompanied' an ICT4D project, which viewed ICTs as tools for democratic development.

The research initially set out to follow an 'innovative' SMS-based citizen monitoring and evaluation platform, discussed in chapter seven as 'the ICT4D project', and to embed the findings in a broader understanding of mobile phone use and citizen participation in Togo (see also Breuer et al. 2017; Breuer & Groshek 2016). The project was developed by an international development consortium in the context of a national decentralisation and good governance programme. It was implemented in Sokodé between 2015 and 2017. Like many other projects, it came to a standstill when tensions rose after the so-called 'troubles' that took place between August and October 2017.

The idea was that a local committee, presided by the mayor, developed questions for surveys about municipal themes. During a period of five days, citizens could subscribe to the system by sending a code word to a toll-free number and replying to the survey questions, sent one-by-one to them by SMS. The results were then to be analysed by the committee, and their recommendations were to be considered in the decision-making processes of the municipal office and serve as feed-back for the citizens. Ideally, this system would improve citizen participation and contribute to democratic development. As this study makes clear, meaningful participation in a politically repressive environment is a complex and challenging process, especially if it does not emanate from the community. Consequently, this study is an ideal contrast case in the field of ICT4D. It encourages researchers and practitioners to depart from the communication ecology of a specific society, before projecting and applying models in the spirit of progress (see also Keja & Knodel 2019).

In this study, I prefer to use the terms civic-ness and civic engagement, instead of the more static term citizen participation. This is not only because I question whether participation of citizens can be guided and moulded to the extent that it is appropriate to use this term, but also because I question more fundamentally the existence of the citizen in Togo. This is part of a much larger debate on civil society and civic engagement that is described in chapter six.

I approach 'the civic' in this work in a broad sense; the civic as an awareness of 'being in the world', linked to being heard and having a sense of responsibility for one's direct environment, much like Freire's pedagogy of freedom (Freire 2001). My approach also borrows from the conceptualisation of citizenship by Isin (2008). Isin and Ruppert (2020: 8) regard being a citizen as an embodied experience in which a person acts to claim rights. Consequently, in viewing people in Sokodé not as necessarily as citizens, their civic-ness can be found in the ways they relate to the world around them, or their connectivity to it, not confined to (a conception of) the state. In the vein of Isin's (2008) call for a focus on *acts* of citizenship, one of the major thrusts of this study is the exploration of the manner in which civic engagement is enacted in relation to new ICTs in an environment where people have internalised constraint.

Agency, trust and mistrust as complex social processes

Concepts like trust and mistrust have been examined in ethnographic studies that describe people in societies in which mistrust has been internalised (Carey 2017; Heitz Topka 2013). These authors describe various conscious and unconscious strategies that people use in order to 'navigate' their lives and social realities. Social navigation is a concept introduced by Vigh (2006, 2009) to offer an explanatory frame of agency in highly unpredictable and ever-changing social settings. A differentiation is often made between constrained and enabled agency, in which structure-agency dialectics play a large role (Giddens 1984). Though the debate has moved beyond these dialectics into more dynamic conceptualisations, Giddens' work remains important, especially his differentiation between material and social components of structure.

In conceptualisations of agency in the social sciences, the idea reigns that actors can exercise agency under all circumstances – even a prisoner has power over his life, for instance to accept or refuse food. Creativity, which can be considered crucial to agency (Emirbayer & Mische 1998), is considered a basic, indelible human condition. The context of this study is one in which agency is highly constrained, and I argue that this powerlessness is linked to economic hardship and political repression. In a way, constraint seems to be internalised to the extent that people do not really notice it anymore. The perceptions and actions of people in Sokodé are embedded in what Johnson-Hanks (2005) referred to as 'routinized state of uncertainty', and even more accurately how de Bruijn and Bot (2018) described the 'experience of enduring hardship' in a society under duress.

This study questions the extent to which people have agency in this environment, which might seem contradictory initially. I do not intend viewing the people of Togo as victims of their circumstances. While considering the question of why they do not structurally and visibly revolt, I focused on the many aspects of power dynamics and the way these impinge on the creativity of individuals on the micro-level, especially when it is connected to 'civic' acts. This allowed me to get not only an idea of the complex struggle that people have on a daily basis, but also of the importance of dignity in the face of this.

In this routinized state of uncertainty, many people are dependent on each another for their survival, and often also depend on people whom they cannot trust. In section 3.5 this is explored with the scenario of David being dependent upon Felix, and then breaking free from Felix, losing his dependency through certain actions. Studies conceptualising trust are based on a presumed rationality (Hardin 2004; Putnam 2000), which often includes an assessment of 'risk' (Coleman 1990; Gambetta 1988; Luhmann 2000; Sztompka 1999). However, in this instance, David's short-term situation probably deteriorated, as he was no longer Felix's protégé.

Rational choice perspectives can be questioned, as trust does not merely seem to be a matter of choice (Heitz Topka 2013). Placing an emphasis on an experience-based reality (Stern 2004), approaches of trust that indicate the agency of the one who trusts seem to be more applicable to describe the processes in Sokodé. Following this line of thinking, intentionality and implicit expectations often figure as qualities of trust (Förster 2014; Heitz Topka 2013; Lagerspetz 1998; Meijboom 2008; Pederson & Meinen 2015). Förster (2014: 58) describes trust as nodal point where actors develop a shared intentionality to expect and fulfil expectations, whereas Meinen (2015) emphasises the trickiness of trust.

The reflections of Lagerspetz (1998) on trust as a 'tacit demand of respect for the expectations of the other on us' are far more subtle than a socio-political survey that measures trust with questions such as 'on a scale from 1 to 5, do you tend to trust or distrust people on the street/your neighbours'. The definition of trust in the latter approach seems to be shallower than the former, though the former may be more difficult to pin down. By identifying and scrutinizing different spheres of trust, using participant observation, it is possible to get a better understanding of the power dynamics in the process of information exchange, which influence and are influenced by this process. For a comprehensive anthropological exploration of trust, the work of Heitz Topka (2013) is useful. She departs from a "Simmelian notion of trust that combines 'good reasons' for trust with the suspension of uncertainty" (Heitz Topka 2013: 301).

In an environment in which trust seems to be a complex affair, as can be said for Sokodé, it is helpful to consider for a moment the terms mistrust and distrust, which are often omitted from the analysis (Carey 2017; Hardin 2004; Heitz Topka 2013). According to Hardin (2004: 3–4), mistrust is used in situations where people have doubts about the other person that prevent them from trusting the other, whereas distrust reflects a more embedded feeling that the other is not reliable, an opinion that people have reasons for. In her work, Heitz Topka (2013: 312–317) developed the image of a fork, in which mistrust precedes either trust or distrust. This is a processual description, in which unfamiliarity is assessed, and a judgement of trustworthiness is suspended. This temporary suspension of uncertainty as the main element of trust can 'overflow' into a judgement of distrust through familiarising oneself with others and assessing their acts.

Unlike Heitz Topka, Carey (2017) takes uncertainty as a given, and takes mistrust as organisational principle of a society he studied in the Moroccan high Atlas. Intriguingly, he considers mistrust as a concept related to trust, but not necessarily its opposite. Placing Simmel's 'wandering stranger' within the core of intimate relations, he argues that familiarity alone is insufficient ground for trust, as there is no definite connection between our idea of a being and the being itself. Carey states that the acceptance that one can never be sure whether even one's most intimate contacts are telling lies or not, provides a certain "rugged autonomy and moral equality that assumes other people to be both free and fundamentally uncontrollable" (Carey 2017: 10). Furthermore, Carey makes the case for treating trust and mistrust as two separate conceptual fields, even though the concepts are intertwined. Though Heitz Topka's fork offers the possibility of describing trust as process, this does not exclude Carey's assertion, and I employ bot perspectives when I indicate situations or processes of distrust and mistrust in the context of Sokodé.

Hahn (2008) emphasises the ambiguities that are present in everyday life in African societies concerning new technologies. Especially in this context of economic deprivation and long-term political repression, it is important to study the introduction of a new medium that is able to strengthen and establish people's networks and connectivity. The connectivity that I describe in the current work consists of and is constrained by both sociality and materiality, and it can be found in the ways in which people relate and connect to each other, to social and institutional structures and to the world at large (Amit & Caputo 2015; Bell, Kobak, Kuipers & Kemble 2018; Castells 2004; de Bruijn & van Dijk 2012). This study elucidates the experience of agency by people in Togo in a constrained environment, the possibilities they have of using their social networks, creating new constellations and connections. These processes are always on the border between intimacy and publicness, and are coupled with ambiguities (Geschiere 2013: 69–70). The ambivalence that is prevalent in mobile communication, intimacy, connectivity and civic-ness that form the core themes in this work, is integral to sociality in Sokodé and beyond.

1.3 Doing research with young local development leaders

Being watched: The white, female anthropologist

In anthropology, the unequal power relations between the researcher and the researched have been widely discussed and analysed, especially since "Writing Culture" by Clifford and Marcus (1986). They questioned the neutrality and objectivity of the researcher, and other inspiring accounts followed (Archambault 2009; Mosse 2006; Pollard 2009). The setting of my research finds its roots in historical inequalities and prejudices, and I question to what extent my own mind is, or even can be, decolonised. However, an inordinate amount of attention to the personal circumstances and relationships of the anthropologist, who is, after all, her own research instrument, can easily lead to the critique of the study being an egocentric endeavour. However, I deem it necessary to reflect on my own position, as it is part of the context of the data collection.

Just as anthropologists cannot fully control their own perceptions and assumptions, the ways in which research participants perceive the researcher are also beyond control. Even though I experienced and always tried to present myself as an independent researcher and not an integral part of the ICT4D project in Sokodé, my position was not neutral. In different instances, my position could be viewed as being a part of the development machinery: being flown in as development expert, giving recommendations in 'steering group meetings' in the European head office and the German embassy in Lomé. Walking the fine line between self-censorship, voice and constructive criticism, I could not judge which of my ideas would be captured by the 'people in suits', in their context of conference rooms, PowerPoints and refreshments[1].

The independence I envisaged was also at stake in my interactions with the municipal officers who were occupied with the ICT4D project that was part of a larger decentralisation project that included the renovation of the marketplace. This became clear when I visited the *grand marché* in Sokodé with a municipal officer, who deployed me as a representative of those who came to renovate the market. He explained to me that my visit was an excellent opportunity to reassure the market women that they were not forgotten, which was the exact reason why I had been shying away from being associated with the renovation project. The comment of a good friend, indicating that my presence meant that he and

---

[1] An insider told me that after one of my presentations, one of the development practitioners had found my presentation very interesting, however commenting that "Roos comes from a different planet".

the city were not forgotten, increased my discomfort. Was I viewed as a type of white saviour, or did I view myself as one? I do not have any definite answers regarding my personal relationship to (post)colonial sociality and the perceptions and expectations of others in this regard.

My ideal of entering more or less equal relationships in the field was probably only attainable in my own imagination, or in a textbook on reflexive anthropology (Johansson 2015: 56, 60). After much deliberation, I decided to anonymise the names of most of the people whose stories figure in this book and omit family names. This is mainly done in order to protect them from outsiders, because most of them know each other and will recognise some of the stories (Nippert-Eng 2010: 19). This also counts for most of the politically sensitive conversations, especially when it concerns more public members of the local community, like municipal officers and radio broadcasters. However, in some cases, people explicitly demanded that they be identified with their own names, which I honoured, to respect their voice.

On the subject of privacy, it is important to ask the question – who is supposed to protect whom, and for what. Had I contributed to the animosity between the young men I was dealing with, by not following the rules of how women and men should behave? Ethical guidelines mostly deal with protecting participants, but my own vulnerability towards male participants was just as urgent. This could also be linked to the need to protect my family's stability; an intimate subject that is rarely described (Brown & Dreby 2013; Clark & Grant 2015; Johansson 2015; Kulick & Wilson 1995).

Regularly called out and approached as '*la blanche*', I have traversed the city socially as a childfree young woman in 2010 – 2011, a pregnant woman in 2015, a wife and mother with a child at her breast, and a woman alone. Each position provided access to different kinds of information in different sections of society. In some cases, I did not want to receive certain information, as I would have had to cross my own personal boundaries, while I also obtained certain information by employing my femininity. This delicate balancing act has had a large impact on the lens through which the data was obtained, which is an aspect that is given too little attention in the social sciences.

In an analysis of the circumstances under which she was sexually assaulted by her research assistant, Moreno (1995: 183) discusses the idea of creating a kind of family around the female anthropologist, that offers her protection. In some ways, the group of people who have come to interact with me and protect me, can also be seen as family. Even so, the family has had a hard time over the years, with the mutual distrust and insecurity increasing – there has even been a divorce. Nonetheless, the fractured family is still there, and as Felix and his friends often exclaimed among themselves: "the family is sacred".

Doing research with young leaders in community development

The core group of participants in this research consists of about twenty people, mostly young men, whose lives have been followed between 2015 and 2019. The relationship with six or seven among them, including Sweet Mama, dates to 2010. One of the main participants is Dao, a young man with a bachelor's degree in Sociology and a large network in community development projects in Central Togo. I got to know Dao as my research assistant in an earlier research project in 2010–2011 on children's perceptions of health in villages around Sokodé. In later years, his many roles included that of collaborator, advisor and close friend. Our collaboration was especially close at the start of the data collection, but in our process of reciprocal knowledge exchange, he steered me towards independence. Dao knew every important person working in local development organisations and associations in Sokodé, which greatly facilitated the research. In one way or the other, most of the people I met were related to one another.

The neighbourhood Komah, south of the city centre became my base in Sokodé. Through a Canadian-Togolese couple I had met in 2010, I found my first house in Komah in 2015, where I shared a compound with a young Togocel agent, Brice, and an older woman. A compound is a cluster of buildings in an enclosure, such as the rooms or houses of an extended family. A local NGO was based in the same compound, where I got to know a young woman called Stéphanie, who had studied sociology with Dao. The house I stayed between 2016 and 2019 was owned by Sweet Mama, and was located near the Komah market, not far from where Johnny and Dao lived. Sweet Mama kept a small shop, selling juice and ice, and I had also known her since 2010. Behind her house, Mohamed rented a few rooms in a house where he lived with his wife Rachida and their children. It was in 2015, when I needed a safe mode of transport thanks to my growing belly, that I got to know Mohamed. At the time, Mohamed owned a garage and hired himself as a personal driver whenever the occasion arose. He introduced me to his family, and while spending time with him and Rachida, I learned about the marriage issues of young couples in Sokodé.

Periods of intense data collection between 2015 and 2019[2], when I was physically present in Sokodé, alternated with periods of more shallow contact, mainly through WhatsApp messages and images, but also through WhatsApp calls, phone calls, E-mail and Facebook. During my first stint in Sokodé in 2015,

---

[2] These periods were from February to March 2015, May to August 2016, April 2017, March 2018 and March 2019. Considering an earlier stay from December 2010 to February 2011, nearly a one year-cycle has been followed.

Dao and I decided to set up a research team with Freddy and Johnny who were high school friends, whom I got to know in 2010, just like Désiré and Moussa, whom I also followed throughout the years. They were all in their late twenties, early thirties. Freddy and Johnny collected most of the 66 mobile phone biographies, in which people talked about all the mobile phones they had owned, from the first to the most recent. These biographies are part of the 'cultural biography of things' as described by Kopytoff (1986). In 2015, Johnny had a job as a teacher at a private school, and Freddy, who had trained to be an electrician, was struggling to find a job. Over the years, Moussa and Freddy moved to Lomé to find a job, whereas Désiré and Johnny stayed in Sokodé.

Figure 1: Johnny and Freddy interviewing each other.

In 2015, Dao brought four young men together to collect quantitative data for the 'mobile communication logs'. Antoine and Jef were working for local development associations, Patrick in the forestry police and Said in community affairs. They registered all incoming and outgoing calls and SMS messages for 100 persons during one week³. Methods that resemble my 'mobile communication logs' are 'digital days' (Caribou Digital 2015) and 'mobile diaries' (de Lanerolle, Schoon & Walton 2017, 2020). In 2016, Silvi came over from Frankfurt to support me for two months, as foreseen in the funding plan. As an anthropology student and outsider with no social obligations in the field, she was able to conduct many in-depth interviews in a short time without much guidance. The co-construction of knowledge that I idealistically envisaged with the research team, mainly took place between Dao and me, although several focus-group-like exchanges with members of the research team had a profound impact on my analysis.

Similar to Said and Patrick, Dao had also been part of one of the friend groups that Felix was often hanging out with in 2015 and 2016, which had seemingly 'dissolved' in 2018 after the poisoning incident. One of the friends had left the country, another had moved from his family home to his own house with his wife and baby, and had 'less time' to hang out, having become the head of a household. A third friend had stopped seeing the others entirely on the advice of his family, as one of his family members had publicly accused Felix of trying to kill him. This was something that the friend could neither prove nor ignore, so he had decided to keep his distance.

Though I always strived to include equal number of men and women in my research, I soon noticed a male bias in the information gathering process. In an environment that already posed many obstacles for me, I often could not resist taking the easier way and adding dozens of lengthy in-depth interviews with talkative, relatively young men. In choosing to be at least partly guided by the opportunistic sampling of my informants, and using the development project as another entry point, it proved more difficult to have meaningful exchanges with women compared to men.

Therefore, in 2016, I asked Dao and Silvi to focus on conducting interviews with women, and the research team of LaDySir collected an additional 20 interviews with women in Sokodé, Kpalimé and Tsevié. I slowly eased into simply 'being there', and becoming more satisfied with my female connections. One particularly helpful move was to accept Sweet Mama's invitation to move into a room in her house in 2017, 2018 and 2019. In these later visits, I sought and came to encounter a different kind of depth in my everyday interactions with the women around me, for instance in the shared sorrow about the loss of a

---

3 For the mobile communication logs, the 100 individuals also answered questions about their religion, ethnicity, gender, education level and the number of phones they owned (see appendix 1).

baby, the sighs about the behaviour of our husbands or partners, and about living up to the expectations of society. These moments of female solidarity have given me more insights and lessons about everyday life in Togo – and life in general – than an interview setting could give.

I developed a special interest in people's reactions in everyday interactions, especially when their interests or mine were clearly at stake. This was not confined to their reactions to my questions, but in every exchange I could follow, I focused on the information that people did and did not share, and the manner in which they framed it. Dao and I discussed and analysed such situations, and I relied on his interpretation whenever I did not know how to deal with certain social situations, to the extent of the exact words I could use in order to avoid irreparable harm to my relationships. Slowly I started to read between the lines, though in many ways I remained an outsider, raised in a completely different context. The most insightful moments were caused by my often-painful mistakes in sharing personal information about myself or others. These subtle and sometimes obvious ways of concealing and revealing information were so intriguing, that they became integral to my research.

1.4 Overview of the book

The first three chapters set the background, describing the specific and unique social structure in Togo, in which mistrust is a leading concept. The incident of Felix's poisoning shows that when it comes down to it, the commonly held belief is that no one is to be trusted. This sociality is the foundation on which ICTs influence society. While Felix's poisoning might seem like a disconnected incident, it is in fact at the core of the research, providing an entry point to analysing how several layers in society are being affected by new ICTs, and of the various ways in which this is expressed. Chapter two focuses on sociality in the social, political, economic and spiritual environment of Sokodé. It describes a constrained environment that has been internalised. The introduction of the mobile phone has not been without consequences, as the increased possibilities to connect with others bring about an increase in self-reflection. Through these new technologies, people in Sokodé become more aware of their deprivation. In some countries, this has brought about civic protest, in other countries, people turn inwards. This chapter demonstrates the ways in which Togo is a society in duress, and the manner in which the political landscape defines the communication landscape.

Chapter three is dedicated to understanding the consequences of the introduction of the mobile phone, and frames this along the public-private continuum. How do the young people who are at the heart of this research access information, and how do they perceive the role of mobile phones in this regard? The systemic view of information, which focuses on the interpretative process, is taken as a point of departure in an analysis of the trustworthiness of information. Considering mistrust to be an organising principle of society entails a flexible understanding of the value attached to information, and in this sense, information in Togo can be considered to be highly intimate. In a society where political silence is the basis of communication, metaphors, secrecy and privacy are a prerequisite for social navigation. The mobile phone has become part of this delicate information landscape.

Chapter four describes the initial effects of the mobile phone on social life in Sokodé. Firstly, the mobile phone seems to be an economic tool, which is integrated in society. It is highly visible in the public domain and offers various possibilities. The communication landscape of the mobile phone is conceptualised from an economic and materialist perspective. By viewing the mobile phone through this lens, this chapter emphasises that the introduction and integration of the mobile phone is not a political process in the first place.

Chapter five explores the consequences of the introduction of the mobile phone on social relations. This chapter posits that the introduction of the mobile phone was a very crucial moment in the history of communication in Sokodé. The phone changes people's lives, bringing about a plethora of new dilemmas concerning connectivity and availability. In a society in which information is often exchanged in encoded and indirect ways, mobile communication is also interpreted in a variety of ways. Silence, in the form of an unanswered call, can bring about suspicion and mistrust, as well as a call from a stranger. The mobile phone changes the balance of freedom and control within couples, between parents and children, and older and younger generations. This chapter reveals the ways in which power relations at the family level, and 'small politics' are impacted by the mobile phone.

Chapter six explores the possibilities and forms of civic-ness and civil society in Togo, which eventually leads to engaging with the question of whether civic engagement is present in a society in which freedom of expression is constrained, and if yes, the ways in which this engagement takes place. The chapter describes the structures that exist for people to claim their place, their being-in-the-world, for them to further themselves and their communities. It also shows how people respond to an environment in which this type of development is only possible under certain conditions and details the social mechanisms that are in place. Finally, through an analysis of a series of street protests and its aftermath in late 2017, this chapter delves into the ways in which people raise their voice, the channels that they use to do so, and the manner in which the national authorities react to 'dissident' voices in what is perceived as being an opposition town. This provides an alternate perspective regarding the possible forms of civic engagement that can be experienced and expressed in this environment.

The starting point of chapter seven is the premise that people's discontentment remains private, and that their expression is not political. Consequently, the argument is that if they are forced to give their opinion, such as in the ICT4D project considered in this chapter, their participation is not very meaningful. I argue that people do participate in these projects, but these projects are disconnected from political realities. The chapter further explores whether local community development WhatsApp groups offer a way out of this impasse, prompting civic engagement. The chapter concludes with two biographies of young people who are constructing their lives with their mobile phones in hand.

In chapter eight, the conclusions depict how the construct of the state, and the possibilities and ways of information exchange leads to a docile form of civic-ness with limited space for voice. Several aspects of everyday life reveal why Togo has not delved into engaged processes in the civic aspect of life upon the introduction of new ICTs, and why young people choose to remain silent.

2 Keeping the faith in enduring economic and political hardship

2.1 Introduction

> With our politicians things cannot work. Millions, billions, they will continue to eat. We don't know where we are and we don't know where we are heading. You never know what will happen tomorrow. Per year, you cannot save 1,000 CFA, so after 40 years you don't even have 40,000. Right next to you lives a millionaire – but we are in the same country. (Interview with Abdulahi, 4 March 2015)

Abdulahi said this to me when we were sitting on the edge of his bed in his small room. In 2010, I got to know Abdulahi through his older brother, whom I had met in *Hotel Central*, where he was staying with his Canadian wife at the time. They were spending their holidays in the proximity of his family, before returning to Canada. Together, we took some trips in the surrounding areas, accompanied by Abdulahi. Though his older brother supported him in setting up a business, the young man did not manage to secure a source of income. When I returned in 2015 and in the years thereafter, Abdulahi was sincere in his desperation and depression. His life story contains two main conditions that are crucial for a better understanding of the context of this study, as this case is not an isolated one. Firstly, his precarious economic condition clearly has a structural character, and secondly, he grew up witnessing a political system in which only a select, privileged group of individuals is having access to power and wealth.

This chapter depicts the context of economic hardship and political repression in which people in Sokodé navigate the uncertain territories of communication. It explores the mechanisms of everyday life in a society that has internalised a silence, at a time when a new means of communication is introduced that allows people to send messages instantly, and seemingly without human intermediaries. Structural constraints to people's agency in Togo, and the city of Sokodé in particular, are revealed, providing an insight into important political, socio-cultural, economic and spiritual factors. The second part of the chapter deals with the media landscape that distributes 'official' and 'newsworthy' information in Sokodé, concluding with a bottom-up description of the telecommunication business, from sales points through collecting agents to the network providers and their links to the state.

2.2 "With our politicians, things cannot work"

The state and citizenship in postcolonial Africa

Anthropologists have studied African sociality and political organisation for a long time; from the organisation of the Nuer by Evans-Pritchard in 1940 to current efforts to come to terms with the decolonisation, not only of the African continent, but also of the domain of African studies. As Piot (2010) notes, the African continent has been a place where theories about 'the state' have been amply developed, where the periods of colonisation, independence and the end of the Cold War have led to specific forms of states, ranging from authoritarian to democratic states. Among the scholars who contribute to the decolonisation of African studies, Piot uncovers structures that perpetuate as well as shape our perspectives. It is imperative to move away from Western notions of sociality, as they blur the analysis of social change in African societies.

Unlike others, Piot (2010) identifies a rupture in the political history of state formation in West Africa not in the period when independence was declared in the 1960s, but after the end of the Cold War in the 1990s, when people in different African countries called for multi-party democracy. Political organisation in the independent African state can be considered to be a continuation of the colonial system. As Mamdani (2005) has argued, race and ethnicities can be historicised as political identities, based on and reproduced by colonial institutions. This has had an enormous impact on the relation between states and peoples in Africa till today, and between different groups of people within the African state.

Based on the South African scenario, Mamdani sketches a racialized form of citizenship, in a colonial legislative system that differentiated between 'race' and 'ethnicity', in which races were treated as citizens, falling under the system of civil law, and African natives were designated as ethnicities, falling under 'traditional' or customary law, ruled by customary chiefs. Throughout this book, the denomination 'customary chief' is preferred over 'traditional chief', as the twin notions of tradition and modernity have contributed, among others, to the 'othering' of people and societies who are not Western – akin to a colonial gaze (Baumann & Briggs 2003). Another part of colonial legacy is the dichotomy of civil and customary law in the judiciary system, which is still perceptible today in many African countries. This system has not only contributed to social inequalities between citizens and 'denizens', but also between different ethnic groups, who competed over land rights – first-comers versus late-comers. This is also evident in the Togolese context in which the autocratic leadership not only relies on the support of local chiefs, but also twists the 'customary' system to their advantage with new decrees that enable the appointment of new customary chiefs with close ties to the ruling political party (Gardini 2012).

In this complex network of power, the ruling national political elite also has its links in every large company or institute, and people must engage with this system to get what they want, which feeds a type of highly unequal collaboration. The population has no real voice, and it is often only through people's connections with the local political elite that they have access to institutional services. The disgruntled yet resigned reactions of the people I interacted with in Togo when I asked them about the local political institutions in place are illustrative of this reality. Sweet Mama would shriek: "The municipality, what have they done for us, nothing!"

Subsequently, this validates Mbembe's (2001) take on the postcolony in which the 'subjected' have come to internalise the authoritarian epistemology to the point where they reproduce it themselves in all aspects of their everyday lives and sociality; the 'intimacy of tyranny'. Yet another part of this intimacy of tyranny exists in the void left by political institutional life. Piot (2010: 12) calls this the 'greying' of the area, where state institutions withdraw from their responsibility to provide basic services, and people's faith is in the hands of NGOs and churches that choose the 'target groups' that receive support and those that do not. This 'greying' is based upon what Mbembe refers to as 'grey zones' where the desperate poor try to survive under deplorable conditions, abandoned by the state and the international (Mbembe 2003: 34).

In their article on enduring hardship in a society 'under duress', De Bruijn and Both (2018) discuss the normalisation of crisis, in which violence and deprivation contribute to a sociality in which uncertainty and misery are the norm rather than exception, and are passed on from generation to generation. This is also true of Sokodé and many places in Togo. In such areas, the authors state, an eruption of extreme violence with either warlords, the army, or both entering to terrorise the population, is only part of a continuum of violence simmering below the surface. In the same vein, the uncertainty of poverty, which is also an embodied experience as described by Kalfelis (2015), leaves deep imprints in society. According to Cooper and Pratten (2015), developmental interventions overlook issues of uncertainty, mistrust, jealousy, that enrich social science thinking on development and social change. The political and economic situation in Togo, and Sokodé in particular, contribute to a certain atmosphere of resignation in everyday life, interspersed with short periods of popular uprising and violence. As authoritarian regimes gain traction in our world, it is important for scholars to examine situations like the one in Togo, which are increasingly the reality for many people.

Living under the watchful eye of the Gnassignbé 'dynasty'

The political landscape in Togo can be described as autocratic rule, with a central role for the army (Kohnert 2015). After overthrowing the first president of independent Togo in a coup d'etat, General Gnassignbé Eyadéma ruled the country from 1967 to 2005. After the death of General Eyadéma Gnassignbé in 2005, people were hopeful that the political situation in Togo would change just like during the 1990s, when people were protesting on the streets to call for democracy. However, the army put his son Faure Gnassignbé in power as president. The hope for political change was violently beaten down by the security forces during the elections that took place later that year. At least 700 people died, another 40,000 fled the country, and amidst the social upheaval and violent repression, Faure was declared winner of the elections (Kohnert 2008). Ever since, human rights organisations have tried to bring to justice the army officers who were implied in the human rights violations in 2005, but they have not been trialled. Faure 'won' the elections again in 2010, 2015 and 2020. From time to time, people take to the streets to protest, and even peaceful protest rapidly turns into violent clashes with the security forces; shorter periods of violent repression alternate with simmering forms of low-intensity repression.

During his lifetime, mythical powers were attributed to Eyadema Gnassignbé, which only increased when he survived an airplane accident in Sarakawa in 1974 (Toulabor 1986; Piot 2010). Even years after his death, he is still referred to as 'the father' or '*le vieux caiman*', and Faure as 'the son', to name but a few. Most people in Togo are not only reluctant to utter their names out loud, but also to talk about anything directly related to politics. One never knows whether mentioning them might create problems. The silence of common people regarding the political situation of the country does not contradict the protests that erupted in 2017, neither does it stop people from expressing their discontentment about the lack of employment, the poor quality of health and infrastructure, basic amenities and the general state of the country. Nonetheless, people exercise the utmost care when it comes to choosing whom to trust and who not to trust – especially when the people in question are public figures, occupying communitarian or political positions.

On many occasions, people explicitly stated that they were not involved in anything connected to 'the politics of politicians', and these statements revealed that any subject could be considered political. Till today, people remain fearful of expressing their opinion in public, because 'they' can knock on your door in the night if you have been openly critical. Though the reign of Faure has known less violence in the number of deaths, the repression has not ended yet. While the recent protests have created a comparatively volatile atmosphere, in which people are more often inclined to state 'enough is enough', this does not mean that there is more openness. There are certain ways and situations in which people feel relatively free to criticise the authorities for the malaise in the country, but not without looking over their shoulder, lowering their voice or talking in metaphors. The majority of the people I knew expressed that they did 'not have the time' to vote or were 'just not interested' in politics. This 'coded information' indicates the severely restricted communication structure in a constrained environment, which is extremely important to consider while studying the communication landscape in Togo.

While most people tried to avoid the subject of politics altogether, some radio broadcasters and journalists whom we interviewed expressively voiced that they were 'tired of the regime'. However, this was not very different from what close friends prudently voiced, or what I read in between the lines during my interviews. People are fed up of the dictatorial regime, while being intimately connected with it (see also Mbembe 2001).

Political divide – and rule along family lines

On the local level, there are many complex factors that contribute to tensions between the ruling regime and the inhabitants of Togo, played out in subtle or obvious politics of divide-and-rule, state interference in customary chiefdoms and land conflicts (Kohnert 2008). The employment and promotion of *Togolité* can be seen as part of a divide-and-rule politics with the Kaybe ranked highest as 'most autochthonous group' (Toulabor 2003; Kohnert 2008). Toulabor and Kohnert suggest that the ruling clan has closely watched the use of the concept of *Ivorité* by Togo's big brother Côte d'Ivoire, privileging the Kabye at the expense of other groups or individuals based on their perceived non-autochthony, questioning their 'rights' to power (Toulabor 2003; Kohnert 2008). This is reflected in the numerical predominance of the Kabye in the security services. At a certain point, two thirds of the army consisted of persons of Kabye descent, and there was an even higher number among the generals (Kohnert 2005).

The same counts for higher positions in public and semi-public institutions, but as 'anything can be political', this is not limited to these sectors. For example, almost every Togocel office around Sokodé has a person of Kabye descent as director. According to our inquiries, the front office is also dominantly Kabye; the Kotokoli girls who work as intern, complain that only the Kabye girls get contracted after their internship. What matters here is not so much whether this is a factual reality or not. The experienced reality is just as real, and reveals a sentiment of 'ethnic favouring', which is a matter of major concern when tensions rise.

It is difficult to disentangle political motives and powers from the resentment between different ethnic groups, and between 'Northerners' and 'Southerners' in general. Among certain groups of Southerners, the resentment dates back to the assassination of the first president Sylvanus Olympio, originating from the South, by General Eyadéma Gnassignbé, originating from the North. It is suggested that a part of the Northerners only support the present regime out of fear of facing a bloody revenge. At the same time, I have been told by people in different parts of the country that the revolution will never come, as 'we Togolese are simply too afraid to die'. The Kotokoli are said to be the exception, and they are seen as the only 'real' competitors for political power. As several people from the South expressed: "We run away when we see blood, but the Kotokoli are not afraid, because they are warriors".

It must be noted that tensions are never far away, not only fed by the lack of political change and sub-regional and global developments, but also by non-human influences as well as feelings of jealousy in this environment of stark economic inequalities. The tendency of the nation's political leaders to frame the tensions in the country as an ethnic (north-south) or religious (Muslims-Christians) conflict, is more likely a politically informed strategy to divert attention away from the fact that large sections of the population seek political change after 50 years of reign by the Gnassignbé family. I refrain from focusing too much on ethnic and religious differences, as it diverts attention away from the larger picture of a minor ruling class that refuses to cede power, which is a point also strongly made by Piot (2010: 32).

In everyday life, ethnic differences are mainly played out in half-serious jokes. There is also a constant call for unity from all sorts of actors, not in the least by political parties such as the ruling party UNIR and opposition party PNP. However, during the street protests in late 2017, the ruling party did play the 'religious' card, when the Minister of Justice asserted that people had shouted "*Allahu Akhbar*" upon setting fire to the commissariat. Though he was stating this as part of the larger international discourse about 'fighting Islamic extremism', the local consequences cannot be underestimated. In early 2018, I heard for the first time a serious undertone when a Zed-man talked to me about the differences he felt among Muslims.

Besides the familiar strategy of divide-and-rule, opposition in any form – political or non-political, organised or spontaneous, civic or social – is severely hindered by the regime via different strategies: from administrative hurdles and complicated regulations for associations that challenge the existing power structures to bribery, intimidation and violence. These strategies are sustained by a fine-meshed network, an informal surveillance system that originated during the previous regime. Self-censorship and concealment pervades the communication landscape in society, being both a part of the system and resulting it.

Most of the strategies mentioned above are played out in a hidden sphere, and they are only captured by rumours and personal accounts of people who were either bold enough or trusted me enough to share their stories with me. In an interview at a radio station, one of the directors told Dao and me: "There is always someone who studies your actions" (Interview with radio director, 9 June 2016). He suggested that the persons who 'study his actions', are also 'studied' by others higher up in the intelligence service. He illustrated its effect with a radio debate during election times in 2015, for which several local opposition members and a member of the ruling party accepted his invitation, but the latter finally did not show up. The director lamented this situation in which politicians of the ruling party cannot speak freely: they always must look up to the highest level – the president himself – before they can express themselves. He stated: "This is no real democracy. Democracy cannot do without opposition".

A middle-aged Kotokoli man, born in the Tchamba prefecture worked for an NGO and freely discussed his political ambitions with me in 2011. Some years later, he had been appointed a position of director of a semi-public institute in Lomé. In March 2018, when he was in Sokodé for an inauguration of a state programme, he came looking for me in a gigantic four-wheel drive to have dinner at a hotel in the outskirts of town. We were alone on the barely lit terrace and he showed me his different WhatsApp groups after I had told him about my research topic. He shrugged while commenting on the different UNIR groups in his account, and said that while he did not agree with many of the exchanges in these groups, his hands were tied. As director, he did not have much choice but to toe the line of the ruling political party. Had his appointment been a way to silence his voice, as a mutual acquaintance had told me? Then again, in order to get actively involved in the higher echelons of political opposition, a person needs to be ready to make sacrifices that greatly affect one's privacy and that of one's inner circle, entering into an environment in which barely anyone can be trusted.

Economic deprivation and despair

Reports by supranational institutions such as the African Development Bank (AfDB), World Bank and UNDP, state that 60 percent of the population in Togo lives in poverty, of which one third in extreme poverty (AfDB 2014). Though the definition of poverty lines fluctuates with the changing interests of international development politics, these statistics reveal that the economic power of people living in Togo is weak. However, they do not uncover the conditions under which people make the most with what they can and their self-perception of their poverty. The social implications of poverty have received scholarly attention in Lewis' seminal 'culture of poverty' (1969) and in more recent publications (Chambers *et al.* 2000; Hahn 2011; Kalfelis 2015; Mullainathan 2011).

The stories of some of the people I met carry a sense of despair that can hardly be expressed in words, therefore describing people in Sokodé simply as 'desperate beings' does not accurately convey their struggles or do justice to their dignity. Poverty is not only about having only one meal per day with children sharing a bowl of porridge or *gari*, and postponing payment of bills till the very last moment, when the electricity is nearly shut off. These are only symptoms. Poverty seeps into one's system, showing up in the deep insecurity of what tomorrow will bring, a deep resignation or sense of lethargy, and requiring flexibility to deal with unexpected situations. It is the constant struggle of trying to get by and have a little savings, until a person falls sick or dies in the family, and hospital bills or funerals must be accounted for. Time and again, it is a matter of finding the strength to start from scratch again, hoping for better days to come.

The wish '*courage*' is expressed every day in several situations, just like '*ça va aller*' [it will be fine]. Though this expression of hope is most often heard, there are enough situations in which people reacted with '*ça ne va pas*' [it is not fine] to a sincere question of how things are going. Abdulahi, who was introduced in the beginning of this chapter, openly struggled with his desperation. Often, he struggled to leave his room, and every time we met he lamented about his condition: at his advanced age (in 2015 he was 37 years old), he still lived in his parental house and did not have a stable income to marry and start his own family. He had once dreamt of opening a workshop as a woodworker, but he had not managed to do so, and abandoned the idea. Instead, he took on petty jobs, such as digging out or cleaning latrines. Abdulahi's total lack of prospects had a paralysing effect on him, and responding with '*courage*' was not even close to a solution for his permanent gloom. Without readiness to fight, he observed:

> Here in Togo it is chaos – no one will say something, everyone wants for their own pocket. The one who finds something to eat will tell you that things are alright. That is the problem in Togo. I also just look for my own bread. It's just that I wish there should not be war in Togo, like in other countries such as in Libya. (Interview with Abdulahi, 4 March 2015)

This quote also reflects the link between the political atmosphere and economic deprivation. The economic deprivation that many inhabitants of Sokodé experience is stark. People try to make ends meet by starting a small business and doing petty jobs, but the profits are minimal. Most incomes are not stable enough for families to send their children to school and stay healthy. People are dependent on their extended family, neighbours and social network for their survival and to move ahead in life. According to Marantz (2001: 1–10), these micro-solutions and micro-economic approach to life are part of an informal social security system that flourishes in African societies. The system is based on interdependence and takes the approach of the individual being a web of relationships.

The concept of solidarity does not cover the various types of assistance encountered in this African society, partly because this concept is based on the individualist assumption that Piot (1999: 1–26) described, that does not do justice to the context in Sokodé. The threads in the web of relationships are not evenly distributed, nor is their thickness the same, and I noted that some of the threads are made of inexplicable fabric. People are conceptualised in different ways, depending on their place in the family, clan, ethnic group and neighbourhood, and their social and economic situation. Since the basis of this is in the relationality of human beings, concepts of interdependency and subsidiarity might offer an alternative perspective. Subsidiarity emphasises the importance of smaller and larger societal relationships such as the family, religious and other associations in the functioning of society. The higher levels of the social structure enable the lower levels to serve society and connect individuals and the society.

In general, older people occupy a higher position in the hierarchy compared to those who are younger, and men are placed higher than women. Paying respect to another follows these lines of hierarchy. At the level of the household, this means that women normally ask their husband for permission before leaving the house, and men announce to their wives that they are leaving. Although there is often no question of refusal, people generally do not leave without expressing their wish to leave; for instance, guests "ask for the road". The response is mostly the wish "go-and-come-back". Another example on the family level is that older brothers can offer protection and support, but they can also demand that younger siblings help with chores or tasks.

Having connections with people in key positions gives one a relative advantage over others who do not have these connections, though people also know that they cannot completely rely on 'big men'. This is the case not only when it comes to customary institutions like the chiefdoms, but also political institutions like the prefecture or the municipality, and in fact any possible establishment. It is considered good to have connections within the security forces or the police, so that one can call upon them in case one has run into trouble with their colleagues. Getting close to wealthier people implies that there might be a chance to benefit from their wealth in exchange for one's loyalty or labour.

Abdulahi's situation captures the complexity of the system of subsidiarity. His family did not totally lack resources. His older brother had made a living in Canada and visited his family in Sokodé on a yearly basis. Though both the older brother and Abdulahi did not share much information with me about their relationship and other exchanges and issues on the family level, the older brother had supported Abdulahi in the past with starting a business, and his support continued: the scooter that Abdulahi used in 2016 was also a gift. However, this support did not seem to increase Abdulahi's financial stability.

From another perspective, the obligations on the older brother to fulfil the expectations of his social networks in Sokodé weighed heavily on him. Towards the end of December 2010, when I spent some time in his company, he was often compelled to pay expensive bills in bars, because anyone who was a passing acquaintance, expected him to pay for their drinks. Some people did not even join his table or inform him, but asked for their drinks to be added to his bill. He was visibly uncomfortable each time he realised this when the bill was handed to him. At times he was upset, but he also seemed resigned to the situation since it would harm his reputation if he made a fuss over it. Furthermore, since he continued to visit these bars, it must have meant that he had a budget for buying drinks. This case is an example of the rights and responsibilities that come with hierarchies, showing that the responsibility of 'patrons' can be as much of a burden as the subordinate position of the people who have turned to them for support. However, even though they are often called upon for help, people higher up in the hierarchy do seem to have more autonomy because of their position – at least they can simply buy themselves a new smartphone of considerable quality if their old one is broken.

2.3 Subsidiarity and the weight of social inequalities

The wish to go on adventure

One of the ways to break out of this system that some people described to me as being prison-like, is to migrate or, in local terminology to 'go on adventure', though the bonds that connect people continue to remain powerful, as was the case with Abdulahi's older brother. When unfulfilled, the wish to go on adventure can at times weigh just as heavily on an individuals' mind as the system from which one wants to be free. This wish to go on adventure has been described by a range of scholars in recent years (Alpes 2016; Collyer 2007; Dougnon 2008; Ferguson 2006; Klute & Hahn 2007; Nyamnjoh 2010; Piot 2010). As Nyamnjoh (2010) stated about Senegalese boat migrants, going on adventure is not a new phenomenon. This type of mobility fits in a sub-region where it is common for youngsters, especially men, to move to other places in order to make some money and gain life experience before returning and getting married.

Sooner or later, almost every person I met asked me about the possibilities of moving to Europe, requesting detailed information about the ways to make it to Germany, other European countries, Canada and the United States, similar to the experiences noted by Alpes (2016) and Piot (2010). Piot's (2010: 77–95) fascinating chapter 'Exit Strategies' is entirely devoted to the US Green Card lottery, a phenomenon which my informants also dreamed of, whereas China, India and Middle Eastern countries such as Kuwait or the Emirates were also on their mind. The idea of 'adventure' is deeply embedded in society, and many people leave to try their luck outside the country. However, most people in Sokodé make their way to Lomé or other big cities and smaller places in Ghana, Burkina Faso, Nigeria and sometimes Gabon. Around the 2000s, there was a peak in groups of teenagers, from 12 years onwards, leaving for Nigeria and to a lesser extent to Ghana. They were often convinced by traffickers, and they left with or without the consent of their parents (Buchbinder 2012; Plan 2005).

The return of the youngsters from Nigeria every December is a social event: people along the tarred road from Tchamba to Sokodé nudge each other as groups of packed, dusty motorbikes pass by. In December 2010, I witnessed some of these young men returning, sometimes with 12 or 13 year old boys riding pillion. They draw a lot of attention, covered in dust, coming from faraway places, bringing along stories and possibly presents for their relatives. The motorbikes are the safest way of transporting the money these youngsters have saved – it is much easier for robbers and custom officers to force them to hand over their banknotes than their motorbikes.

Like many young people whose stories have been recorded by anthropologists over the years (Alpes 2016; Piot 2010), Abass, a young broadcaster I had got to know in the context of the ICT4D project, was yearning to leave Sokodé. At one point, he had gotten in touch with 'a contact' who had connections in Dubai, and a first group of five youth had apparently arrived in Dubai. Abass had used all his charm to secure a loan of a micro-credit organisation to set up his hairdressing saloon. However, after he had transferred the sum of money, his contacts kept on postponing appointments, until he had to acknowledge that his plans had failed, and he had to find a way to return the loan. In one of our conversations, he sighed:

> This is what Sokodé lives. People are buying sheep in the preparations for the Sacrifice Feast, and papa asks 'what do you do for me?' because I have nothing. (Conversation with Abass, 16 April 2017)

The inability of youngsters like Abass, who live in the family compound, to make a financial contribution to the household, brings about small and big conflicts, and the resulting shame contributes to an underlying sense of stress and gloom. Since these young men and women feel they have no other choice, the despair they feel pushes them to undertake dangerous journeys such as through the desert and the sea to find better prospects. Though an entire field of studies is devoted to the subject of migration which I have only briefly addressed here, it came up in our conversations so many times that it can be considered an obvious part of the context in which mobile communication is embedded.

"The African does not want to see his brother advance"

One of the push-factors that makes people long for migration is captured in the oft-quoted expression "the African does not want to see his brother advance". According to my understanding, this expression is founded on poverty, the system of subsidiarity and the potentially devastating force of jealousy, all of them being part of the uncertainties of life as captured by Cooper and Pratten (2015).

Relatives or close contacts call upon people who are better off for favours of various types, which greatly contributes to their financial instability. In most sections of society, saving money is not an easy task; people who manage to save a little bit of money, lose all their meagre savings when a close relative falls ill. In the worst-case scenario, the member dies, and the family has lost their beloved one, money and – if the person was working – a source of income. There is always the worry that family members will come asking for money, in the face of multiple needs, like health issues, an overdue rent to be paid, an application that has to be filed for a bid for employment in the public sector, ceremonies, feasts and more, as described by various scholars (Geschiere 2013; Cooper and Pratten 2015).

Besides open requests to share one's material possessions, there are also cases in which people face more explicit thwarting, which often have to do with jealousy. For instance, a reseller of second-hand bags told me during an interview in July 2016 that her shop had been robbed twice. Thieves had taken most of her stock in second-hand bags that she regularly buys in Lomé and resells in Sokodé. She lamented that most of her neighbours were not concerned that she had to start from scratch again. According to her, people wish to see that things are not going well, rather than being happy for someone when she is getting ahead. This is related to jealousy, which probably also played a role in the alleged poisoning of Felix, an incident introduced in chapter one. Felix readily showed off his snazzy smartphone and sleek motorbike to others, and when he explained to me that no one could be trusted in this environment, he also referred to the envy of people around him.

To further illustrate this, consider Freddy. One of my key informants, research assistants and close connection, Freddy took great care with his appearance, always dressing in clean, well put together clothes. He took pride in this, and I imagined it was also a way for him to keep his morale high. He remarked that no one could assess his misery because he was well turned out, though he added that it made people less inclined to help him. However, they could not make fun of him either. In this regard, no matter the position one has in the social hierarchy, everyone seems to navigate between compassion and pity on one side, and jealousy on the other. It goes without saying that this assessment heavily influences the extent to which people share information with one another.

The person as constituent of Relation, ancestors and spirits

This section begins with the premise on which my analysis of the connectivity in Sokodé is based followed by a focus on the constitution of this connectivity. Not only anthropologic traditions find their roots in Western societies, I am also shaped by them. Therefore, it is challenging to distance the study from 'Euroamerican' conceptions of self and society, elucidated by Piot (1999: 1–26). However, the conviction that this does not exonerate me from the responsibility to explore, is also a deeply rooted one. Not only Piot, but also others, such as Riesman (1986) and Jackson and Karp (1990) argue that the person is considered to be a part of her relationships, in various African societies. In fact, people exist only in relationship with others.

For Piot (1999: 1–26), who argues that the non-existence of individualism in a society like Togo remains little understood, this assessment is only the start. According to him, theoretical models based on structural functionalism, Marxism and practice theory are based on Western conceptions of self and society, in which individuals compete for power or control over others, strive to fulfil their self-interest and maximise profits, own property and have independent agency. Though such models do contest the existence of individualism in African contexts, they approach the clan or ethnic group *as if* these were the African variant of the Western individual: "the group as individual-writ-large" (Piot 1999: 16). What Piot found among the Kabye in northern Togo goes beyond this: A person is not considered as being separate from the relationships in which she is a constituent, but instead is *situated in* a multitude of relationships. This is illustrated in the jokes shared by a Togolese-Canadian couple that I met in *Hotel Central* in December 2010, one of whom introduced me to his younger brother Abdulahi. The partners frequently reminded each other: "Your knee is my knee... your foot is my foot..." continuing with other body parts. Applying Piot's findings, this multitude of relationships not only consists of human beings; but also extends into the world of ancestors and spirits. These non-human actors substantially influence and have intentionality toward the individual, and vice versa. This is an approach of the self as diffuse and fluid, being multiple and permeable, imbued with the presence of human and non-human others (Piot 1999: 19).

It is imperative to note the importance of invisible non-human actors and spiritual life in Togo, such as studied by Piot (1999), Hamberger (2013), Keyewa (1997), Kreamer (1995), Lallemand (1988) and Keita (1984). The theme cannot be ignored, as it plays a large role in people's calculations of whom to trust, the level of privacy they want to interact with others at and whether to answer certain phone calls or not. It is also part of people's explanatory framework to make sense of the world. For example, a meningitis outbreak south of Sokodé in 2009 was explained in terms of sorcery: a 'nightly airplane' had crashed in the area, spreading the disease and claiming many victims. On the road to Sokodé in May 2016, Mohamed explained to me that such 'airplanes' are the form of transport used by sorcerers. Several decades ago, Geschiere (1997) showed convincingly that witchcraft and politics are closely interlinked in postcolonial Africa and are more similar to Bayart's 'politics of the belly' (1989) than social scientists initially thought.

Non-human influences, other than sorcerers, who are human during the day and operate in a non-human form during the night, include spirits, who reside under trees or in other places, and people's ancestors; the tombs belonging to a clan are considered to be sacred and only initiated people are allowed to enter. People maintain strong ties with their ancestral village, even when living in Sokodé, and many frequently return to the village of their clan, to attend ceremonies and maintain links with their ancestors and living family members. When misfortune befalls them, some people consult a traditional healer to get an insight into the situation: have they accidentally upset a spirit by spilling dirty water on the street, have they sold land against the wish of their ancestors, or has there been a fight over a woman with an older cousin who happens to be a sorcerer? It is widely believed that especially people with whom one has close ties can hurt a person, and motives can often be attributed to jealousy, as was the case with the incident described in the introductory chapter. In many cases, when an illness would not heal easily, people would mention their relative success vis-à-vis their peers and relatives, and link their illness to jealousy, a reasoning that is mentioned in numerous studies (Lallemand 1988; Piot 1999; Patel 1995).

Some people attach more value to 'tradition' than others, as reflected in the persistence as well as partial abandonment of initiation ceremonies. I use the term tradition tentatively here, as it is a catch-all term often used by people in Sokodé when they explained these issues to me. Sweet Mama for instance, who frequents an evangelical church, often said that the only one she knows is her God, who is enough for her. She also told me that the trees of the Komah market had refused to be cut down, shaking and putting their roots back in the ground, before they finally 'gave in'. The contradiction merely exists in official discourses; for in Sweet Mama's lifeworld, these matters simply coexist. The influence of non-human actors on fortune and misfortune cannot be fully known, and experiences and events in this area remain inexplicable to a large extent.

Interconnectivity with the Other

More than ever before, new media have given us the possibility to be in one place with our mind and in another place with our body. Never has this been so omnipresent. There are indications that our brains and brain activity have significantly changed through the constant stream of information that intrudes into our daily activities to such an extent that it has become one of our predominant daily activities. The constant alertness triggered by the immediate desire to know whether a new message has come or not, has an effect on our system (Przybylski & Weinstein 2013; Hadlington 2017). The mobile phone has left no region of the world unaffected; even the most remote people are a part of this network that is pregnant with information.

Most Western scholars – I include myself here – might consider this constant interconnectivity provided by new technologies a novelty. However, throughout history, people in different parts of the world have been living in a world with invisible threads connecting them with other human and non-human beings, physically close or separated by large distances, ancestors, spirits, and something larger that some describe as god. Understandably, the technology offers new possibilities, though it does not necessarily bring us closer to non-human actors. However, in Sokodé, they are believed to make use of these new technologies to manifest their influence on living human beings. Though the technology is new, in most African societies the seemingly unlimited possibilities of interconnecting do not necessarily change people's world views profoundly – it is mainly very practical to be reachable through a phone.

The idea of the 'collapse' between time and distance as an effect of mobile communication, was also noted when other technological novelties saw the light, such as when cars or railways were introduced (Gewald, Luning & Walraven 2009). But even long before technologically advanced machinery was invented, the collapse of time and distance has been experienced in astral journeys and trances, documented during many occasions that could be described as spiritual, other-worldly, realities. In order to understand the realities of the people with whom I have worked over the past few years, the legacy of Enlightenment must be overcome. This not only calls for a reconsideration of the emphasis on empiricism and rationality, but also requires a critical examination of the public sphere.

An interconnected system, in which the visible and the invisible are of equal importance, places ethnographic methods in a different light. After all, though postmodernism has brought about shifts in the ways of perception, science still attaches more value to reason than to intuition after Enlightenment and Descartes. This would be a colossal mistake if we are to understand what it means to be human, for the invisible part of the world, in which non-human actors play their many roles, can only be intuitively approached. Shamans, priests, marabouts and other spiritual persons serve as mediators between the tangible and the mystical.

If the social sciences and humanities adopt a world view in which non-human actors are important, the implications for our methodology are profound. I personally do not know of any study in which ancestors have been consulted about the research questions, though this is not necessarily the way forward. The way forward is played out on a far more subtle level, even beyond decolonisation debates (Boswell & Nyamnjoh 2016; Fanon 2008; Mbembe 2015; Wa Thiong'O 1986). Glissant's concept of Relation – with a capital R to emphasise that it is a distinct concept – offers a framework for considering decolonial identities beyond the dichotomy of resistance and submission, using these as starting points for recognising a shared world of infinite differences. In the words of Glissant: "Relation is the moment when we realize that there is a definite quality of all the differences in the world" (Glissant, Diawara & Wings 2011: 9).

Vokes and Pype (2016) proposed to study what they call 'chronotypes of media' might do more justice to examine mobile communication in an ethnographic setting, in order to trace the entanglements of time and space in various social and political lifeworlds. Citing Clifford, who defines the chronotope as "fictional setting where historically specific relations of power become visible and certain stories can 'take place'" (Clifford 1988: 236 in Vokes & Pype 2016:

3), they understand the chronotype as a performative concept. This concept allows an analysis of the ways in which media assemblages and their performative effects are embedded within structures, and the impact they have on people's agency, their social lives and their interconnectivity with others. When employing the perspective of a person as diffuse and fluid, imbued with the presence of human and non-human others, interconnectivity is already implied. The introduction of the mobile phone in Sokodé has impacted this interconnectivity, in a setting that continues to offer little perspective to young people.

2.4 The city of Sokodé and its media landscape

Sokodé at first sight

At first sight, Sokodé shares many similarities with other small African towns, with two markets, the *grand marché* and the Komah market, where there is both the hustle and bustle of buyers and sellers, and social interactions. People greet each other, exchanging small talk before moving on to the next stall, women sell small foods like tomatoes and lettuce, and men run the bigger *boutiques* surrounding the marketplace. In the square between the grand mosque and the grand market, and at other crossroads in town, motor-taxis or 'Zemedjan' gather to wait for customers.

As can be seen on the map in figure 2[4], only the few main roads in Sokodé are tarred: the national highway number one, leading from Lomé in the South to Cinkassé in the North, the road to Bassar to the Northwest and the road to Tchamba to the Southeast. The road towards the prefecture is also tarred. All the other roads are laterite or earth, prone to erosion in the rainy season. 'No man's land' or uncultivated shores of the small streams and rivers are often polluted with litter, whereas the streets are relatively clean, which the authorities at the town hall would immediately attribute to their cooperation with an international development partner.

The bus station is close to the *grand marché*, and throughout town, there are designated places along the road where shared taxis and minibuses depart. A deserted stretch at the southern entrance of Sokodé, where the weeds arise between the asphalt, is a silent remainder of the failed attempt to move the grand market and bus station elsewhere, in order to 'decongest' the traffic in the city

---

4 This map is based on a map of the scenario in 1994 (Barbier & Klein 1995: 137), with landmarks that I added.

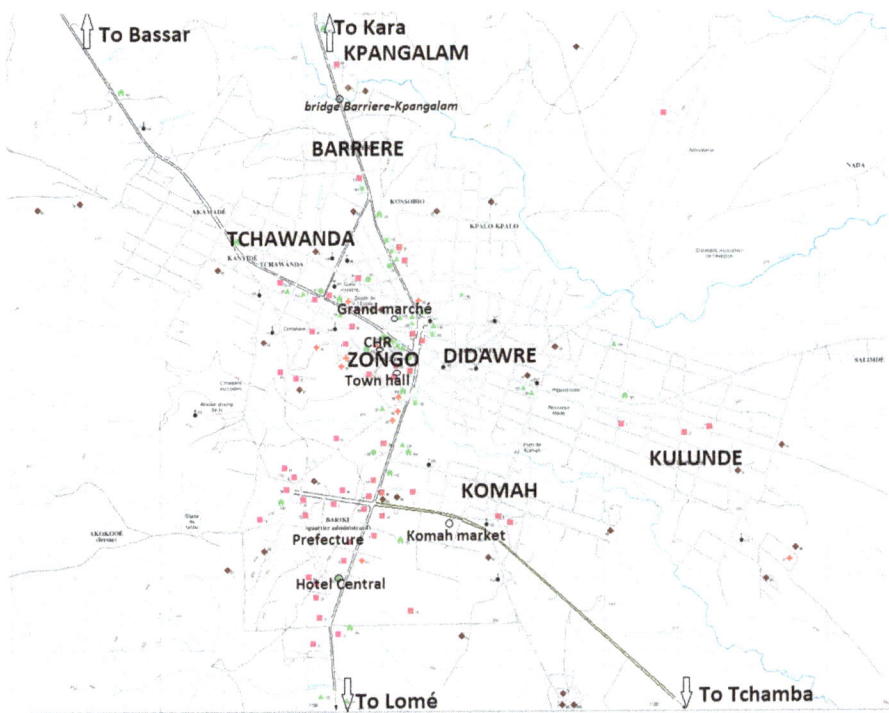

Figure 2: Map of Sokodé.

centre. Alongside the national highway that runs through Sokodé, the many signs are a testament to the multitude of national and local development associations and NGOs in town, of which only some are successful enough to establish long lasting partnerships with (inter)national donors. Between July and early September, the city appears less busy, as many people leave to cultivate the fields. In January 2017, a factory for the transformation of soya and peanut was opened by Faure Gnassingbé, but there are hardly any industrial activities in Sokodé, and the economy is dominated by the transport, commerce and artisanal sector.

Along the national highway and on the main junctions, large billboards of mobile phone operators dot the landscape. With their green colours, Togocel and Moov are highly visible in urban and rural spaces, as can be seen in the photo (figure 3). Smaller signs indicate places where consumers can buy prepaid airtime for their calls and SMS, and internet airtime. Almost every bar or shop, however small or remote it is, has a sales point for airtime.

Figure 3: Streetview with Togocel and Moov sales point.

On the 'shoreline' of public and private spheres (Nippert-Eng 2010: 4), friends and acquaintances meet in the many bars in town, the little restaurants along the roadside where people have a meal and the courtyards of houses where people drink home-brewed *tchouck*, a local beer based on sorghum, or *sodabi* which is distilled alcohol. In Kabye villages, *tcouck* is made by women in turns, and a calabash bowl turned upside down on a stick in front of the house means that *tchouck* is available (see also Piot 1999). In the city of Sokodé, there are also neighbourhoods with relatively more Kabye and other Northerners, who serve this local beer. Their courtyards serve as meeting places for people to drink beer and have a chat.

Sokodé's population is relatively young similar to other places in Togo. More than half of the roughly 100,000 inhabitants of the city are estimated to be below 20 years old (Direction Général de la Statistique et de la Comptabilité National 2011; UAID 2001).[5] Pupils are in school, while mothers and girls sell food

---

[5] Though statistics from the region are notoriously unreliable, a fairly reliable estimate was made by UAID in 1997 (2000) in which Sokodé's population was estimated to be 76,000. In 2000, the town hall made a projection of 144,000 inhabitants for the year 2010, based on a yearly growth rate of 3 percent between 1998 and 2000 and 4.8 percent between 2000 and 2005 (UAID

under some trees towards the edges of the school terrain. The soccer fields next to these schools often serve as training grounds for the multitude of neighbourhood soccer teams. Large trees that provide a lot of shade draw people to sit together beneath them and have a chat, though neighbours sometimes complain that the people gathering there talk too loudly. Moreover, people are careful not to evoke the wrath of the spirits who live in the trees. Besides the trees, all the places mentioned above are embedded in social and spiritual frameworks, with general and specific sets of rules. The public spaces in Sokodé exist by the grace of the proprietors or custodians of the land, human and non-human.

The multi-centred city of Sokodé

Sokodé can be seen as being part of the remotely global area that Piot (1999) described, where people hid from the slave raids that characterised the uncertain times between the sixteenth and eighteenth century. Present-day Sokodé began as a trading post along the kola route in the sixteenth century, as several groups of traders settled in the area. The Germans, who 'pacified' the area during military expeditions around 1890, after they had signed treaties with several coastal rulers and founded Southern Togoland in the 1840s, built their administrative quarter on a hilltop adjacent to Didawré in 1898 (Barbier & Klein 1995: 12). The French settled in after the First World War, and till today, the administrative function of the quarter is retained, including the prefecture.

In present day Sokodé, the historical traces of the agglomeration of several villages can still be discerned. These villages were merged together, partly because of the expansion of the town, and partly because of their own transmigration to town, which is why Barbier and Klein (1995) call Sokodé the 'multi-centric' city. The central quarter of Didawré is predominated by the Kotokoli, and the descendants of the villagers who have settled towards the exits of the city, still live around these places – most Bassari are at Akamadê on the road to Bassar and most Tchamba reside in Kulundé and Komah, on the road to Tchamba (Barbier & Klein 1995: 81). People meet each other during the Friday prayer at the grand mosque or in church on Sundays. The presence of Islam is unmissable in Sokodé, with several hundreds of mosques in the city, many of them constructed with the support of Middle Eastern countries (Tata 2006: 132). Togo's main

---

2001). The government's official projection of the number of inhabitants for 2016 was 103,300, which was 3,200 persons less than Kara, the second largest city after Lomé.

imam also resides in Sokodé, where over two thirds of the population, mostly Kotokoli, are Muslim.

The Kotokoli or Tem, now the major ethnic group in the region, find their roots in the groups of traders that moved from present-day Mali, Niger and Burkina Faso such as Mandinka and Hausa, and Gurma chiefdoms (Barbier & Klein 1995; Froelich, Felixandre & Cornevin 1963; Keita 1984). Kabye are the second major ethnic group in town and are distinct from the Kotokoli and need to be considered separate instead of being grouped together, as most demographic sources do (Froelich et al. 1963). Kabye and Losso groups from the region around Kara have arrived towards the end of the nineteenth century, first as forced labourers for the German colonial administration, and later as migrants in search of better pastures (Piot 1999: 40 – 43). Some groups of sedentary Fulani live in hamlets at a small distance from other villages. Besides these groups, there are larger groups of Tchamba and Bassari in Sokodé, who are both from the region. Smaller groups that reside in Sokodé are Adja, Ewé, Ana and Ifê, who are from Southern regions, and other Northern groups, like Nawda, Lamba and Moba (Barbier & Klein 1995).

In the city centre, modern materials have largely replaced the traditional adobe houses that can be found towards the periphery. Quarters like Zongo and Didawré in the centre of the city have a high population density, and further away from the centre, the houses are more scattered. Like most cities, Sokodé expands in an anarchic way (Barbier & Klein 1995). The land was originally in the hands of the chiefdoms and then became a commercial asset in recent decades, and most of the land has been privately sold. This contributes to the difficulties faced by the local administration to construct public services, such as schools and public toilets. There are also land conflicts, which can be related to the enmeshment of customary and 'modern' land rights, but also to arguments of autochthony like in other parts of the sub-region (see Geschiere & Nyamnjoh 2000). For example, there have been continuous struggles over the ownership of some parcels of land in the city centre of Sokodé, or 'Didawré', as the neighbourhood and sometimes the entire city is referred to. This case has also been mentioned by Barbier and Klein (1995: 25). While one family asserts that their ancestors were the first settlers, the other family bases their claim on an ancient German land registration document. Till date, the dispute has not been settled.

The compound of the spiritual chief is situated in Didawré, while the 'royal courtyards' of the two most important customary chiefs in Sokodé are situated in Kpangalam in the northern part of Sokodé and in Komah, south of the city centre. Komah is also the quarter where I was based during my fieldwork, as described in paragraph 1.4, and therefore, geographically it is an important part of the research field.

The field: Connected presence

The conceptual contours of the research terrain can be mapped in the complex influence of the mobile phone on locality; in its promise of constant accessibility, and in the connected presence that is being 'called upon' by the mobile phone. As has been described by many, the boundaries between 'home' and 'away' have become increasingly blurred through new ICT (Geser 2004; Gergen 2002; Katz 2006; Pelckmans 2009). The experience of physical distance has altered, and social media and mobile phones have heightened this blurriness further.

'The field' is a highly problematic term, as it presupposes a space, occupied by relatively fixed elements, in which the researcher can move in and out. It does not do justice to the dynamic character of societies and individuals in societies such as the Togolese, nor does it reflect the ambiguous position of the researcher. In his description of the physical environment of children, LeVine (2003) does not describe the field as a geographic space – he describes it in terms of the space between the mother and the child, and 'familiar items' such as the child's bed. The relationship between mother and child and the field of tension between distance and closeness are constituents of the field, much more than the geographic location in which this relationship unfolds.

Following this conceptualisation, where and when can this field of mobile media be located, if at all? In one perspective, the field is where my informants want it to be, a place between their hopes and dreams. In another perspective, the geographic location and the given context are realities that greatly influence people's lives and lived expectations and are also part of the field. The study of Miller *et al.* (2016) about social media is relevant in this regard as social media in the Togolese context is almost entirely accessed through mobile phones. They argue that it no longer makes sense to study social media as a distinct field, but rather as "another place in which people live, alongside their office life, home life and community life" (Miller *et al.* 2016: 7). Nevertheless, this does not mean that locality has lost its importance. On the contrary, the mobile phone is paradoxically a means of localizing.

Mobile phones arguably contribute to a 'sense of place'. De Lange (2010: 35) argues that the question 'how are you' has been largely replaced by 'where are you'. De Lange's 'sense of place' and its connection to the concept of 'home' has shifted over time, as evidenced by the body of literature on belonging (Bouman 2003; van Dijk *et al.* 2007; Fortier 2000; Probyn 1996). For diaspora communities, the mobile phone has greatly contributed to securing and maintaining a sense of 'home' because they can stay in touch with their beloved ones abroad daily (Nyamnjoh 2014; Paragas 2005; Tazanu 2012).

Like Licoppe's 'connected presence' (2004), de Lange (2010: 138) states that the mobile phone helps to create 'co-presence': an imagined sense of nearness with others. By having the mobile phone at arm's length – placed on a table or carried in one's bag or on the body, familiar people are 'always in the pocket' (De Gournay 2002: 201–204 and Fox 2006: 13 cited by de Lange 2010: 138). Drawing from Berger and Luckman (1966 cited by Licoppe 2004: 138), Licoppe states: "Eventually, the relationship assumes the metaphoric form of a 'continuous conversation', consisting of a multitude of interactions, united in time through the construction of shared expectations and routines, and of a common world". The mobile phone is especially interesting to study because this 'connected presence' has become much more pronounced. Of course, people have always been connected to their loved ones, even if this connection was not physical. The 'novelty' of the mobile phone is that it emphasises the connectedness of the mind to the detriment of the body. But there are limitations to this medium of communication that is especially interesting as a subject of study.

The constant communication flow with people who are not physically present has brought about significant change; not only in people's lives but particularly in the way ethnographic fieldwork is done, demonstrated among others by Pelckmans (2009). Pelckmans' rich description of the pervasive influence of the mobile phone in anthropological research offers a variety of challenges. In the present discussion of 'the field', the most relevant challenge faced is the increased blurring of boundaries between 'home' and 'away', if these were ever separate 'spaces' at all. Even before the rapid spread of the mobile phone, many anthropologists had 'more or less continuous' contact with their key informants through letters, telephone or E-mail (Hannerz 1998: 249).

Nonetheless, even when I was not physically present, there have been times in which my daily contact with people in Sokodé was immediate and detailed. For example, I was asked to justify who else gave me information about a road accident in Sokodé that happened moments before I knew of it. The 'absence presence' coined by Gergen (2002) was possibly most pervasive when I was physically away from Sokodé, scrolling through WhatsApp messages and reacting to them. In this context, the idea of multi-sited fieldwork (Hannerz 2003) has an increasingly complex connotation; it is probably more appropriate to talk of more and less intense periods of data collection, regardless of the locality of the anthropologist. However, this does not mean that locality has lost its importance. One evening in 2015, Dao and I went to a hotel to make use of their WiFi in order to check our WhatsApp messages. Hundreds of messages filled my phone and mind, and the meaning of these messages was transformed to fit into a specific context, bound by time, space and sociality: the exchange between Dao and me, sitting on our plastic chairs in a hotel in Sokodé.

The media landscape in Sokodé

It is noteworthy that in Sokodé, people have gone "from no phone to cell phone" (Orlove 2005: 699). In such a context, a mobile phone is not a better communication tool, but rather 'a tool that makes telecommunication possible often for the very first time, opening up entirely new spaces and possibilities' (Archambault 2009). Moreover, the society's strong roots in orality have a big impact on written and visual forms of communication. When describing the media and telecommunications landscape, this reality has to be taken into account.

Before the widespread availability of the mobile phone, when the need arose to communicate an urgent message, a letter had to be written, posted at the post office and people had to wait for days or weeks until they had a response. The other option was to travel to the village, or send someone there, to bring back news. For most families in Sokodé, the mobile phone as technological novelty does not fit in to an evolutionary pattern from fixed phone to mobile phone, from letter to telegram and fax to e-mail, with a variety of other media available like newspapers, radio and television.

Even considering the existence of 'traditional' media, they are rarely accessible beyond Lomé; there are hardly any newspapers to be found, though radio stations are popular. Sokodé has six official local radio stations, of which two are Christian. Radio Tchaoudjo is the most established radio station, and is popular with the older population. Radio Central and Méridien have a younger public, whereas the two Christian channels Radio Thérèse and Radio Albarka are popular among the Christian population for the songs and sermons. Radio Thérèse streams direct broadcasts from the Vatican while Radio Venus has a firm base in the eastern part of the city, being a neighbourhood association. The non-confessional radio stations get some state support, but the taxes they pay are higher than the support they receive. As several local radio producers lament, it is difficult for them to broadcast the realities. They do not have the means to employ journalists in different parts of the country, and they often receive information about events after they have already taken place. This is why they sometimes choose to use the format of a debate or discussion about a newsworthy event that has taken place – it is the only 'newsworthy' avenue that remains available to them when the information is outdated.

Radio producers, journalists and others whom we interviewed over the course of the years, have explained that they cannot be too critical in their broadcasting. If they are openly critical regarding politically sensitive issues, their radio station would be shut down under the pretext of non-payment of certain financial dues. Consequently, press freedom is considered problematic in Togo (see Freedom House 2016; Reporters without Borders 2016). Most journalists and broadcasters practice some form of self-censorship, limiting their political statements out of fear of being shut down, prosecuted, incarcerated or facing even worse consequences. "We do not do politics" is an often-heard phrase in Togo, not only among broadcasters but practically among all sections in society.

The national television channel mainly broadcasts information on the activities of the head of state and other highly placed government officials attending ceremonies or opening new promising projects. For people who have not experienced their living circumstances improve over the past decades, the narrative about the advancement of the country is a lie. In the words of one of the broadcasters: "Only the death announcements are true" (9 June 2016). Though the inauguration of the new national airport in April 2016 was all over the news, it is very difficult to find objective information about events such as the eruption of violence in Mango that took place in the same month, in which several people were killed. In fact, another broadcaster assured me that Beninese news coverage on this subject was more accurate than Togolese. This is one of the reasons that people prefer to watch France24, TV5 Monde or RFI, where news is believed to be more trustworthy. The French bias – for instance, abundant information about the French presidential elections – is taken for granted, with some people in Sokodé making cynical remarks like "We are still following the motherland", especially in relation to the lack of vision of Togolese leaders.

Few people in Sokodé trust that public information about national or local events is trustworthy when it is transmitted to them via official state channels such as television and newspapers. Considering the meagre availability of independent information, a low literacy rate, and a general 'tiredness' of decades of Gnassignbé rule, it is not surprising that many people do not actively seek out news to stay informed.

This book covers the period in which the mobile phone became widespread in the provincial opposition town of Sokodé. Rapid technological changes in the field of communication are continuously taking place, and the introduction of the mobile phone is one of the major changes. Between 2005 and 2010, people in Sokodé gradually started to own their first mobile phones; among which Nokia handsets with strong batteries were popular. At the start of the fieldwork period in 2015, the common ways of communicating using the phone were phone calls, beeping[6] and sending SMS messages. Android devices and internet connections were rare. However, during 2016, most of my contacts obtained a smartphone, and by 2017, WhatsApp had become the most popular medium of communicating over the mobile phone. WhatsApp is a mobile based messenger service,

---

[6] Beeping indicates missed calls to convey specific information.

and is conceived of as social media platform in this book, as it fits common definitions such as the one cited in *The SAGE Handbook of Social Media Research Methods:*

> Social media are web-based services that allow individuals, communities, and organisations to collaborate, connect, interact, and build community by enabling them to create, co-create, modify, share and engage with user-generated content that is easily accessible. (McCay-Peet & Quan-Haase 2017: 17)

WhatsApp has become essential in everyday communication for the people in Togo, even though social media platforms like Facebook are also used. So will other technological applications and changes also be appropriated and play their role in society.

Messages are sent and received instantly through social media, and people actively use these platforms to stay informed about current affairs. At the same time, they are aware that the trustworthiness of some of the messages can also be unreliable. For instance, when photos circulated of a teachers' strike in 2016, one of the members of a large, local development WhatsApp group cautioned members of the group to verify the source of the photos, suggesting that they were taken in a different city and not in Sokodé. Along with the trustworthiness of information shared via traditional media, the trustworthiness of information on social media is also a matter of concern. This is one of the reasons why a solid social network is so important in Sokodé in people's access to information; one can always double check information with well-informed contacts. The last paragraph of this chapter zooms in on the telecommunication business in Sokodé, from small vendors of airtime to state control of the market.

2.5 Making a living in the telecommunication business

Sweet Mama's business: From hairdressing and phone cabin to ice and airtime

The life story of Sweet Mama is in a way indicative of the everyday struggle of residents to make a living in the Togolese environment, though she might be considered more successful compared to others in this regard. At the same time, her story reflects the developments in the telecommunication business.[7]

---

7 Most of what is written here is derived from the only official interview I conducted with her on

Sweet Mama was born Isabel on 22 February, 1968, on a Thursday. She grew up with three siblings in a city in the region of Kara, where she went to school at 7 years old. When she was in CE1, at 9 years old, she lost her father, and she continued her education elsewhere. About her childhood, she remarks that her mother suffered bitterly. She came back to her hometown in 1990 and moved to Sokodé in 1991. She lived in Kara from 1992 to 1994 and in Lomé from 1994 to 1997, where she trained in hairdressing. She came back to Sokodé in 1998, where she opened her hair salon, and proceeded to obtain four official diplomas between 2001 and 2007. In these years, she was an active member on the board of the local hairdresser association, and she had countless apprentices. Some years later however, she quit the profession. She says that it was no longer profitable; instead of receiving 1,000 CFA for a treatment, prices dropped to 500, whereas the price of the shampoo went from 500 to 1,500. Besides, the price for the hair ointment Barka that she used went up from 2,500 CFA to 5,000 or 6,000. She concludes: "So hairdressing fell down. But my children are everywhere. They opened at least ten salons; in Lomé, Camboli, even the hairdresser in front of the house is an apprentice of mine" (Interview with Sweet Mama, 2 August 2016).[8]

After she closed her hair salon, she transformed the garage into a shop. She first sold balm and soap, but the balm changed colour after a while. This did not necessarily mean that it was spoiled, but people did not buy it anymore, and she lost a large sum of money. Following this setback, she slowly turned her shop to a small alimentation store. In 2016, she considered buying a car and turning the shop into garage once more, because "nothing works anymore". However, she had also purchased a second-hand fridge the same year, and in 2018, her ice business seemed to be working, alongside sales of her homemade juice, wine bottles and whiskey sachets.

In order to 'spread the risk' by undertaking diverse income generating activities, she was also active in the telecommunication business. When she arrived in Komah in 1998, their house was one of the few houses in the neighbourhood

---

her veranda on 2 August 2016, supplemented with observations and conversations over the course of the fieldwork, a large portion of it during my stays with her in 2017, 2018 and 2019.
8 When I asked Sweet Mama to tell me about her life, we were in a relatively official setting compared to the spaces we usually interacted in: I had come to her house with my notebook and it was different from our usual 'hanging around'. Whenever we hung around, she hardly talked about her married life or her children, but on sharing her life history, their absence was even more evident. Though I could have added details about certain dramatic life events here, I decided to respect her silence, as these incidents are simply 'none of my business'. I return to this encounter in chapter three.

with a fixed phone, and she soon decided to have a second fixed phone and open a phone booth alongside her hair salon. In the same interview, she says: "The pulsation was at 100 CFA, the benefit was more than the cellular phone! The consummation at the level of the agency was 100 CFA and we would get 50 CFA. So for them it would be 30,000 and for us 30,000. Togotelecom was really interesting – I had recuperated the money for the cabin within five months. So people called for 80,000 and I had to pay 36,000 to the agency."

People used her service not just for outgoing phone calls, but also for incoming calls. She or one of her children would then walk to the house of the neighbour for whom the phone call was intended, to ask her to come to the booth in order to receive the call at a certain pre-determined time, or in some cases to convey a message. For such incoming calls, she gained another 50 CFA of the person who received the call.

For the owners of phone booths, the arrival of the mobile phone meant a decline in revenues. Sweet Mama purchased her first personal mobile phone in 2002, and in 2004 she started selling 'top-up' cards for Togocel, which became 'transfer' when Moov entered the market. She is now a sales point [*point de vente*, in short PDV] for both Togocel and Moov, the two mobile phone operators in the country. The revenues of a PDV are minimal. With every 10,000 CFA that is sold by the PDV, the PDV has a profit of 500 CFA. This is more than the profit for the agents, who sell much larger quantities. Sweet Mama sells at least 20,000 CFA per week during the school year, so she earns 1,000 CFA per week with this business, which can buy her some plantain, yam or oil.

During the holiday months, the business is down. There are many students between 18 and 25 years old who rent a room in town by themselves, without their families. During the months of July and August, they leave the city to spend time with their family, work in the fields or join a family member in Lomé, to earn some money to finance their upcoming school year. During these months, she calls her Togocel agent to transfer 10,000 CFA to her, and the airtime sometimes lasts more than a week. In our interview, she explained: "The pupils pay 200, 200, 200, you see it is nothing, but this is what makes the airtime finish quickly. The airtime I put there [on the phone] now, I have it ever since, because yesterday, Sunday, Tuesday, the airtime was still there." In her perception, the students are the real consumers of airtime, as they call, chat on WhatsApp, and send messages: "They call their parents in the South or in the Grand North at any moment" (Interview with Sweet Mama, 2 August 2016).

Risks and benefits of the airtime transfer business

Practically every shop, bar or restaurant has an airtime sales point or PDV, which means that one never has to cross more than 100 metres in the centre of a town in order to find airtime. Most people buy airtime with their regular PDV or points with whom they have an ongoing relationship, but if the urgency arises, they buy with any PDV.

For PDVs like Sweet Mama, the benefits might be low, but the start-up deposit is also relatively low. Generally, PDV's have both 'airtime transfer phones' and personal numbers for the two providers, similar like their customers. PDVs are most often individuals, though there are shops or bars where the phone can be given to a trusted person to temporarily run the transfer business. However, this is not without risk, because this person needs to be reliable, and needs to be skilled enough to limit erroneous transfers. Therefore, in practice, the 'business phone' is mostly in the hands of one person.

Some of the PDVs hand over their phone to the client to enter their phone number, before they enter the airtime and the hash and star keys that go with the transfer code as one of the ways to avoid mistakes. Others type the number in their phone and show it to the client to confirm that the right phone number is entered. If a mistake is made – a rare occurrence – and the airtime is accidentally sent to another number, it is considered the problem of the client and they must pay for the airtime anyway. But the client can refuse to pay, which can adversely affect relationships and income generation. In some cases, both the buyer and seller share the damages. For personal numbers, there is a specific code for transferring (a part of) one's own airtime to someone else's phone, so in case an amount gets lost, the buyer often calls the 'wrong' number to plead for the airtime to be sent back to their phone. However, in such cases the receivers usually refuse to do this and thank God for the unexpected present they received.

Regarding mobile money transfers, the amounts are transferred are much higher, as are the risks and this is illustrated with an unfortunate incident involving Rachida, Mohamed's wife, who is around 30 years old. In March 2017, in the last month of her pregnancy, she had to be hospitalised, and she asked a person of confidence to act as agent for her business. The person had made a mistake with one digit of a phone number in a mobile money transfer of 150,000 CFA, and the entire sum of money was lost. Like most sales points, she was not insured for any loss. In her case, the trade-off between possibly losing a large sum of money or losing her customers upon her hospitalisation did not work in her favour. However, as such emergencies are always unexpected, it is difficult to speak of a miscalculation, since nothing had been calculated here. Worse than the loss of money, she lost her baby after what was practically a full-term pregnancy and returned from the hospital empty-handed.

"Alhadi, yes, 10,000": Togocel and Moov sub-contracted agents and PDV's

In their initial years in the market, Togocel and Moov offered special promotions of a phone and SIM card, to entice people to start using mobile phones. Foster (2016) notes a similar development for the company Digicel that is active in 33 countries in Oceania, Caribbean and Central America. The company sells subsidised smartphones and uses a variety of tailor-made price plans for the world's poorest consumers. Foster quotes Mirani (2013 in Foster 2016: 7), stating that in the saturated telecommunication market, getting existing users to spend more money is one of the little ways left to expand their profits.

In September 2013, Moov launched Flooz, a mobile banking system, and Togocel followed with T-Money by mid-2016. Everyone with a Moov SIM card could subscribe to the system at a Moov agency, by bringing along their identity card and filling in a registration form. They then enter a special code, and they are subscribed to the system. People can send amounts between five and 300,000 CFA. The system also permits payment of salaries, but due to its novelty, this is not yet used on a large scale. A map on the website of Moov shows roughly between 50 and 70 agencies in smaller and larger Togolese cities, where people can withdraw their money. Togocel is believed to be less reliable than Moov. However, the payment of electricity and water bills through T-Money are expected to become a reality soon, and this comes at the expense of Moov. It is expected that these possibilities will be more widespread in the coming years.

Togocel is more powerful than Moov, but their business models are similar, and reflect those of telecommunication companies in the sub-region and worldwide. There is one official Togocel office in Sokodé that handles sales, assistance, information and advice, on the national highway that runs through town, in the neighbourhood Barrière, near to the city centre. Most customers come in to buy a SIM card or restore their number or all their contacts, after they have lost their SIM card. The office that is run by a sub-contractor of Togocel is in the heart of the city. This office employs a team of agents, who are responsible for the airtime transfers and collecting the money of their PDVs within one or two days after their request. In 2015 and 2016, I interacted a lot with one of the agents, Brice, who rented a room in the compound where I also stayed.

Like Brice, the agents are generally young men and women who traverse the city and surrounding areas on their motorbikes to collect money from their PDVs (see figure 4). They can be reached day and night by their PDVs whenever they run out of airtime to transfer to their customers. The usual amounts are most often 10,000 or 20,000 CFA. The agents need social skills to deal with their customers and to recuperate all the money in due time.

The motorbikes and helmets, featuring the green Togocel logo, are provided by Togocel through the sub-contractor. Whenever there is a problem with a motorbike however, the agents pay to repair it. Brice outlined possible scenarios when an agent does not have the money for repairs: they visit their clients by foot or use a motor-taxi, which they pay for, or they ask a colleague for a ride. Brice has his own helmet, because he says that the Togocel helmet is of low quality, just like the motorbikes themselves (see figure 4).

Figure 4: 'Togocel' and his motorbike.

On average, the agents earn a fixed salary of 40,000 CFA per month. Over and above that, for every 5,000 CFA they sell to their clients, they earn 25 CFA. In February 2015, Brice explained that he earned about 2,000 CFA daily over his salary, but as agents pay for their own gasoline, he spent about 1,100 CFA per day. At the time, he managed to save 300 to 500 CFA per day. However, he did not have access to his salary, as he had asked for an advance payment of several months, and got himself a loan with a six-month salary as collateral. He had used the money to support his father with his mother's hospital bills, and his younger siblings with their studies and rent in Lomé. In 2016, he had set up a shop dealing in second-hand clothes that he ran in the evenings, until the owners told him to find another place to rent.

Crucial to the work of a telecommunications agent is the ability to maintain smooth relationships with the PDVs, which is not always evident at the outset. When an agent is perceived to be unreliable, other agents are easily called upon to do his work, and 'steal' the market of their colleague. This unreliability can manifest in numerous ways. Perhaps the agent was not quick in sending new airtime, or did not collect the money at the right time or address the sales point correctly with the right form of address. In the environment of Sokodé, where mistrust reigns, a flaw is easily found, and relationships tend to change quickly. When this happens, some PDVs turn to another agent. The work of the agent of recuperating money requires the right mixture of patience, humility and boldness towards the client and their employer, who pressures agents to bring cash back to the agency in due time.

At times, Brice expressed his bitterness about the disparity between the corpulent Togocel managers who moved around the city in green, luxurious four-wheel-drives, and his own aching backbone that had to endure the countless bumps on the road, spending hours every day in the heat on his ramshackle motorbike, without health insurance or social security. However, he tried to maintain a calm facade in front of his superiors, as he knew that innumerable youth were eager to replace him in case his short term contract was not renewed.

State control of telecommunication companies Togocel and Moov

In a country that is run by an autocratic regime, it is not surprising that the people at the top of the economic hierarchy are in close collaboration with the ones in the highest echelons of the political hierarchy. In many cases, the two are intertwined to such an extent that they cannot be distinguished. In recent years, Togocel is considered the richest company in Togo, and Togocel sponsors major events in the country. The director of the company is reported to be a close relation of the current president. Togocel sponsored the ruling party's election campaign of 2015, and it is widely believed that it paid many bribes during this period. A human rights activist in Sokodé who gathered evidence on prohibited practices during the election campaign, mentioned as example the use of a Togocel four-wheel drive for the UNIR campaign in villages around Sokodé.

Togocel is a subsidiary of the national telephone and internet provider Togotelecom that is fully state-owned (Togosite.com 2015). Since 2009, Togotelecom provides fixed phone lines and offers a 'mobile fixed phone' with Illico. Though these telephones are mobile, in practice they are commonly used as if they are fixed lines, left at home, as mentioned earlier in this chapter. Togotelecom also provides the infrastructure on which the networks of the two mobile phone companies depend. Moov is the only independent company that has a foothold in the strictly regulated Togolese market.[9] Having the benefit of the protection by the state, Togocel has been slightly more popular than Moov since the beginning, though most of the population owns SIM cards from both operators.

One of the reasons for subscribing to both networks is the unreliability of the communication structure in Sokodé. The telecommunication network is especially unreliable in the rainy season, which is frustrating for people who want to reach others. In some cases, this means spending hours pressing the 'call' button and hoping that the quality of the connection remains good once the person is finally reached. This is especially stressful for people when there are emergencies and the networks are down. With regard to the unreliable internet connection, sending documents to international donors is one of the matters that several development workers mentioned as a stressful affair.

In the days that internet connections and Wi-Fi were rare, Dao and others sometimes saw no other option than to travel to Kara, 70 km north of Sokodé, to send an urgently needed report. Though the quality of the internet connection has improved a lot in the late 2010s, there is a lot to be desired. Airtime frequently disappears much quicker than people anticipated – especially Togocel's internet airtime can apparently 'vanish' altogether, which is one of the reasons why people say that "Togocel are thieves". The dissatisfaction of the end users with the telecommunication companies, especially with Togocel, seems to be a constant factor.

In 2014, word spread that the state was opening the market for a third operator, and rumours circulated about a bid by Orange. Apparently, the negotiations did not yield positive results, because five years later, Togocel and Moov were still the only two operators in the country. Though the government does not have a stake in Moov Togo to the same extent as it does in Togotelecom and Togocel, the government has a strong control over the sector.

From the beginning, Moov Togo endured several obstacles created by the government. Between August 2009 and January 2010, the government even

---

[9] Telecel Togo was introduced to the market in 1999 and later became Moov Togo, run by Atlantique Telecom. In 2005 Etisalat, the Emirates Telecommunications Company, acquired a 50 percent stake in Atlantique Telecom, increasing it to 82 percent in 2008. During a takeover of West-Africa's Moov agents, Maroc Telecom finally took over Moov Togo from Etisalat towards the end of 2015.

shut down the network, leaving around 400,000 to 600,000 owners of a Moov SIM card without recourse to a solution. About 2,000 people protested in Lomé, but the impasse was only broken in December 2009, when Moov signed a treaty with the government, with the provision that 30 percent of the investors would be local investors (Aghu 2009; Da Silva 2015). In 2014, the government fined Moov with 1.332 billion CFA, because of non-compliance with the agreement. It was noted that Maroc Telecom finally settled the issue after tedious negotiations with the government when taking Moov over in 2015 (Afreepress 2015).

The control of the state is not limited to the services of the telecommunication companies. During especially tense times such as national elections, political turbulence or social unrest, the phone networks can suddenly be disabled, as has been the case in the past, reported by The Guardian (Koutonin 2017). Disabling parts of the telecommunications network is also a strategy employed by the ruling regime to stay in power in several other countries, such as China, Egypt, Tunisia and Turkey (Howard, Argarwal & Hussain 2011). In Togo, this is also one of the myriad ways in which the current regime stays in power. Nonetheless, a national disruption of communication networks is clearly not a long-term solution; it can fan the flames of popular protests and is disruptive for a country's economy. For instance, the digital network shutdown in Egypt cost the country at least 90 million dollars (Howard, Argarwal & Hussain 2011: 12).

Though personal data protection is not a visible matter of concern in daily life in Sokodé, people take it for granted that the government has the power to wiretap their mobile communication (see Seli 2012 for a comparison with Chad). Some believe that all phone calls are recorded, and that this happens for their own safety; for instance, when a woman is raped, her assailant can be traced easily.[10] When I brought up the subject of identification that is required to register for a new SIM card, people explained this to me as a safety measure that works in their favour. These answers are readily offered compared to answers about politically sensitive issues, such as expressing one's fear and discontentment about the authorities wiretapping phone calls. People 'play it safe' by giving the socially desired answer, because there is too much at stake to lay their cards on the table. Nonetheless, there are times that the contestation against state control surfaces strongly in society, like during the turbulent second half of 2017. In this regard, Jef, one of the members of the local research team and anthropologist by formation, said:

---

[10] The pretext of protection of women is a strong, recurring theme, which returns in chapter five.

> Identification is a good thing to avoid crimes, theft, and the like, but it can also lead to espionage; they know everything you do, so the freedom of the individual is not respected. The services also do not really explain the users to what end this is done. (Interview with Jef, 1 July 2016)

Clearly, there is a lot of not-knowing, and people are obliged to base their ideas on the little information available. In this context of mistrust, people also do not have the slightest expectation of receiving correct information of others, because everyone knows that there is a lot at stake.

The all-encompassing power of the state becomes clear in the many links between the government and Togocel, and the obstructions that Moov faced as independent operator. The networks are not only down when there is abundant rainfall, but also during critical political events such as the street protests in late 2017. People do not believe that their communication through the mobile phone is 'safe' or 'private', as most of them grew up in an environment in which political leaders are capable of doing anything to remain in power.

2.6 Concluding remarks

This chapter illustrated the circumstances of young people in Sokodé, both those who were born in Sokodé and those who migrated there for their education, or so that they could save some money. Various aspects of a society in duress, including the political, economic and social environment were described. The passive despair of some of the people who feature in this chapter, indicate that duress has become internalised. From an emic perspective, some people may no longer realise that they live in a constrained society that limits their agency.

In this environment, people take great care to conceal their personal intentions, out of fear of the bad intensions of other people, including non-human influences. A level of mistrust prevails in all relations. In times of increased political tension, ethnic and religious differences can become more pronounced. However, there are also social and political impulses to focus on similarities, like the case of the opposition party PNP that managed to mobilise thousands of people to protest the current regime in August 2017. For the moment, the Gnassingbé regime manages to stay in place, even though people are exhausted after fifty years of their rule, backed by the same clique of army generals, and a multitude of strategies to silence political opposition.

In Togo and Sokodé specifically, society seems to offer few opportunities for common people to further themselves and their communities. In this environment of economic deprivation and political repression, people's interdependency is imbued with mistrust. This prevailing scenario is not only reflected in social and political life, but also in the possibilities and forms of communication. It is evident that the political climate has a determining role in the communication landscape in this country.

However, the introduction of a new technology like the mobile phone gives the habitus a 'blow', as people become more aware of their misery. In some countries this triggers protests, in other countries people react by turning inwards or fleeing, whether this means physically drifting to another country, or mentally drifting away. To borrow Piot's (2010) term, 'exit strategies' are limited in Togo, and resignation and sedation are more common coping strategies than revolt and outright violence. This is the foundation for the analysis of the consequences of the introduction of the mobile phone in the social fabric.

3 Private and public information and communication

3.1 Introduction

On one of the simmering evenings in early 2018, in which the rain refused to fall, Sweet Mama asks me to join her on the rooftop to "catch some wind". She walks to and fro, lighting her steps with her phone's torch. She points at the dimly lit streets and remembers how the streets were all empty in the days following the arrest of Imam Hassan in October 2017. Apart from the military patrols, not the slightest sound could be heard during those days, as she and her son stayed inside the house for three consecutive days. She then points her torch at the building opposite her house, which used to be the office of a development organisation when we first met, seven years ago.

She continues speaking and begins telling me about a woman who often came to the office during lunchtime to spend time with her lover. One day, after the woman had parked her motorbike and greeted her, a man came and tried to take the bike. Sweet Mama intervened by asking him what he was trying to do. He reacted by making a scene: he had found out that his wife had a lover, and as he had paid for this motorbike, he was claiming it back. Firmly, she told the man to take his hands off the bike, as she did not know who he was. Sweet Mama made it clear to him that her only interaction had been with the woman, whose greetings Sweet Mama had interpreted as a sign of confidence. For Sweet Mama, this implied that she would keep an eye on the bike. Sweet Mama told the man that this was all that she knew, and the rest of the story was none of her concern. The man saw no other option than to back off. She stops talking. We stare into the night for a while, and then she says she wants to go to bed, as it is late.

I knew Sweet Mama well enough to know that she did not share this story with me just for the sake of telling me a story. There were evenings when I returned home almost at midnight, sharing a drink with friends in a bar in town, which was not considered appropriate behaviour for a married woman. I interpreted her story as a subtle way of reassuring me that my whereabouts were none of her business. However, both of us never attempted to clarify whether I had understood her correctly. This chapter deals with this exact field: the communicative space between interpretation and the unspoken.

This chapter disentangles some of the complexities related to access to information in Sokodé. The restrictions of the structural aspects notwithstanding, communication and information exchange are constant factors in human relations, which raises the question of how the ways in which people get access to information, and the role of mobile phone in this. The meaning of the term information is clarified and a perspective offered regarding everything that is exchanged, verbally or non-verbally, intentionally or unwittingly. In this chapter, this is linked to intimacy and privacy, hidden from the public sight, because social change emerges from individuals as much as it does from the structures and networks in which they interact and are a part of.

3.2 The intimacy of information flows

Information technologies and social organisation

The assumption that new ICTs automatically make for better informed citizens, who then act based on this information and claim their rights, is rather misplaced in a context like Sokodé. Common conceptualisations of information as 'knowledge communicated' do not completely capture information flows in Sokodé. The differentiation between information and knowledge is much more complicated than I can explore here, but it is worth citing Dretske (1981: 91–92), who argues that "knowledge is information-produced belief". Going beyond the perspective of information as knowledge communicated, I employ a system-relative approach, in which information can be framed as "the observer's construction or a mental difference that makes and/or finds a difference in the external world" (Maturana and Varela 1980; von Foerster 1980, 1984 in Capurro and Hjørland 2003: 374). This is close to Bateson's famous definition of information as a 'difference that makes a difference' (1972: 459).

In this systemic approach, information is a relational concept that includes the source, the signal, the release mechanism and the reaction (Karpatschof 2000: 131–132). According to Capurro and Hjørland (2003: 376), Karpatschof "forces us to shift the perspective from information as an object to the subjective mechanisms that account for discrimination, interpretation, or selection". This can also be related to Gleick's (2011) description of the technique of information flow, in which he demonstrates that information is multi-interpretable. The moment that information is interpreted, people start to act according to their interpretation. In this regard, it can be linked to the interpretative or evaluative aspect of agency, or the angle of 'evaluation' in the Chordal Triad of Agency by Emirbayer and Mische (1998).

Selection can be seen as main element in the communication process. In his thinking about information and communication, Luhmann (1987) defined communication as the unity of meaning offer, information, and understanding. In this theory, there is no transmission of information between the sender and the receiver; there is some 'thing' the sender loses upon sending it, making in fact a suggestion for selection. According to Luhmann (1987: 193–194), information is not identical to the sender and receiver, but it is constituted through the communication process. Information is often multi-interpretable, and the mobile phone has arguably added several layers to this multi-interpretative process of making sense of reality that can be called communication. As people can no longer rely on all their senses when they are in the act of communicating through their mobile phone, the possibilities of misunderstanding or 'misinformation' increase.

Following Brown and Duguid (2000: 107) who attempt to unveil the 'myth of information', information technologies by themselves do not shape social organization. They argue that it is not shared information, but shared interpretation that binds people together, which feeds back into the systemic approach to information and the communication process as understood by Luhmann. This 'shared interpretation' reveals many features of human sociality, a concept embraced by anthropologists (Long and Moore 2013; Amit 2015). I follow Long and Moore (2013: 2) who define sociality as "a dynamic and interactive relational matrix through which human beings come to know the world they live in and to find their purpose and meaning within it".

This also means that the mental and emotional processes that are involved in the transfer and interpretation of information in Sokodé are intertwined in a complex manner with larger societal structures and processes, in which mistrust and trustworthiness play a central role. As discussed in the introduction, in Sokodé, mistrust serves as a guiding principle of social organisation (Carey 2017). In such contexts, the trustworthiness of information becomes a point of contention, especially if it involves 'public information', though whether any information in Sokodé can be classified as public information remains a question. The value attached to information in Sokodé is relative and depends on the relationship between sender and receiver.

Access to 'official' information does not guarantee transmission

When it comes to information that is considered to be more public than private, government decisions and decrees are often disseminated to the customary chiefs and the highest levels of local authorities, the prefect and the mayor. Decrees and official information designed by the municipality or prefecture are shared with the local radio stations, customary chiefs and religious leaders. After the religious part of the programme of the weekly prayer is finished, the mosques, cathedral and other churches usually dedicate some time to public announcements. The position of actors such as customary chiefs and *Comités de Développement de Quartier* (CDQ) [neighbourhood development committees] that have been set up in recent years, with an intermediary role with regard to certain types of 'civic' information flows are further examined in chapter six.

Firstly, with a focus on written information, there is the risk of omitting the importance of orality in society (Hahn & Kibora 2008). Secondly, the content of information that is publicly accessible fluctuates, because of instability and unpredictability. For instance, the time for a bus ride from Sokodé to Lomé fluctuates because road construction companies work on the national highway and because buses can break down at any time. The prices of products on the market change not only per season but also depend on the wealth of the buyer: the wealthier the buyer, the more she will be charged. Furthermore, news about strikes and protests, such as the teachers' and pupils' strikes in 2015 and 2016, and the general protests in 2017, can be manipulated by political actors, or anyone with a mobile phone who is member of many WhatsApp groups.

To illustrate my arguments about access to official information, the municipality's budget is considered, which was posted on the announcement board of the municipality building at Sokodé, of which I took pictures in April 2017 (see figure 5). Setting aside the receiving end of information, the trustworthiness of the sender and the message is the third, focal point in this assessment of access to 'more public' information, whether written or not. In the current analysis, it is not as important to know whether this trustworthiness is perceived or factual, since this cannot even be disentangled in an environment dominated by mistrust. Trustworthiness of information is a matter of concern because persons in lower and higher positions alike do not necessarily react to the content of questions. Instead, as noted before, their answers depend to an extent on their assessment of the intentions of the person posing the question, along with their own interests.

Even though this is a general observation about the communication process, which faces constant mediation (Peterson 2008), particular mechanisms are exposed in the context of Sokodé. This partly relates to the lack of transparency and accountability, with significant effects on the management of institutions, companies, associations and groups, from the national to the local level. The implementation of programmes or execution of public works are more often than not delayed, faced by a lack of materials or means in an environment that leaves ample room for mismanagement and the disappearance of funds. When viewed together, these factors make it difficult to determine what would be considered public information according to different sections of society in Sokodé, that have differing levels of access to information. Moreover, the point that the value attached to a message depends on its perceived trustworthiness, calls

Figure 5: Participatory budget of the municipality of Sokodé.

into life a notion of information that implies an inherent instability, a concept I revisit in the conclusion.

Another example is the municipality's budget which does not take into account the major role of gatekeepers or intermediaries. It serves here as an example to cast doubt on the claim that any person entering the town hall, regardless of their position, would be able to obtain the same information, following the same process. This is also the case when it concerns persons entering private institutions such as banks or mobile phone operators. If someone visibly does not 'belong' in such a place, by not complying with the unwritten rules of being properly dressed and pretending as if one understands the basics, the individual will only be given some extent of information.

If someone has a higher social position in society or personal relations with people within an institution, the person will be treated with privilege. For instance, I could easily obtain the Community Development Plan (PDC) for 2015–2019 (Mairie de Sokodé 2014) from a municipal officer, who copied it on my USB-stick during our interviewed in his office in March 2015. However, in this specific situation, my position cannot be ignored. In this case, I was treated as representative of the international development consortium to whom the officer swiftly presented an official version of the project's proceedings. The stakes are high: the municipality is financially dependent on development projects. To add one more layer, some male interlocutors were driven by more intimate interests and hopes when they readily provided me with parts of the information I asked for.

A final set of important questions are connected to the 'receiving end' of this public or official information, for example, the municipality's budget. To be able to access this information, the first requirement is that people are aware of and care about its existence, in the frame of its relative importance vis-à-vis other information and vis-à-vis their own needs and expectations. Secondly, interested people need to know how to locate it, find the means to make the physical displacement and then access it while dealing with possible gatekeepers. Irrespective of the problem of trustworthiness, it requires the right knowledge and capacity to interpret and make sense of the information.

This last point relates to a particular 'noise on the line', which Serres ([1980] 1982: 79) regards as necessary part of the relation that is involved in the communication process: people interpreting information to suit their own interest, which can alter the original intent of the information. To illustrate this, the example of Mamah will be considered, a repair man and broadcaster, who mainly listens to the radio in a transactional manner, hoping to get information about NGO or governmental projects or workshops which he can participate in to benefit from investments or per diems.

In February 2015, some days after we both had attended a two day workshop organised by a development project, I visited him in his shop along a noisy part of the national highway running through town. I asked him for his opinion about the workshop. He was talkative, but the engines of the passing trucks, the heat, and the moving baby inside my belly prevented me from understanding his words. When I finally managed to make sense of his answer, I was intrigued: it was centred on the per diems (for an overview, see Samb, Essombe & Ridde 2020). My own interpretation of those days was entirely different from his interpretation, drawing my attention to the obvious fact that the process of information transfer between sender and receiver is highly complex.

The development project is not of interest at this stage; it is important here to underline that access to information is akin to an empty shell when it is not coupled with a kind of 'translation' or 'awareness raising' about that piece of information – assuming that the sender is keen on conveying a particular message. After enquiring, I noted that the same is true for public announcements after religious gatherings: the majority of the members in the assembly do not pay much attention, but rather fiddle with their clothes, looking around for acquaintances to speak to. This gives credence to the notion that access to information does not guarantee its transmission, one of the assertions on which the key argument in this book is based.

Navigating information territories and hierarchies: Rights and responsibilities

In a context in which many issues remain unclear, one has to navigate prudently to get closer towards one's aims. Having the right kind of information, for instance about the availability of a market stall or a small shop, is of utmost importance. Social hierarchies are rather strict; the highest echelons of society, like the chiefs and local elites, are consulted and receive information, but this does not automatically trickle down to 'the population'. As evident from the example above, there is no such thing as 'public' information, indicating accurate information about certain processes, projects or institutions that can be easily accessed by the population.

It is almost without exception that people have a mediator, an uncle, older brother or other person who is higher up the hierarchy, who knows which persons to approach to get information, employment, support or other benefits. 'Not having someone' is really considered to be unfortunate. There seem to be fewer restrictions in information sharing between people on a similar level; peers, friends, family members, people from the same clan or ethnic group. In chapter four, I show that calling behaviour correlates with this; people mainly call their closest contacts. However, each level has its own internal hierarchical logic. Within families, different members are responsible for different domains, though 'traditional' structures and roles have been – and will always be – subject to change. For instance, the young father in the household who runs the local affairs of his uncle in Europe knows about the processes at the bank, the grandmother keeps herself updated about the well-being of her children and grandchildren and gathers the family members in case of problems. Only certain designated people in the family deal with administrative matters, such as acquiring a birth certificate at the level of the municipality.

In the decision-making and accountability structures within the household and in society in general, seniority and gender play a large role. Generally, the oldest people in the household are key when it concerns information that is considered important. One of the particularities of most ethnic groups in Sokodé is that a maternal uncle often plays a larger role in a person's life than their father. The example of Dao and several members of his family, all of whom I have known since 2010, clarifies the subtle ways in which family information is hidden and disclosed.

Dao was raised by his grandmother, and I met the two of them in 2010 through one of Dao's maternal uncles, who had greatly facilitated my research project at the time. One morning in July 2016, when I called this uncle to inquire about his health, he told me that his mother was ill and that he had taken her to the hospital. Later that day, I sent a message to Dao to wish him strength with his grandmother. Though Dao always reacted to my messages, he did not react to this one. When we met some days later, he subtly made me understand that he had not received the information before I had sent him that message. Now that Dao had talked with his grandmother on the phone, he gave me the opportunity to 'rightfully' speak about her illness with him and offer my compassion. Though it was never expressed outright, I interpreted his initial silence as a sign that I had overstepped in being the messenger of information about his grandmother's state of being.

Dao in return, when he fell sick, did not inform his uncle and grandmother. In fact, he only informed the person driving him to the hospital and back for his treatment. Dao's grandmother found out four or five days later, on her regular calling round to keep up with the state of her family's well-being. As Dao's maternal uncle visited his mother every other day, he got to know about his cousin's illness only a week later. When he saw me, he directly asked me about Dao's state, and he expressed his unhappiness with the fact that Dao had not let him know, as he could have offered help to his cousin, and he asked me the exact directions to Dao's house, who had moved there some months before.

This case illustrates some of the subtle ways of hiding and disclosing information at the family level. While Dao's uncle probably did not want to alarm Dao, Dao in turn also did not want to alarm his uncle. His uncle expressed his unhappiness about Dao's silence, because he wanted to support him. Possibly, this could have been the exact reason for Dao not to contact his uncle, since he already owed him a lot. Moreover, Dao's uncle's interest in 'teaming up' with me might have been keeping in mind the possible opportunities I could also offer his young nephew. No matter what the case is, the most important family updates come to the fore sooner or later, because of the regular contact with Dao's grandmother, who is in this case the *mater familias*. She plays a large role in keeping the family together, although this almost romantic ideal of the role of grandparents in a Sub-Saharan African context can be questioned. Hierarchy in family relations is not set in stone and is very context dependent.

When there are major events in the family, such as cases of life and death, ceremonies to be conducted, marriage or divorce and the (re)payment of dowry, the family gathers and discusses the strategy to follow. For example, a case will be considered in which a mobile phone had a large impact on the decisions in a family meeting, narrated by Stéphanie to me in June 2016. The meeting dealt with the problem of a daughter whose husband accused her of cheating, and then asked for a divorce. The woman denied the allegation, and the family went along with her side of the story, until the husband showed some of the text messages on her phone, which provided ample proof. Instead of pleading with the husband to take his daughter back, the father decided that she should be beaten. The outcome would have probably been different without the phone, similar to Archambault's informants' testimonies (2016). It again indicates the hierarchical structures that are followed in decision making processes. In the examples mentioned above, there are certain ambiguities of disclosing and revealing information that are apparent and these fit well in a framework that considers the private and public elements of information.

Information as private affair

It has become clear that information in Sokodé is embedded in a complexly encoded communication structure. To clarify, this chapter does not delineate different 'types' of information such as public, private or personal, as this would not do justice to the given context. Instead, the communication landscape is viewed as blurred and includes overlapping domains of information. Therefore, although I do employ terms such as 'personal' and 'private' information, there are no clear boundaries to the exact content of the types of information. The aim here is to shed light on the mechanisms of information sharing in the constrained context of Sokodé, and not on the content of information.

In Sokodé, sharing personal information and information about one's thoughts or emotions is often considered a private area. Information in Sokodé is not necessarily neutral, nor fixed. As shown above, the act of information sharing reveals something about people's intentions on a meta-level, where communication entails much more than spoken or written words. Real requests are often posed in an indirect way, and direct questions are generally not understood as being direct. For instance, asking only out of interest how a certain procedure works, or asking for details about a certain product, must be done with the greatest care, and the person addressed will often reply with the expectation that one wants to undergo the procedure or acquire the product.

As noted earlier in this chapter, the common expectation is that there is a hidden personal reason or need behind a question, which the receiver will try to uncover in order to make sense of their social relations. This 'reading between the lines' is important for social navigation; too much openness can even be outright dangerous in light of non-human powers and political sensitivities. Under the constrained conditions described earlier in this chapter, it makes sense to take care to reveal one's intentions only if the need arises.

As can be construed from the context in which 'the African does not want to see his brother advance', many people do their best either to avoid envy, or to protect themselves when they know others envy them for their success. The more information others have about one's weak spots, the easier one can be harmed. Furthermore, as also mentioned in section 2.3, having too much compassion and pity can also lead to difficulties. One of the interpretations of Sweet Mama's attitude, is that too much curiosity toward someone else's business can only lead people into trouble in one of two ways: being compelled to help or giving rise to feelings of jealousy. People take this into account when sharing information, they consider private. For instance, when people plan to travel, they do their best to conceal their exact travel dates. Only a handful of intimate relations will know of it. During travel, these contacts are usually in constant touch, and updated about the progress.

The same 'secrecy' is held regarding people's future projects, such as starting a small business or constructing a house. The reason for this is that revealing one's plans carelessly might bring misfortune, and the plans may never materialise. Firstly, announcing one's plans in public would be like defying God, who is considered as being the only one who knows what tomorrow will bring. Concealing one's intentions is based on the importance of maintaining goodwill of both human and non-human actors. It is linked to the fear of arousing the jealousy of neighbours, sorcerers or spirits. This is also the reason why people prefer to move their belongings after dark, so that others cannot see one's material possessions.

However, there would be no point in driving around in a BMW if no one is present to admire the car and the owner. In other words, people go to great lengths to show off their prosperity resulting in material and immaterial affairs – once the process to acquire or construct their material possession has been completed, or at least assured. Secrecy about this process is not an absolute goal, but more of an aspiration. This is because people in Sokodé live in such interconnected constellations that it is practically impossible to conceal their aspirations, but more importantly, people simply need others to be able to realise their goals. Besides sufficient resources, most personal projects can only be successfully executed when they are based on reliable information, access to the right persons and support of one's network.

Partially similar to the context that Vigh (2006) studied before he coined the term social navigation, the inhabitants of Sokodé navigate political, social and economic insecurity and instability that is part of the environment on a daily basis. The art of concealing and revealing information at the right moment can make or break relations. This is the explanatory frame of Sweet Mama's storytelling: she takes the chance that her message gets through and reassures me, while she manages to protect her inner world that is none of my business.

3.3 Phones in the public-private continuum

Degrees of privacy: Private-public continuum

The difference between public and private is increasingly blurred, and the difference could possibly only be theoretical. However, anticipating the further exploration of the civic in chapter six, Habermas' (1991) conception of civil society as 'bringing a private issue into the public' might be of use here. The private-public continuum that I discuss here, offers a framework to consider the disclosure and uncovering of information on multiple levels, in diverse situations and serves to refine the systemic approach of information described in section 3.2.

Every society has forms and levels of privacy, in which the game of disclosing and uncovering certain information about oneself to others is played. It is noteworthy that the more common theme of privacy and new media that deals with data protection on a more individual level, is not at stake here. What is at stake is privacy on a more systemic level, *in relation* to others. Here, privacy deals with the issues that people hide, about which they lie and what they disclose to others, whether mediated or face-to-face. It is about trust between people and trustworthiness of information, varying from one context to another.

What is considered private and what is public differs according to the social context and person. Both privacy and publicness are fluid to a certain extent and are constantly negotiated. The use of the concept of privacy by Nippert-Eng (2010) is useful in my consideration of privacy. She considers a continuum of privacy and publicness with the purely private end being "that which is completely inaccessible to others", and the purely public end "that which is completely accessible" (Ibid.: 4). This conceptual sliding scale serves as an analytic tool, but in practice it is impossible to pin down a certain act of disclosing information at a specific point in the continuum. Information is never purely private or purely public and includes elements of both 'ends'. Moreover, people have the intrinsic need to connect to others on an emotional level and sharing private information in one way or the other is the imperative to establish a connection. This theoretical scale should instead be imagined as a multi-layered, overlapping, dynamic and ever-changing patchwork of scales, as any relationship carries countless micro-moments of hiding and unveiling on differing levels.

Nippert-Eng (2010: 5) argues that people are engaged in a constant balancing act between disclosing and concealing, denying and granting access to others, in their need and desire for both privacy and publicness. Generally, concealment is more complicated than disclosure. One of the aspects ascribed to privacy is the extent of control on granting others access to information. By granting someone access to certain areas, one's inaccessibility in other areas is more easily accepted by the other, without jeopardizing the relationship. Some of these processes are unintentional, while in other cases when there is something to lose or to gain, accessibility is calculated.

The mobile phone as private matter in Sokodé

Obviously, notions of privacy and publicness cannot easily be applied from one context to another, and next I distinguish concepts embedded in this particular African context that are relevant to the mobile phone. The challenge in describing private and public matters in Sokodé is evident; firstly, what is private can never be entirely known by another person. Secondly, these matters are often taken for granted, which makes it difficult to focus on them and reveal them. Thirdly, and more importantly, the concept of privacy in Sokodé is based on an entirely different world view than my own, which makes it more difficult to grasp. It was often by transgressing boundaries, when either of the people involved made mistakes, followed by awkward social moments, when the contours of privacy surfaced.

Of course, there is not a single fixed notion of privacy in Sokodé. When discussing the matter with my interlocutors, they ranked family issues, one's personal financial situation and the mobile phone as being among what they consider most private. From this angle, it is somewhat contradictory that the materiality of the phone is so publicly displayed, often being one of the first things that people take out of their pockets and put on the table in front of them – something they would never do with their money. The privacy connected to the phone, then, is found within the device: one's contact list, messages, photos, music, call log, applications, credit and so on. Mobile phones are an especially contested private space, as they can potentially uncover people's most secret connections. Phones are also easily gifted, or lent out to someone whose phone has problems, but people take care to erase their personal information before they do so. In line of thinking with Nippert-Eng, this is an obvious way to control one's privacy: granting others access to some extent with the gift they give but denying them access to the information on their phone.

Answering my question about what they consider to be private, besides the mobile phone, the people with whom I interacted with in Sokodé commonly brought up family and financial matters. Family matters cover a vast area, ranging from the number of children, to the type of relationships with marital and romantic partners, health matters, ceremonies and mediation in strained relations. Concerning financial matters, though people keep the exact amount of their earnings to themselves, other people often find out if someone has gotten their hands on a sum of money, as is also noted by scholars working in the sub-region (Heitz Topka 2013; Marantz 2001). Even though it is a private matter, money is among the matters that can easily be claimed by relatives or friends who have an emergency. This motivates people to invest as soon as they have a certain sum of money. People's wish to invest their money in the manner that they want can be controlled or restricted by their closest family members, especially if it is earned by a young person.

Sharing phones: "No one can hold my phone"

Sharing one phone with several persons is another interesting aspect in the discussion about the privacy regarding mobile phones. In Sokodé, I did not encounter people who shared a phone, and when I asked about handing over one's phone to someone else to use, I often got the response that 'no one except for me can hold my phone'. The phone is often labelled as a private item, though it is a private item that changes owners once in a while.

Several authors have noted that mobile phones are shared within families, neighbourhoods or villages (de Bruijn, Nyamnjoh & Brinkman 2009; Hahn & Kibora 2008). In Sokodé, in the early years of mobile phone adoption, the first phones that were brought by the diaspora were given to 'brothers' but often served to get in touch with their mothers, who did not (yet) have phones. A young person in the family, most often male, would keep the phone and manage it for their mother. Other family members would occasionally use the phone, but its main role was to serve as connection between the migrant and his mother who did not have the skills to use the device. In some families in Sokodé, this might still be the case, but since the mobile phone has become so ubiquitous, older people have also gotten their own phones, whether they can make use of all its functions or not.

In rural areas, mobile phones were from the start more often shared, as also noted in Uganda (Burell 2010) and Kenya (Komen 2015). This 'sharing' is not about its ownership, which used to be and still is in the hands of an individual. Relatives and neighbours sought to use the number and share it with their contacts in the city or elsewhere. Following this, whenever their contacts outside the village wanted to speak to them, they would call the number and ask for the person, and would negotiate with the phone owner when to call again if it was an inconvenient time. Though this has become less common in recent times because there are more phones available in urban and rural areas, it still persists. In the urban space of Sokodé, getting to know the number of one's neighbour for others to get in touch with a person has not been common from the beginning, as the space has always been relatively more fluid, and people are often on their own.

Nonetheless, the fact that people in the urban area of Sokodé relate to phones as private items in our conversations, does not prevent them from passing it on to a friend who needs to make a call. Jef's statement can be seen as illustrative:

> I rarely like to take the phone of someone else to communicate, because I think that the device is personal. But I can pass it to someone I know and who is in a situation in which he has no units and has an urgency. (Interview with Jef, 1 July 2016)

There are also other moments in which people pass on their phone to others. In an interview with Dao, which we also used to test the interview questions, he explained to me:

> Sometimes a friend has paid a subscription and then says: 'Hey do you want to call someone? I have some minutes left for free'. Sometimes we also put some money together and we come together on a Sunday. We pay for the subscription and call everyone. You chat, you laugh, until you're tired. (Interview with Dao, 17 February 2015)

In this case, Dao and his friends use one of their phones to pay a certain amount of airtime and take turns in calling with the phone. As discussed by several authors (Foster 2016; Hahn 2015), mobile phone companies are aware of the low budgets of their customers, and they market their promotions accordingly. A phone can be shared for a short while, but in a case such as this, the person who is using the phone will be constantly watched, so that it will be difficult to browse through the messages or contact list of the friend's phone. The phone is and remains a private object.

The contents of one's phone can of course also be shared with others at will. One night in May 2016, when I accompanied Brice and Leo to one of their favourite eating places in Komah, Leo grinned and showed Brice a message from a person, I was sure was female. They both laughed out loud and seemed excited to read the message, and Brice prevented me from grabbing the phone as the message was not intended to be seen by me – was it because I was a researcher, a woman, or simply an outsider? The girl had clearly written something that stirred up the young men's interest.

The fact that there are third parties in mobile phone communication is something that people (must) take into account. This can be especially 'risky' in cases when private or even secret information is shared, like sharing one's fantasies or confessing one's love to another. People who are looking for romantic dates calculate the risk of exposure to third parties, which they accept as being part of the process. However, the inexperienced or naïve can encounter problems by sharing pictures or texts that might 'go viral' and which they later regret. On the other hand, not everyone regularly deletes messages on their phone, as it requires an extra action to be taken and because the mobile phone is considered a private item that others should not consult without their permission. Moments of 'intrusion' of this private item in the public sphere are intriguing to observe, as they provide information about social norms and expected behaviour.

3.4 Mobile communication: Private information in public

Privacy in public mobile phone use

The perception of receiving or making phone calls by the people who are physically present largely depends on the activity in which one is engaged. This differs according to the cultural setting, and therefore it is interesting to study moments when people step away from their group for privacy when they receive a phone call. Höflich (2005: 160) posits that most people know the situations that are appropriate for making a call, and the choice of topics that are acceptable in the setting in which they are when the call takes place. It goes without saying that the diversity and fluidity of settings and behaviours is immense, and that these are ever changing with the widespread availability of simple phones and smartphones in the urban landscape.

There seems to be an obvious dividing line between work and personal time in Western European societies, though authors such as Broadbent (2016) have convincingly shown that these boundaries have become increasingly blurred, especially through new ICTs such as mobile phones. Taking the blurred dividing line between work and privacy as an organising principle does not do justice to the Togolese context, and not only because of the estimated employment rate of 55 percent and underemployment rate of 22 percent[11] (DGSCN 2011). Mamah, whose repair business was introduced in section 3.2, was clear about this. When I asked him about his principal activities, he exclaimed cheeringly: "We do not have principal activities here in Togo!" (Interview with Mamah, 25 February 2015). His own example is telling. He is not only a technician, repair

---

[11] Underemployment is a term used for workers whose advanced skills are not being used, or are being underutilized, such as motor-taxi drivers or airtime sellers with a Bachelor's degree (Nkwi 2015).

person, but also a broadcaster and board member of an organisation for the handicapped.

The work-privacy continuum is unsuitable to describe the situation in Togo because of limited employment opportunities, but also because it is based on different perceptions of time, private space, and social networks among others. The management of one's time and one's private space is bound to certain rules. In Togo, this is usually not about time as a fixed thing, as in "I will meet you at three", but about the objective of the meeting. To illustrate this point, when people would be involved in an interview with me, they regarded this time as 'working time' and referred to this when we were interrupted – either by passers-by or a phone call. In my company, they would usually excuse themselves when accepting an incoming call, but whenever hanging around with a group of friends or on a short visit, people would not apologise for incoming and outgoing calls. These are some of the strategies to carve out one's 'private space'.

Depending on the nature of the call, people stand up and walk away, or remain seated while talking, sometimes mentioning the others present and sometimes not doing so. In bars, whenever making a phone call to common friends or girls who were supposed to join the group, the caller often goes so far as to draw attention to the call by raising his voice. On one hand, he – because these people are almost without exception, men – shows his friends that he is 'on it', on the other hand, he employs it as a means of pressure for the interlocutor to rapidly come and join.

In some cases, the tacit conventions about the degrees of privacy in public spaces become evident. One evening in 2018, I was hanging around with Felix and his friends in a bar, when one girl in the group received a phone call. She got up and left the circle, and after she had taken some steps, Felix and another man started to comment on the distance that she created. With every step she took, the comments of the men became louder, and the louder their comments, the further away she walked. Whoever her interlocutor on the phone was, she tried hard to keep both parties separated. Were the men only joking, expressing their jealousy, displaying their masculinity to each other, or did they attempt to discredit her, or even claim her in a certain way? It was probably a combination of several of these points, but it was clearly a difficult moment for the girl to navigate the boundaries of privacy.

In several other social situations, phone calls can be considered as being obtrusive or even offensive. When talking about the less positive pleasant aspects of the mobile phone, people give the example of mobile phone users walking on the streets and only looking at their phone. This is not common like in the Western European public spaces I am used to, but nevertheless, a narrative also exists in Togo about people not paying enough attention to their physical environment and causing an accident. I have rarely observed someone making a phone call while simultaneously walking on the streets in Sokodé. One afternoon in June 2016, I was in Kpangalam, making a phone call while walking in the direction of a woman I did not know. When our paths crossed, she stopped and asked me to give my phone to her. I quickly ended the call, and after trying some arguments that did not convince her, I came up with: "But then I cannot call you to greet you, since I will not have a phone anymore". She finally changed her serious look for a smile, and I took this as a sign that she seemed satisfied with my answer. We both continued our way.

Leaving aside possible interpretations, the encounter underlines the convention that phone conversations are not supposed to be held in the middle of the streets. One man explains that this is 'because the communication can be published'. In other words, one's privacy cannot be safeguarded when the conversation can be overheard by any passers-by. In the rare cases that I saw people receive a call on the road, they looked at the caller identity and usually put their phone back in their pocket, or they stopped and took a step back to shortly answer the call.

It is socially accepted to make and receive a phone call in relatively public spaces after or just before meeting someone face-to-face, when sitting in a bar with friends, driving in a private car or being on a bus. When making a long journey, for instance from Sokodé to Lomé, people stay in contact with their close ones waiting for them and the close ones they left behind, to let them know at what stage of the journey they are. This can be for practical reasons – communicating with the one who will pick them up from the bus station – but close ones also want to be kept updated about the traveller's position, as traveling always entails a risk because accidents are common. In most of these semi-public cases, such phone calls will be short, and answers will be non-specific, as people do not know who else might be listening.

Unknown caller ID: The dangers of anonymity

Several people have at one stage received a phone call from an unknown number which they picked up, which Dao, Freddy, Johnny and I noted during our interviews in March 2015. In such cases, a person who often has a particularly 'proper' French accent, told them that they had received a price and that they should give all their bank details so that a large sum of money could be transferred to them. In an interview with Freddy, a student at the technical college explained that this has also happened to him, but the connection was cut. He quickly went to a shopkeeper to buy airtime to call back. His airtime quickly ran out and he went back to the shop. When he told the shopkeeper the reason for recharging his airtime again, the shopkeeper warned him to not call again, as this was probably a fraud phone call (Freddy's interview with technical college student, 13 March 2015). A car mechanic explained to Freddy that he went to see his big brother with a similar story, as he did not have a bank account himself. His big brother told him that in case he would get another call from the same number, he should report it at the nearest Togocel office (Freddy's interview with car mechanic, 7 March 2015).

In Sokodé, people express that it is important to be wary of calls from unknown numbers, especially when the numbers are long, and some specify "as if they come from outside the country". Among these are phone numbers with more than ten digits, but also 'odd numbers' like four times zero or five times six. The story goes that some of these numbers are used by scammers who try to get someone's personal information such as described above. Other numbers are perceived to be even more dangerous, as there can be non-human powers behind such calls. These phone calls usually occur in the night, and as the narrative goes, when someone picks up such a call and is the first one to say a word, she runs the risk of immediately 'losing' a body part. This 'loss' is not a literal one, but it signifies that the body part goes numb. Several times, people recounted a case in which a person completely disappeared when he picked up the phone, though they often hurried to say they had never witnessed anything like it.

'Death calls' or 'killer calls' are reported for other places in the sub-region, but also throughout Asia and the Middle East (Bonhomme 2011; Emery 2018). Bonhomme (2012: 210) frames a similar Nigerian case of a brother and sister who lose consciousness upon responding to a 'killer call' in the frame of the 'modernity of witchcraft' (Comaroff & Comaroff 1993, 1999; Geschiere 1997). He suggests that new media contribute to transnational rumours, as their very essence makes it possible for messages to spread with high speed across regions and even across continents. He bases his analysis on Goffman's suggestion that phones are 'points of access' through which a user can be reached and that are essentially vulnerable (Goffman 1971: 35). While the service of 'caller ID' on mobile phones has diminished the anonymity of the callers in one's contact list, it has increased people's feelings of ambivalence towards unidentified phone numbers. Bonhomme (2012: 223) argues:

> This routine use of beeping and caller ID makes even more sensitive the difference between identified and anonymous calls. The threatening situation evoked by the rumour stands in sharp contrast to the ordinary social use of mobile phones. From this perspective, killer calls represent the occult flipside of beeping.

According to Bonhomme (2012), the calls should not simply be put in the frame of fear for new technologies, but also in the everyday context of mobile phone use, unstable networks and unreliable mobile phone operators. This counts as much for the Nigerian case he describes as for the operators in Togo, described in chapter two. The main argument here is that such stories fall in a general ambivalent attitude towards mobile phones and their operators, and highlight how people perceive present-day 'dangers of anonymity'.

Four inexplicable stories from Sokodé: "If it wants to happen to you, it will"

Such stories about 'inexplicable' phone calls circulate in Sokodé and form part of people's daily framework in which they relate to mobile phones, this section details four stories among the many that the local research team – consisting of Dao, Freddy and Johnny at the time– and I collected in 2015. The first account by a 55-year old home maintenance worker deals with a person receiving a phone call through a dream:

> I have a friend, named Taibou. When he was asleep he dreamt that he had received a call from his uncle who had deceased several years before. In the dream, the uncle gave my friend the numbers with which he should play the lottery. Immediately the next day, he went to play the numbers of which he had dreamed: at the end of the day, when the results were communicated, he had won 700,000 CFA. (Johnny's interview with home maintenance worker, 15 March 2015)

A 25 year old footballer told Johnny about his strange encounter in Qatar:

> Look, this is my story, I have heard many but this is a story that I have experienced myself, in 2005 when I was in Qatar. I had travelled to Qatar for a football test. After two weeks of hard work, I was walking in one of the streets in the hope of getting to know the city. Then I received a phone call of an unknown number. Being cautious, I did not pick up the phone. Then the phone rang a second time, a third and a fourth time, so at that moment I decided to pick up and what do I hear? It is the voice of a childhood friend from Sokodé, but who had deceased in 1999, way before I travelled to Qatar. I have even played together with him in the neighbourhood team.
> At first when he called me he presented himself and said he is Simone. I recognized his voice and responded 'how is this possible, since he does not exist'. He responded by saying that he cannot give me any explanation, but he can only direct me to a place where we can meet, and also show me his house in Abu Dhabi. And then I said okay, no problem.
> The next day we met in a cafeteria close to his home and without lying, it was our friend Sadat Simone. Suddenly a terrible freezing cold caught me, I did not understand. After a coffee, he took me to his house and said he wanted to travel to Germany for a

deal and would come back in a week, doing everything possible to meet again. After one week, I went to his home and I met other people who lived in the house and when I asked them after Sadat Simone, they replied that there was no one with that name living in the house, since a very long time. Since that day, no more phone call, nothing. At my return, I reported this news to the family, alright it was incredible. (Johnny's interview with a footballer, 10 March 2015)

A 28 year old owner of a small print shop explained to Freddy that he did not like to pick up the phone when an unknown international number calls, and recounted the following story:

> There was a Nigerian called Ibo who lived with his wife and two children in the same compound as where my office was. He was a trader of spare parts for car and truck. So this man was chasing young girls too much, and once he received a call in the night when he was already in bed with his wife. So he jumped out of bed and went out to meet this person. As he had not said a word, his wife did everything to search her husband's phone and she found the number of the last call and other numbers of girls her husband was chasing. When she called one of the numbers, it appeared to be the phone of our secretary. So the secretary also went out with him. The wife immediately recognized her voice and the next day she came to our office and made a scandal with our secretary, who made clear to her that she had nothing to do with her husband. Then her husband came and started to beat up his wife in front of everyone, really it was not well that day. The woman went to the police and summoned her husband and our secretary. On their return, the Ibo asked his wife to leave, to go home! The woman returned to Nigeria.
>
> Some days after the woman had left, her husband the Ibo received a phone call at noon from a strange Nigerian number and when the Ibo picked up, someone called his name and he said 'yes it's me'. The person did not say anything, and the call was disconnected. Instantly, the Ibo started having a great ache in the heart, pain, and as we have a fridge in our service, he asked us for fresh water and after drinking, he told us what happened to him. The next day when we returned to the office, we learnt that he had been urgently evacuated to the hospital the day before as he could no longer speak, and he died the same day. So everyone suspected his wife to have done magic to eliminate him. I was scared because really I had seen it. Ever since, I do not pick up calls of bizarre numbers. (Freddy's interview with Print shop owner, 9 March 2015)

The last story was told by a 24 year old student in civil engineering who did construction work in Kpalimé:

> Once we were at a building site in Kpalimé and we needed water to work. We asked the women next to us if they were willing to help, and we would pay them. So they began. They were two women and a third also came. After a while, the husband of the third woman came to see his wife and told her to prepare a meal as it was noon, and he began to complain: What right do we have to call his wife, and he is a charlatan, and he will not let us finish this project, and we discussed a lot with him until he left with a lot of anger. So the next day was a Sunday, so we took a break. My boss was at home

that day when an unknown, strange number called him. Only zeros, and he picked up the phone. The person did not speak at all, he did not say 'hello' and my boss hung up. Moments after this, he started having headaches and it was a little serious, he had so much pain that they drove him to the hospital where he spent 3 days. Then he felt somewhat better and he was taken home. He went to a great witch doctor who found out that he was bewitched. We do not know when he got it, but the last thing he did before it happened was that he picked up his phone. (Freddy's interview with Civil engineering student, 6 March 2015)

As evident from the four stories, some of these inexplicable events are beneficial to the person concerned, but they can also be dangerous and even lead to death. Except for the footballer's story, the events did not happen to the narrator, but had happened to other people. When reflecting on these and similar stories, most people said that this had never happened to them or their closest contacts. Some added that they do not believe it, but on my questioning how one can generally avoid such occurrences, most people advised me to never pick up the phone when an unknown or 'odd' number calls. As Johnny remarked several times, shrugging his shoulders at my inquisitiveness, as we discussed the results of our interviews in March 2015: "If it wants to happen to you, it happens". According to him, people are afraid of these events as they simply cannot be controlled. As Bonhomme (2012: 226–227) stated, such 'situations of technological anonymity' bring to the fore an insecurity that is experienced in society, one which affects feelings of trust.

One way to deal with feelings of insecurity is the application CallApp, which gained popularity in Sokodé in 2017 and 2018. This is how it works: CallApp uploads the contact list of all its members, and if someone receives a call from a number that is not registered in her own contact list, CallApp displays the caller ID as registered in another person's contact list. When I first heard of this, I immediately imagined the interesting situations that could evolve from the use of this application, not only because I had seen numbers being registered as 'my baby' or 'my wife', but also because of the many numbers that belong to a girlfriend and have names like 'Ibrahim' or 'Eric'.

3.5 The intimacy of information

Entrusting private information through the phone: Moussa's illness

In contacts with peers or friends, the sharing of different levels of information are strongly related with the trust level within the relationship, which is based on numerous factors including one's character, expectations and past experiences, and the nature, duration, frequency and intensity of the relationship. Whenever we spoke of trust, my informants explained to me that trusting someone is a delicate matter, and as noted before, it is commonly stated that 'trust does not exclude control'. Many people I got to know closely, told me at some stage that they do not really have friends, even though they can be surrounded by 'friends' all the time. Sometimes, one or two people may be close friends, but commonly one's immediate family members are trusted more.

People in Sokodé experience difficulties in finding a marriage partner whom they can trust, which is not about financial issues or physical fidelity. Firstly, the belief is that no one can be trusted when it comes to money or goods. One cannot even trust one's spouse – or perhaps partners are among the most distrusted because of the high stakes involved. Both men and women generally distrust their partner's physical fidelity; exclusive rights to the body of the other might be considered a worthy goal, but they are not integral to people's expectations. WhatsApp messages that are sent around 'for fun' or 'to laugh' reflect this attitude. For instance:

> Mouth of woman. A woman comes back to the hotel with her lover. She crosses her husband going out with a *go*. She says: You there, when I told you one day I will catch you. You see, today I have come with a witness.[12]

The trust between partners, and also between friends and family members, is one that is based on a mutual understanding and respect for the expectations of the other, in line with Lagerspetz's (1998) definition of trust as 'tacit demand'. As I noted above, personal information is often shared with specific aims or interests, which can even mean sharing a hospital report of one's blood values. An incident between two young men and me as we interacted on WhatsApp, illustrates that there are cases in which it is appropriate to share highly personal information. This empirical exploration is one such rare moment that provides insight into intentionality and agency of the person who trusts, and emphasises the experience-based approach in this research.

In October 2016, some months after I had returned to the Netherlands from my fieldwork, Désiré sent me a WhatsApp message with the news that our common friend Moussa had returned to Sokodé because he had gotten very ill in Lomé, where he worked in a garage. The next day, Moussa sent me a text message himself, and an image with the results of his blood test was sent next

---

12 Original text: *Bouche de femme. Il y a une femme qui rentrait a l'hotel avec son amant. Elle croise son mari entrain de sortir avec une go. Elle dit : Toi laaa quand je te dis un jour je vais t'attraper la. Voila ça aujourd'hui je suis venu avec temoin.*

through Désiré's phone, and after that, I exchanged messages with Moussa on his own phone. However, the main part of our interaction happened through Désiré's phone.

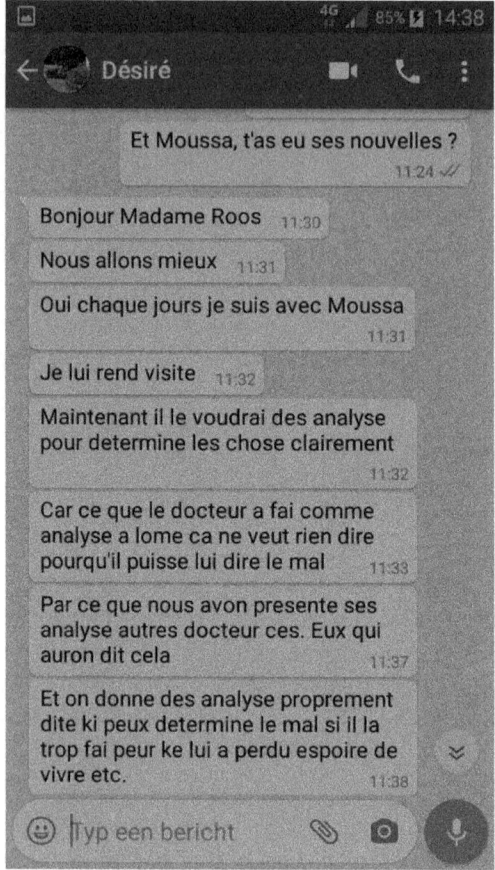

Figure 6: WhatsApp conversation about Moussa's illness.

Some days later, when I inquired with Désiré about Moussa's health state, Désiré explained that it had not improved (see figure 6). A free translation of his WhatsApp messages is as follows:

> Hello Mrs Roos. We are doing better. Yes, every day I am with Moussa. I visit him. Now he would like to have some tests done to determine things clearly. Because what the doctor did in Lomé does not mean anything, so he can tell him what is wrong. Because we have presented these tests to other doctors. They are the ones who have said that. And we give

the proper analysis, which can determine the harm, yes, it has scared him too much, that he has lost hope to live etc.

Désiré listed the different medical diagnostic tests that the doctor recommended. As some sort of 'evidence' of Moussa's illness, Désiré sent me two pictures of Moussa, who did not look good. I asked several questions to understand the situation and then I asked him about the cost of the treatment. He replied that they were looking for 'the most less expensive hospital' [*l'hopital le plus moins cher*] to continue the diagnostics. I urged him to find the hospital with a quick and qualitatively good treatment instead, adding 'I can send through Western Union'. In the weeks that followed, Désiré kept me updated by sending me the results of the medical diagnostics, and Moussa's health gradually improved.

The reason for focusing on our exchange is the particular mix of highly personal, detailed information, and the lack of a direct message. When taking a closer look, this case unveils the same mechanisms as the story of Sweet Mama; the transfer of a hidden message. Désiré never insinuated that I should offer help in any kind, but by giving me detailed information and emphasising that Moussa was suffering, it was obvious that the question was implied in the information provided by him and Moussa.

Like in this case where Désiré took the lead, requests for help are often put forth through a mediator, and they are mostly concealed in extensive descriptions. The sharing of one's medical data requires a certain level of trust by the requesting party, and in this case, the tacit demand is heavy: 'I put my health, my life in your hands'. This seemingly unlimited access to personal information is granted in exchange for something – a promise, a helping hand or financial support. This kind of privacy is highly situational; a similar request would not easily be put forward in the presence of others. The fact that there is no straightforward request leaves space for both parties to maintain a good relationship, as a refusal can be conveyed in silence.

Concealing information as the lubricant of sociality

In certain social situations, remaining silent or concealing information is regarded as being of higher moral standing than unveiling the 'truth'. Archambault (2009) considers the 'invisible realm' of mobile phone communication as a new space where one can exercise one's privacy to a certain extent and consolidate relationships without the interference of relatives, neighbours or others. Nonetheless, she compares phones with fences, "providing only a false sense of privacy. They might help conceal secrets, but they can as easily reveal them by providing proofs of unfaithfulness, through intercepted phone calls or text messages."

These ways of concealing are also mentioned by a 28 year old broadcaster, who talked to me about his WhatsApp use in an interview at a local radio station in July 2016. He only checks his WhatsApp early in the morning and late in the evening. This is not only because the network is too saturated during the day, but also because he does not want to divert his attention to his phone at any moment. He adds that in that case, his smartphone would control him instead of the other way around, as it should be. The main reason, however, is that he is unable to react to all messages immediately, as was also the case with Felix. Nonetheless, others see it when their messages have been read: With WhatsApp, one checkmark means the message has been sent but not yet received, two checkmark means that it has been received and when they turn blue, this means the message has been read. One way to deal with this is to turn this function off, but this means that one can no longer see whether others have read one's messages – the 'privacy level' goes both ways.

If people see that the receiver has read their message but has not yet replied, the broadcaster explains in the same interview that this can lead to unpleasant social situations, in which they reproach the receiver "Am I not important enough for you?" This is also one of the reasons that people would rather respond to phone calls and say "I am on the road" than to say "I am busy". The latter can easily be taken as an insult, displaying an arrogant attitude. In one of our many conversations, Dao patiently explained to me that the question will immediately pop up in which activity the other can possibly be involved, that is so important that she cannot even give attention to her family or friends. Admonitions such as these can be expected when people do not answer a missed call or message within what is considered an appropriate amount of time. In a society where people regularly need each other's help to meet their basic needs, it is important to avoid anything that can give the other the impression of not being needed.

The phone transgresses private and public spheres

For scholars, the redrawing of the boundaries between private and public is an intriguing part of social and cultural contexts of mobile phone use (Goggin 2006: 4). In the words of Wasserman (2011: 151): "Mobile phones challenge us to pay attention to how these popular uses transgress the realm of the private into the realm of the public". Katz and Aakhus (2002) argue that the use of mobile phones has led to a degeneration of the public sphere and with this, an erosion of the private sphere; the public realm is 'invaded' by private talk.

To illustrate an unintentional transgression of private and public spheres in the particular context of Sokodé, I describe an exchange that appeared in September 2016 in a WhatsApp group, with 142 members at the time, dealing with development matters in and around Sokodé (see figure 7).

Figure 7: Mistaken WhatsApp exchange.

A translation of the posts is as follows: "I want you, today we are going out or what do you say", followed by "Excuse me it is a mistake". The response at 17: 51 reads: "God forgive you my brother. What you hide we have known. But we're among family". To which the culprit responds: "Thanks for your advice". This 'slip of the tongue' did not generate much more reactions than the ones displayed. I suspected that this was possibly because this could have happened to the majority of the group members, and they wanted to respect the privacy of the person by staying silent.

Though the unwanted disclosure of private information in such a large WhatsApp group as described above may not be common, almost everyone can recall a shameful or awkward moment caused by or through a mobile phone, related to an unintentional disclosure of information. Nevertheless, to add to the conception of relatively more private and more public spheres, and the increased issues with trust and trustworthiness 'caused' by the phone as unveiled in chapter five, the mobile phone in Sokodé does not solely lead to private talk and impinges upon the public sphere.

On the contrary, several scholars argue that in African societies that they studied, the mobile phone opens up new spheres of privacy, contributing to the creation of intimate spaces that could not have been imagined before (Archambault 2009; Hahn & Kibora 2008; Maroon 2006; Steel 2017). As noted earlier in this section, local discourses in Mozambique for instance primarily evaluate the impact of mobile phones on people's private lives (Archambault 2009). Considering the constrained conditions that were described earlier in this chapter, it is clear that concealing information is essential in everyday communication in Sokodé, regardless of whether a communication act is classified as private or public. If the private-public continuum was to be used as a yardstick, most aspects of life in Sokodé would carry mostly private elements. The mobile phone offers a new range of opportunities to stay in touch and experience instant relief upon learning that a beloved one is doing fine, as discussed in more detail in chapter four.

However, the mobile phone has also increased the opportunities to control and distrust a beloved one. This can bring about additional stress and tension into people's relationships, as was the case with Felix who was sure that his friend had intended to poison him. This relationship reveals the heavy consequences that the mobile phone can bring about when unveiling private information within an intimate relation.

Before Felix found enough evidence to unfriend the young man I decided to call David, their relationship had been symbiotic but largely unequal; David had the dual position of not only being Felix's protégé, but also a personal assistant of sorts, quasi-permanently at Felix's disposal. In March 2018, when David and I had a moment alone, I asked David whether he always responded to Felix's calls. David hesitated for a moment, but then 'confessed' to me that he did not respond when he was drinking the locally brewed *tchouck*, because Felix disapproved of this. David added that Felix simply did not understand that the local beer was ten times more affordable than the bottled beer in the bars. Felix, in return, said that he did not understand why David preferred to drink beer that was brewed under dubious hygienic circumstances, because David could always rely on Felix paying for as many bottles of beer as he desired. In this relationship, both parties, but especially David, were continuously forced to reveal their geographical location, and to explain where they had been or what they had been doing in case they did not immediately respond to a phone call. In this sense, the mobile phone in Sokodé does not allow the transgression of private talk to the public sphere, but rather allows private talk to impinge upon one's private sphere.

At the same time, the mobile phone also allows people to enlarge one's private sphere: there were times that David evaded social pressure either by temporarily not answering his phone or sending a text message to Felix saying that he had a stomach ache. By including his health condition, he risked being confronted again with Felix's disapproving "I told you, you should not drink *tchouck*", but at least this permitted him to retain his privacy. However, the fact that he seemed to have a hidden agenda that undermined Felix's social network – sending his girlfriend photos of him with yet another girlfriend – indicates the imbalance of the transgressions of their respective private information.

As an example of transgressions of privacy, this case emphasises the value of delving into information flows between friends and within families. Mobile communication in Sokodé takes place in the broader framework of information flows, in spheres that are situated along the private-public continuum. The examples above show the importance of embedding mobile communication in a particular sociality. This is also why I am not a proponent of studying these processes merely through the content of people's phones; after all, phones are an extension of people's lives and not vice versa. The analysis of information flows dealing with civic-ness cannot be seen in isolation from the intimate process of sharing information.

3.6 Concluding remarks

This chapter shows that private and public are delicate in an environment of duress. Since the information landscape is under stress, information itself is a complicated issue. The trustworthiness of information in Sokodé is always relative, and the private overrules the public, which means there is a major private element in every communication act. Access is important in this regard; a request for information can be an intrusion in someone's privacy. There is often mistrust regarding the reasons, aims and ends of the request. Not only is the act of information sharing often private, but the quality of information itself in the environment of Sokodé is largely private. There is a layered purview on information, as people tend to give meaning to the information within the information. This turns information into a relative and unstable given.

The mobile phone provides additional ways to exchange information in a highly complex communication landscape. It is because of these complexities, that the mobile phone has a profoundly ambiguous status. In a locality where the exchange of information is tense on a meta-level, this has effects on practical, everyday living. Therefore, it is understandable that the mobile phone leads to more insecurity and distrust since it presents a multitude of information that is not necessarily more trustworthy than information that is passed on through another medium. However, this is not always the case, as there are instances and specific types of information for which social media can be perceived as being more trustworthy than other sources.

With every step a girl takes away from a group of friends when she receives a phone call, she runs the risk of increasing the distance in trusting relationships – what information is revealed by such attempts to conceal mobile phone exchanges? The fine line between one's personal privacy and keeping up a public image of trustworthiness is drawn using social conventions that leave space for much indirect guessing and opacity. However, exactly because of the fragile equilibrium and the great impetus in society to maintain peaceful relationships, the space for manoeuvring that exists to conceal factual information is stretchable and flexible. When Sweet Mama tells me using metaphors that the whereabouts of others do not concern her, she contributes to our peaceful relationship. And then she says goodnight, prays for God's pity and goes to sleep, hoping that tomorrow will be a better day.

4 Economic and techno-social basis of mobile phone use

4.1 Introduction

On a sunny morning in June 2016, Dao and I pay his grandmother a visit. With a gesture, she invites me to sit next to her on her bed. Her hands rest in her lap, and she is happy to answer any questions I have about her mobile phone usage. When I ask her whether she calls often, she lights up and exclaims cheeringly: "I have the flavour of calling, but unfortunately my airtime is often gone. It was only yesterday that I paid 450 CFA, but now it is already gone!"

Dao's grandmother, like other people in Sokodé, cannot imagine living without the mobile phone anymore. The ubiquity of the mobile phone in large parts of the world is a fascinating feature of the phone, even though the conditions of mobile communication in Togo are more constrained than in other parts of the world. It has not caught the attention of scholars, but it is a subject that almost everyone likes to talk and have opinions about.

This chapter discusses the ways in which the mobile phone has become an integral part of everyday life in Sokodé, specifically, the techno-social relations between the person and the mobile phone. Besides the material infrastructure, an overview is given of the social and economic parameters that enable, disable and instigate people to use their mobile phones. This is necessary to contextualise not just a new technology in a Togolese city, but also new kinds of Togoleseness in this city, borrowing from Horst and Miller (2006: 78–79).

Departing from the materiality of the phone, this chapter first considers the idea of the mobile phone as external body part, before delving into the material world of mobile phones in Togo. Besides classifications of different qualities and brands, the chapter describes how the phone was introduced in Sokodé, and the strategies that people employ to limit their communication costs, situating everyday mobile phone use. The chapter concludes by considering the phone as an identity marker. Finally, it returns to the question of the mobile phone as an external body part and the consequences that this has for techno-social relationships in society.

4.2 Techno-social relations between phones and people

Embodiment and technologies: The phone as external body part

In a conversation with Eva, a young woman who rented a room in the compound where I also stayed, I asked her what she would do if her phone would break. She told me she would immediately go to a repair shop to have it repaired, and to underline this, she used the following metaphor: "as if my phone is a part of my body; if there is something wrong with your body, you also quickly go to the hospital for a cure" (Conversation with Eva, 9 March 2015). As it turned out, Eva was not the first to imagine the mobile phone as some kind of external body part or 'area of sensitivity' in the line of Merleau-Ponty (1962).

For the largest part of the day, the mobile phone is within reach of the body if not carried on it. Therefore, I shall briefly describe the paradigm of embodiment. The paradigm of embodiment understands the 'embodied experience' as the starting point for analysing human participation in a cultural world. In the words of Csordas (1993), this means that the body should be understood as "the existential ground of culture – not as an object that is 'good to think', but as a subject that is 'necessary to be'." Embodiment is the underlying basis of this chapter, since it helps connect the materiality of the mobile phone with how humans experience and manage this technological device. It has become an area of sensitivity, just like the blind woman's stick that is an extension of her perception and no longer an external object (Merleau-Ponty 1962: 143 in Rettie 2005: 24). Rettie (Ibid.) views this as an alternative 'phenomenalist' approach, in which 'technology extends the field of action and embodiment is extended to the virtual environment'.

Techno-social relations have interested humans since ancient times, as these relations say something about the human condition. Though a considerable part of the world's population values innovation and embraces new technologies with enthusiasm, at the same time there is a tendency to regard people's rapid appropriation of new ICTs as a threatening development, especially when power and politics come into play. However, there is a third way to perceive technology, found in the works of social scientists like Stiegler and Latour, who have been writing about humans and technologies for several decades.

One of Stiegler's (1994) earlier works, *Technique et le Temps 1*, is based on the premise that people's adoption of and adaptation to technologies are inherently human processes that distinguish us from other species, just like our ability to develop new technologies. In Stiegler's concept of individuation, humans not only shape technologies, but are also shaped by technologies. Regarding society in this way, technology comes before the individual; the individual is born into a technological world that already has a history, which he calls 'tertiary retention'. Tertiary retention selectively shapes individuals and societies. This view encompasses both the enthusiastic embracing of a new technology such as the mobile phone, and the fear or reluctance about potential negative effects of new technologies.

The mobile phone as total social fact

The *fait social total* or 'total social fact' was first developed by Mauss in his seminal essay on the gift ([1925] 1990). It may offer a methodological framework for understanding the different attributions, roles and uses of the mobile phone. Though it was developed in a structural functionalist paradigm that has been rejected by postmodernist theories, the concept has not lost its methodological value (Kasuga 2010). Total social facts can be described as follows:

> In these 'total' social phenomena [..], all kinds of institutions are given expression at one and the same time— religious, juridical, and moral, which relate to both politics and the family; likewise economic ones, which suppose special forms of production and consumption, or rather, of performing total services and distribution. (Mauss 1990: 3)

As shall be clear in this study, the mobile phone envelops these varying fields, and serves as a link between these fields, some of which are overlapping. In recent years, anthropologists have considered a range of subjects under the lens of the total social fact, as varied as pragmatisms (Levine 2016), water (Orlove and Caton 2010) or sports (Wendling 2010). The latter however criticizes the use of the notion of 'total social fact', though employing the notion as methodological tool offers a way out. Therefore, at the risk of merely attempting to 'claiming an anthropological approach' (Wendling 2010: 90), I draw on the example of Orlove and Caton (2010: 402) in replacing 'water' with 'the mobile phone'.

Although the mobile phone could be reduced to a technological fact when thinking about its nature, it has become integral, even essential to many if not most domains or institutions of society – for instance, in shifting public and private spheres, the political and spiritual realm, fashion, in notions about surveillance and freedom, as Katz (2007) notes in his essay on mobile media studies. In this way, the mobile phone is 'total and social in precisely the encompassing sense that Mauss had in mind' (Orlove and Caton 2010: 402).

The functionality of the mobile phone as medium of communication and information can be perceived as a necessity. Besides communicating with other people, this necessity finds its use in seeking information for one's education or employment, consulting news pages, or in the form of distraction, like sharing jokes or watching pornographic images or videos. The mobile phone can be considered as 'window on the world', a place of imagination, which is where the terms 'sense of possibility' (Musil 2017) and 'imaginations' (Förster 2012; Kaufmann 2016; Salazar 2011) come in. The phone can bring people to other places, it can make people 'travel while sitting down' (Archambault 2012), though there is no consensus yet as to whether it increases or decreases mobility.

When sliding the mobile phone in to one's pocket, an individual can theoretically be assured of some sort of 'perpetual contact' (Katz & Aakhus 2002). Even though in physical and abstract ways, the phone could be perceived as the 'glue' in social relations, the mobile phone as a social fact is made possible and also limited by its concrete form. The brand or model of the mobile phone that people own matters, as does the portion of their income that is spent on their communication, and cultural nuances of whether they walk away from a group when calling. In Sokodé, and most probably anywhere in the world, the information that is passed on through the phone is not the same as the information that is shared face-to-face. One of the factors that plays a role is the degree of trust, which is one of the central themes in this work. Another aspect put forth by Ling and Yittri (2002: 139, in de Lange 2010: 138) is that phone exchanges often serve as a prelude to face-to-face encounters. The question that is of interest here is whether communication through the mobile phone is different from face-to-face communication and if so, in what ways is it different. How does the platform influence the content, and vice versa? In this sense, it must be noted that there is no unmediated communication – all communication acts can be interpreted in numerous ways (Peterson 2008).

In the concrete forms mentioned above, the mobile phone is connected in a 'total' way to public and private domains, meeting the human need to communicate, and being an addictive object, while functioning as part of a political-economic aesthetic (as seen in accessories of cases, headphones, screen protectors, chargers, cables, holders etc.). The choices and meanings are no less complex for Togolese city dwellers, who move around with two phones in their pocket: one for their most intimate connections, the other for their broader social network, or a phone each from two telecommunication networks. The individual may or may not have credit on their phone to call or text someone, they may even lack the skills to write a message. The screen may be shattered, the battery worn down; all these elements constitute the totality of the social fact (for this section, see again the comparison with Orlove and Caton 2010: 402).

The total social fact is primarily used as a methodological tool in this work, because as theoretic model, the concept soon becomes problematic (Gofman 1998; Wendling 2010). In this study, the methodological consideration of the mobile phone as total social fact is intended to underline the diversity of aspects connected to the mobile phone that can be studied. Treading different paths to conceptualise the theme does justice to its complexity. The consideration of the mobile phone as 'total social fact' has the advantage of capturing the multiple social domains in which mobile phones are used, as enabling a plurality of 'connectivities'. This pathway follows a line of anthropological thinking that links Mauss' total social fact to the framework of Actor-Networks.

Agency and domestication of the mobile phone

Based on the premise of actor networks, mobile phones can be viewed as the nodes or 'intersections' in a network. Together, they form a kind of social network. This network would be made up of persons as well as things with agency. Along with mapping social networks of people through the mobile phone, this study provides an additional aspect in emphasising the mobile phone as material object.

The main merit of Latour's 'Reassembling the Social' (2005) is the agency it attributes to non-human actors. The theories about actor networks have sought to radically transform how social scientists talk about society's relationship to technologies and other non-human actors. For instance, in studies about the *social* aspect of social media, the agency of things may frequently be overlooked (Adams & Thompson 2011). As *actor* presupposes a certain human-ness, actor network theory (ANT) prefers to speak of *actants* in order to underline non-human agency. Building on Deleuze's rhizomatic approach in a creative way, Latour's (1996) actor network consists of multiple *actants* that are constantly interacting in different levels of connections, which are never permanent.

As *theory*, ANT does not provide a basis for power differentiation between human and non-human actors. By limiting the approach of mobile phone use as 'network', moments of alienation are missing, because distraction is underevaluated in the concept of the network. It disregards mistrust against the system, of people temporarily or permanently not using their mobile phone anymore. As Latour (2005: 143) remarked, ANT should not so much be seen as a theory but as a tool. These insights have sharpened the methodological framework of the current work. This study builds on Latour's concept of 'networks' (2005) in the sense that it 'describes the interaction between people and non-human actors' (Hahn 2012: 182).

Of interest here is what Horst and Miller (2006) describe as appropriation: the dialectic relationship between how people use and perceive their phones, and how their phones shape their lives. Others rather talk about 'domestication' of a technology such as the mobile phone. For instance, Hahn and Kibora (2008) claim that the domestication of the mobile phone in Burkina Faso as a foreign good in an oral society is coupled with ambiguities. The relationship that exists between humans and technology suggests that the mobile phone can be seen as external body. Kenaw (2012, 2016), who has closely worked together with technique philosopher Verbeek (2011), discerns a certain cultural determinism when it comes to the adoption of new technologies in African societies. According to him, the commonly perceived distance between foreign, imported technologies and members of Ethiopian society, silently implies that they would be passive receivers of a kind of superior knowledge that they did not yet dispose of. In order to overcome the dichotomous nature of the terms 'technological determination' and 'social relationships theory', he uses the term 'techno-social dialogue'. He prefers to describe the appropriation process of technologies in an Ethiopian context as 'culture-technology dialogue', which implies a multi-directional process.

In keeping with Horst and Miller (2006), these approaches emphasise that appropriation is based on active exchange. From here, it is a minor step to reach the concept of agency. As I have shown, a growing number of ethnographic studies point at the ambiguity of these 'dialectics' of new technologies and societies. This study can be seen in this light, linking new technologies to the question of development and social change from an *emic* perspective. The unstable political, economic and social context of Togo lead to a situation in which people must 'navigate' the webs of their relationships with care. As mentioned in the introduction, for this analysis it is useful to apply Vigh's (2009) conceptualisation of agency in a complex, ever-shifting social context, which he labelled 'social navigation'. However, as stated by de Bruijn and Bot (2008), the hardship of the environment is engrained in the experience of people in their everyday lives and is not external to them.

Taking into account the inner lifeworld of my informants, the mobile phone is a new, foreign technology that is appropriated in the social realm, and the most intimate 'friend' that can be imagined. In this case, the denomination 'foreign' is not limited to being an imported good that is manufactured outside of the country, as is the case in countries such as Togo, but foreign here also refers to an unfamiliarity, a 'strangeness' to the self, that seeks to be hosted. Though Hahn and Kibora (2008) emphasise this foreignness as contributing to the ambivalent domestication process of the mobile phone in Burkinabe society, I would add that the domestication of any complex technology is coupled with ambiguities on the social and the individual level. There are obvious cultural and individual variations in material and economic accessibility to technologies and supporting infrastructure among other factors, which is a recurrent theme throughout this study, but especially in the current chapter.

This study considers the ways in which people interact with the numerous possibilities that mobile phones have opened up as an ongoing process of appropriation, in which culture and technology are in constant interaction. When focusing on people's practices in this multi-directional process, it is important to refrain from essentialising and reifying the mobile phone. The lens of research is focused on the ever-changing contours of this appropriation process, which takes place in a specific setting.

4.3 Material basis of mobile phones in Sokodé

Classifications of mobile phones in Togo

In order to understand techno-social relationships between humans and phones in Togo, it might be useful to connect Stiegler's tertiary retention to Hahn's discussion of appropriation and globalisation. Hahn (2008) draws attention to the uncertainties in African societies as new technologies are imported in their daily lives. In the era of increased globalisation, locality has arguably become more important than ever. One of the ways for people in Togo to indicate the 'foreignness' of products are the geographic indicators for the various mobile phones and other non-food products on the market: for instance 'venu' (having come) is used for second-hand mobile phones and other goods that have come from 'the West'. These products are usually considered to be of high quality. Phones of lower quality fall under categories such as 'Chinoiserie' and 'Dubai', which also refers to their (imagined) places of origin. As the name already says, the *Dubai* phones are believed to be sent from Dubai and these can be bought new or second-hand in small shops. The *Dubai* phones have better quality than the phones that are described as *Chinoiserie*. *Chinoiserie* are the cheap, low-quality phones with many features such as camera, radio and memory card. These phones look fancy but usually do not last long. If one is unlucky, the camera stops working after some weeks, and most of the time if the phone falls, the screen scatters immediately.

However, the exact geographical origin of products is not deemed to be important in the majority of cases; *venu* from the United States, Canada or Europe, it is all the same. When asked about the country the phone is manufactured in, many people also believe that the phones that come from Europe are also manufactured in Europe.

Apparently, it is rather difficult to distinguish between original phones and replicas, though there are some indicators that can facilitate the distinction. Firstly, a phone that can take only one SIM card is usually original, which is often equated with the phone being a *venu* from Europe. Secondly, the weight of the phone is telling; usually the lighter the phone is, the lower the quality. Thirdly, the price is usually an indication; most people believe that the quality of a phone rises with its price. Of course, there are individual variations, for instance someone believed when it is difficult to insert one's SIM card, it is more probable that the phone is original.

During the first weeks of my fieldwork, I focused on people's categorisations of different mobile phones. At times I showed my Nokia 108 dual SIM, bought in the Netherlands, and I asked questions about its quality. Generally, people first asked me where I had bought the phone, in order to find out more about its origin. When I asked them to guess, they doubted, and usually proposed to open the phone to check the battery and the place to enter the SIM cards. Most people then guessed that the phone could well be *Chinoiserie* because of the dual SIM. Some of them simply read the 'made in Korea' printed on the battery and 'made in China' on the phone.

This experiment was not used to indicate how uninformed or exotic people in Togo are (see also Piot 1999) – as if people in other regions in the world would be better at guessing where their goods are manufactured – but rather to see how people try to determine the quality of the goods they want to buy with the little information that they have. The way in which my companions in Sokodé tried to investigate the origins of my phone provided a background for two ideas: firstly, the distinction between *venu, Chinoiserie, Dubai* is not clearly defined, or for that matter goods from Nigeria, India or elsewhere. Secondly, if the categorisation exists at all, it should rather be seen as a slippery guiding line, one of the uncertain factors to consider when trying to buy goods with the best price-quality ratio.

Nonetheless, when compared to buying a handmade fan for stoking the fire in the kitchen, buying a mobile phone is trickier, not only because it is more expensive, but because the technology is more complex. The lack of knowledge about assessing the technical features of mobile phones can result in people buying a smartphone with not enough storage capacity or with other shortcomings that they discover only after they have bought the phone. One way to deal with one's lack of expertise to determine the quality of a product is to trust another person's judgement. In this society, where trust is so volatile, having to rely on others can be a precarious balancing act.

Obtaining and maintaining phones

People's memories about the different phones they have owned serve to apply the biographical approach to the mobile phone in Sokodé. Though not everyone remembers the exact number of phones and the different brands and features of all the phones they have owned, people remember their first phone without exception. Most people also have vivid memories of the price of the first phone they bought and the SIM kit that went with it, like an evangelical pastor whom I met in 2010 and again in 2015 and 2016. When I interviewed him in 2015, he recalled that his first phone cost about 100,000 CFA (about € 150),[13] and the SIM card cost 19,900 CFA at the time (Interview with a pastor, 25 February 2015).

In the mid-2000s, mobile phones became affordable to a larger section of the population in Togo, though not the destitute. Prices for a promotion package were as high as 35,000 or 50,000 CFA, which salaried employees could afford, having saved money and borrowed a bit from family members and friends. Nowadays, people can buy brand new phones for 5,000 or 6,000 CFA, and a SIM card for 500 CFA (under one Euro). In Lomé, there are even new phones for sale for 2,500 CFA (about € 3.80), although the quality might be questionable. Nonetheless, such prices do mean that new mobile phones are now within reach of most sections of society.

Most of the people who shared their mobile phone histories with us have had about three or four mobile phones since their first one, but others cannot recall how many phones they have had. Many of their phones have been lost, stolen, sold or given away, though most were simply too worn out to use any longer and were beyond repair. One in every two or three phones that is in use, has minor or major issues. This can vary from a crack in the screen or the back falling off the phone, to a malfunctioning screen, failing sound or other issues. As people simply do not have the means to buy good quality gadgets, they settle for less and deal with the bad condition of their phones as best as they can. When a phone breaks down, most people are not angry or disturbed because of its condition, but because they are not reachable. Some will immediately go to a phone repair shop to inform about the problem and the price of the reparation, whereas others directly buy a new one.

---

13 The exchange rate is 655.957 CFA for 1 Euro. The CFA franc has been fixed to the Euro.

Mobile phone biography of Dao's grandmother

This chapter began with the interview with Dao's grandmother and I return to it because it is illustrative of the collection of mobile phone biographies. Many of the subjects that will be touched upon, figure in the story of Dao's grandmother, who was in her eighties at the time of our interview (7 June 2016). Her case serves to demonstrate the material aspect of how people use their phone. Sadly, after a long period of deteriorating health conditions, she passed away in the second half of 2017, when turbulent events were taking place.

Dao's grandmother was born in the 1930s in a Kabye village to the south of Sokodé. Her older sister gave her to a man from a village close to Kara [for marriage], and they had several children. After her husband died, she remarried and had more children. She used to sell maize, charcoal and traditional mustard that she produced herself. At the time of the interview, she did not get out of her house a lot, because of vision problems. Since she was not so mobile anymore, most of the family members came to visit her, especially after the mass on Sunday, but also on other days.

When I asked her how she used her phone, she answered that she only used her phone to make calls, and she did not know how to use the different functions of her phone. When we discussed her mobile phone biography, she and Dao entered into a light-hearted discussion about her phones, and he joked that he knew more about his grandmother's phones than she did herself.

When Dao still lived in his grandmother's compound, he accompanied his grandmother every Sunday after church, to help her to call a number of family members and other people if necessary. This had to do with her eye issues, but it was also connected to technological skills. Since Dao is no longer in the house, another child from her family who is still a student took over his task to be by her side. Whenever her phone rang and the student would be around, she would ask the student to check who was calling. When I asked about possible problems she encountered with the phone, she explained that there was a problem: sometimes people said they had called her, but she had not heard the phone ring. Again, Dao clarified the situation to me that her phone easily switched to vibration mode, without her knowing or understanding that this had happened.

There used to be an Illico fixed phone in her house. In 2005, one of her sons paid for two Illico fixed phones, because the family judged that it had become too dangerous for her to cross the road to Sic's phone cabin to make and receive calls. When the phone broke, the son brought it to Lomé but it could not be repaired and did not work anymore.

Dao explained that another uncle of his had won a Nokia in a lottery in 2008 and gave it to his grandmother. This was her first phone. However, when one of her grandsons visited her, he silently took the Nokia home with him. Another relative saw him with his grandmother's phone and confronted him about it. The cousin explained that 'he also wanted a phone'. The other said that this was not the right way to acquire one and took the phone back to grandmother. Till the day of our interview, the young man had never returned to his grandmother's house to greet her again.

After the Nokia, grandmother got her daughter's old Samsung, a midwife who converted to Islam because of her husband's religion, but the Samsung did not last beyond 6 months. Towards the end of January 2016, she got another one from one of her sons, which is the Samsung she was holding in her hands. First, she used the Moov number that her son had put in the Nokia, but the grandson who had seized the phone, had thrown out the Moov SIM card. Then one of her grandsons who is a soldier paid for her to have a Togocel SIM card. She was happy with Nokia, as its battery life was quite good; the battery lasted up to five or six days.

Though Dao's grandmother began her phone ownership with an Illico fixed phone, she began using the phone at the same time as the majority of the people whose mobile phone histories I transcribed. Most people started using a phone in 2004, 2005, and the majority received their first phone as a gift from a relative or close friend.

Phones as a gift

Since the 2000s, the '*frères de l'Europe*' [brothers from Europe] have provided a steady supply of phones as gifts to their loved ones,[14] along with supplying second-hand or '*venu*' phones for the small phone shops that mushroomed in the late 2000s (see figure 8).

Gift relations have captured the interest of anthropologists for quite some time, which is why I focus here on details about the phone and phone airtime as gift. I refer to Mauss' seminal work '*The Gift*': "the objects are never completely separated from the men who exchange them" (Mauss 1990: 31). His conception of the inseparability of the gift and the giver is especially interesting in the context of techno-social relations. As mentioned above, people with close connec-

---

14 It must be noted that these relatives or close friends abroad also live in regions other than Europe, such as the United States or Middle Eastern countries like the Emirates or Kuwait.

Figure 8: Phone shop 'Super boys'.

tions in Europe, the United States or elsewhere get a large supply of phones. For instance, the young man who was in charge of collecting the rent of the house I lived in 2015 and 2016, explained to me that he had never bought a single phone. Among other activities, he oversaw the affairs of a number of relatives and connections living in Europe. He emphasised that he never asked for a new phone, but every year his paternal uncle living in Sweden brought a new mobile phone for him to use.

These gifts are not just connected to generosity or to help the receiver. Instead, it is often in the interest of the giver to connect to the receiver. The direct connection that is established with the receiver of the gift often serves another relationship: that of the migrant with their mother, who is usually older and not always keen or able to comfortably use a mobile phone. Moreover, this aligns with the custom of having a mediator in many relationships.

When an individual really likes the phone of a friend, she can continuously emphasise that she likes the phone, until the friend gives it to her. It is rare for someone to refuse such a pressing request. One of the reasons for this is the conviction that one can never fully comprehend the desires and personal situation of another individual. If the person insists on being given a certain object, it must certainly be important for the individual and it would be rude to reject the demand. Of course, everything depends on the relationship; the gift should serve a specific aim. Often, these exchanges fall under what Piot (1999) describes as *ikpantu*, a friendship with obligations of exchanging – for instance buying *tchouck* – and providing for the other in times of necessity.

In other cases, friends agree upon a price for the phone ("alright, since you want it so much, I can give you this phone for 12,000 CFA"), or give it away when they have found another phone they like even better and can spare the old one. As stated before, phones circulate extensively between friends and family members, whether coupled with financial transactions or not, and as gifts that 'encourage' a girl to accept an invitation to go out with the giver.

Children from rural or other urban areas often move and live with a relative in the city to continue their education from high school onwards. This is mainly because high schools are scarce in rural areas, but it also aligns with the prevailing idea in the sub-region that children will be more obedient and focused on their education when they are mentored by a responsible person, other than their parents (see for example Verhoef & Morelli 2007; Bledsoe 1990). Most children return to their village during the holidays from June to September to work in the fields of their relatives. When they have reached a certain age, their parent or relative who oversees the fields can give them a mobile phone on their return to the city. Parents or caregivers are often also the ones who send small amounts of airtime to the students, so they can maintain contact with people in the village.

In June and July 2016, I interviewed all the members of the research team, who had worked with the theme and who shared some interesting reflections. In one of these interviews with Jef, we discussed the value of mobile phones in society. He expressed his amazement at the mobile phone being such an attractive object, which he illustrated with the story of his aunt in the village. He regularly calls her to enquire about her well-being, and he recalls a period in which she repeatedly asked him to bring her a mobile phone on his next visit. When he finally came to the village, instead of bringing a phone, he offered her a note of 10,000 CFA, saying that she could buy her own phone. She refused the note, and he did not see another option than to buy a mobile phone for her. Though the phone he bought cost only 8,000 CFA, which was less than the 10,000 CFA he had presented to her, his aunt was thrilled with the gift. She explained to him that she would be reminded of her nephew every time she would use her phone, which she found more valuable than the money he had tried to gift her.

Evidently, when it comes down to it, it is not just about the monetary value of the mobile phone, but the value represented by the phone: the ties that are strengthened between individuals, families or groups. The gift of a phone is not only an effective way to strengthen connections, but also a way for the receiver to showcase the fact that she has good connections, which generally has a positive impact on her position in society.

4.4 Everyday mobile phone use

Length and moments of calling

The patterns to do with calling or sending SMS messages during the day, as collected in the mobile communication logs, can be seen in the bar chart below:

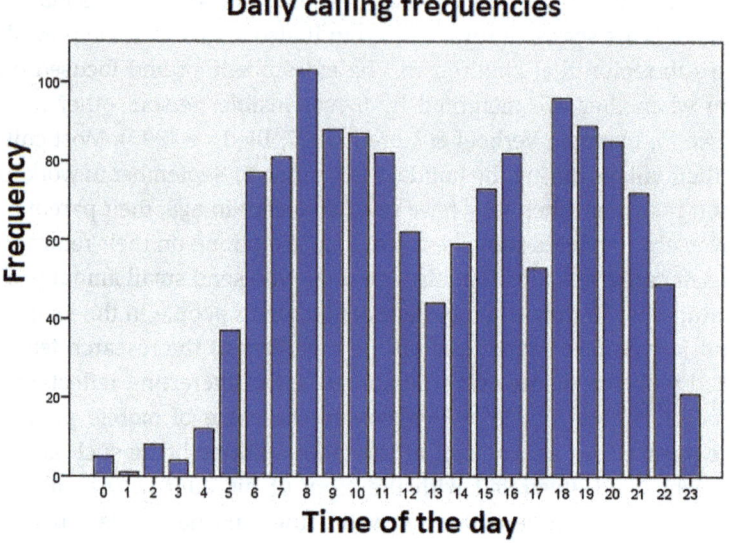

Figure 9: Daily calling frequencies.

This chart reflects the daily rhythms of life in Sokodé; for instance, it can be understood that most people go to bed between 10 PM and 11 PM and wake up between 5 AM and 6 AM. From the broader data, there appear to be slight variations between men and women; women for instance have less phone traffic between twelve and one, whereas men have less phone traffic between two and three. This can be explained by the activities they are engaged with: women commonly prepare the meal. Furthermore, there are no real fluctuations in calling times with one's partner; this is done throughout the day. People hardly report work-related phone calls during lunch break, roughly between one and three, which are also the times that they call their friends and family relatively lesser.

Besides the short, practical calls with one's inner circle, people give in to the urge to call their loved ones for a few minutes when they have not heard their voice for some weeks or months. In 2015, the most popular day to do this was Sunday, as Togocel's minutes cost 40 CFA instead of the usual 80 CFA. After another tariff change in 2016, every night between 21.30 PM and 5 AM, Togocel's minutes cost 40 CFA instead of the normal 80 CFA. An example of calling in this regard is the calling behaviour of Désiré, whom I often visited in his house in Kpangalam, and with whom I regularly kept in touch even in times of physical absence, as became clear in section 3.5. In 2015, Désiré called his maternal aunts every other Sunday for a few minutes, to enquire about their well-being. Regardless of the price change, he continued to make more calls on Sundays in 2016, and explained it like this: "The communication does not cost too much according to me. But everyone has their own way of seeing and doing things" (Conversation with Désiré, 28 May 2016).

Clearly, the timing that people choose for their non-urgent phone calls are heavily influenced by the costs, but also by their perception of the costs as evident from Désiré's quote. Though the content of people's calls is not significantly affected by the time of day, the information transmitted is usually very concise so that the calls are as short as possible and the expenditure as low as possible. People usually try to plan their longer conversations according to the costs and certain promotions. For example, there was a period when people paid only 500 CFA for 'Moov zone' for a conversation up to one hour on Saturday night between 11 PM and 5 AM. Some people know more about the different promotional codes and are up-to-date on their information compared to others; Freddy for instance was an expert when it came to the different codes of Moov – information he readily shared with his friends and family. Unlike Désiré, Freddy judged Moov to be more economical than Togocel. I set the context for one of the longer conversations between Freddy and Johnny, whom I have also known since 2010, like Désiré. To situate the friendships, Freddy and Johnny did not interact much with Désiré and Moussa, even though they got to know each other and me through two German volunteers.

The friendship of Freddy and Johnny was a tight one, even though Freddy had gone to Lomé by the end of 2015 in search of a job in his field and Johnny stayed in Sokodé as teacher. One Saturday evening in August 2016, when we had gathered in Sokodé, Johnny said that he would call Freddy in Lomé when the time had arrived for the lower tariff, so that Freddy could be there with us and know what he was missing out on. When he called, he told Freddy that he had a surprise for him. Freddy did not seem surprised at all when he heard my voice on the phone and he chattered away for about fifteen minutes, before I passed Johnny's phone back to Johnny, who then passed it on to Désiré, who has not spoken to Freddy in a very long time. In the end, Johnny took over the phone again, listened to Freddy for a while and said bye.

After the call, Johnny told me that he sometimes got an earache because of listening to Freddy for hours, and that he sometimes put his phone on the table and occasionally mumbled "yes" or "mmm" to give the appearance that he was listening. Such inattentiveness would be commented on if the conversation had been face-to-face. These are bits of information that cannot be known when one is on the phone.

Costs for calling and social hierarchies

Clearly, wealthy people and people who are higher up in the social hierarchy, like for instance Felix, usually spend more money on airtime than poorer people. This is not only because they are able to do so, but also because they are expected to call others more often than vice versa. This is a social obligation; the people with a higher position on the social, professional or economic ladder are often 'beeped' by those in the lower levels who indicate with their beep that they want to be called. There are of course exceptions: if the receiver of a call owes something to the caller, the caller generally does not expect the receiver to call back after she has seen a beep – people do everything to avoid such phone calls. Also, if someone urgently needs a service, she will have to call the other, even if she calls higher up the social ladder.

Most of the people with whom we spoke do not have a large budget to spend on mobile communication, as they do not have a stable income, but relatively they spend a lot of money for their communication. As Foster (2016) argues, personal discipline is intrinsic to the model of pre-payments for mobile phone airtime. To maintain discipline and handle one's precious 'minutes' with care is a great challenge in a society in which migration is deeply embedded and calling 'the village' is a regular duty. It is normal to stay in close connection with an extended network of loved ones, friends and acquaintances close by and further away, and there is always someone who urgently needs a call. Dao's grandmother illustrated this when I asked her whether she often made calls. She lit up:

> I have the flavour of calling, but unfortunately my airtime is often gone. See, it was only yesterday that I paid 450 CFA, but now it is already gone! [...] If I have not heard from my children for two or three days, I call them. [...] I receive between five to ten calls per day, and almost double on Sundays. (Interview with Dao's grandmother, 7 June 2016)

With an income as low as 30,000 CFA per month, people recharge 200 CFA or 450 CFA airtime on their phone(s) every day or every other day (about 0.30 to 0.70 Euro). This is a large portion of their household expenditure. In rare cases, people skip a meal to buy airtime, but some confirmed this had only happened to them in cases of 'emergency' like sickness or death, or, referring to Foster (2016), in cases in which they were unable to be disciplined.

Assuming a person who earns 30,000 CFA per month spends a minimum of 200 CFA every second day, she spends a minimum of 3,000 CFA per month (4.57 Euro), which is ten percent of her income. In contrast, Western Europeans generally spend about one percent of their income. Moreover, 4.57 Euro is extremely high compared to the prices in Europe; for five or six Euro, there are plans for 300 minutes per month and unlimited calling minutes are not uncommon. In 2016, even if a phone user in Togo would make her phone calls only on Sundays, when the Togocel tariff was 40 CFA per minute instead of the regular 80 CFA, she would pay 18.29 Euro for her 300 minutes, which is about three times as high as in Europe. Though most of the users in Sokodé do not spend more than 200 or 450 CFA per day, if at all, others with a relatively stable, higher income say they can use about 1,000 CFA per day.

Dao's expenditure in 2015 provides an idea of the expenses of people with a relatively higher income. Like many agents working on an international project for a local development association, Dao earns between 100,000 to 120,000 CFA per month. He can spend up to a quarter of his salary on communication costs. On a monthly basis, he buys 12,000 CFA airtime for his Togocel number from a specific seller he knows. The advantage of their acquaintance is that Dao can get his airtime on credit and pay some days later if he does not have the entire amount of money at hand. On top of this, he spends at least another 5,000 CFA for his Moov number with another acquainted seller. Whenever his airtime is finished during the month, which happens most of the time, he buys new airtime on the spot. In total, this can amount up to another 30,000 CFA per month, which he judges to be very high. Most of his calls are work-related. Since he is among the agents who work in the villages to implement a development project, villagers contact him all the time, and he is obliged to call them back.

This example emphasises the fact that the costs of making calls in Togo are high. Moreover, if one is lucky enough to be employed, it must be noted that communication costs are generally not covered by employers. Though a person like Dao's grandmother would not spend anything close to Dao's mobile phone budget, she also makes more calls than she receives. In the case of Dao's grandmother, her children and grandchildren come by her house to greet her at least once or twice a week. As noted above, if she would not be up to date about the well-being of one of her close family members for two or three days, she called them to enquire whether everything was alright. In this way, she was an important link in the sharing of information in her family.

People sometimes ask others to buy airtime for them; for instance, a child, younger sibling or someone's driver is given a piece of paper with the phone number and some money and sent out to buy airtime. Not everyone requests just about anyone to run this errand for them; this request follows specific social conventions and power relations.

The power relations discussed in chapter three are reflected in behaviour around mobile phones too. Airtime or even phones can be sent to someone as a gift or requested as a gift. In love relationships or marriages, men are the ones who provide for the women and not the other way around, the latter could even be taken as an insult. Therefore, girls are in the position to ask their boyfriend to send them airtime, among many other material goods. Stéphanie is an unmarried young woman I got to know in 2015 when she was 26 years old and was spending her days at a small local NGO, hoping for a new project to generate some income. In an interview in June 2016, I asked her whether her boyfriend also sends her airtime. She replied that her boyfriend always calls her, and not the other way around. Therefore, she is not in a position to ask him for airtime, as he will be suspicious and ask her: "Then who do you want to call?". This pattern also emerged in the mobile communication logs: almost without exception, men seemed to call their wives or girlfriends and not the other way around. If the woman would be the first one with the need to contact her partner, she often beeped him so that he could call her back.

Strategies to limit communication costs

In general, people in Sokodé have at least two SIM cards; one Togocel and one Moov. The reason that is most often given, is that people have friends and relatives on both networks. However, it also pays off to acquire a second SIM card of the other network, because the costs to call between the two networks are relatively high.

People who have only one SIM card are an exception; ownership of three or four SIM cards and mobile phones is not uncommon, as mentioned above. Usually, people have at least one phone that can carry two SIM cards. Most of our informants had at least two telephones. The persons who have bought an Illico 'fixed mobile' phone with a Togotelecom SIM card at the time of its promotion generally leave this phone at home, and only use their Illico when they are at home in the evening time, when the prices are lower. As discussed in chapter two, Togotelecom encompasses the fixed telephony system and infrastructure.

People deal with the high costs of mobile communication by limiting the time of their calls: Most calls are very short and do not exceed one or two minutes. People quickly check whether their loved one is doing fine, or they pass on brief messages. I was intrigued by the impatience of Brice, the young Togocel agent with whom I lived in the same compound in 2015 and 2016, and who knocked on my door to hang around with me practically every evening in 2015. He was always ready for action whenever he had a phone conversation, his finger positioned on the off button to end his phone call exactly the second that he deemed talking was no longer an absolute necessity. Whenever I called someone in his presence, he used to make wild signs at me to end a call immediately after the essential had been said.

The phone logs indicate that people in Sokodé receive calls more frequently than making them, which is a reflection of my qualitative data in which people say that Sokodé knows many 'brothers' who live outside of the city, country, continent. It seems as if most people own a phone mainly to be called, to be reachable by others – and not to initiate a call themselves. The costs for calling are simply too high and calling just to greet someone is considered a luxury. Most of the calls last less than one minute, though work-related phone calls sometimes last long. There are people who call just to convey their greetings in the morning or evening, but this is usually not done on a daily basis – except for very close relationships such as one's partner or parent.

Some people who have switched to smartphones explain away their investment by saying that their communication is less expensive. They are pleased with social media such as WhatsApp and Facebook as these services enable them to communicate with their peers and family for a low price. Most people with few resources but who have managed to get a smartphone, also manage to come online once every few days. In some cases, a friend sends a SMS message asking the person to come online so that they can chat, which is less costly than SMS or calling.

For the work-related calls, it is important to indicate the costs too. In some cases, the people higher in the workplace hierarchy receive a monthly sum for work-related phone use, but since these people are expected to be the ones calling, all persons lower in the hierarchy beep them whenever they need to exchange information. This means that the allowance for their airtime – if they receive it at all – is almost without exception far from sufficient for the calls that their subordinates expect them to make.

In some cases, an employer offers employees the chance to subscribe to a collective mobile phone plan, which makes calling between the numbers registered in this plan cheaper. One accountant for instance has a younger sister who works as nurse and who is responsible for a regional health mobile phone plan. She added him and his wife to this plan so that they can benefit from lower calling costs. This indicates that it is of utmost importance to have close connections with people who are close to those who pull strings.

Like many people in Sokodé, a man who works for a local NGO has few of his brothers and sisters in Ghana. In an interview I had with him at his NGO in March 2018, he told me that he learned one day that the son of his brother had disappeared, and no one knew where he had gone to. Finally, some years later, the son returned. The man said that he has been relieved ever since, although he never came to know the entire story, because the costs for calling were too high. He hoped to travel to Ghana later that year or the year thereafter, which is when he would hear the entire story. This is not a common occurrence, as other individuals or families would possibly spend the money to know more about what happened, if that was their priority. But that is exactly the point – there is only a limited number of minutes available to discuss many things, so people only choose subjects that are their utmost priority.

Since people generally only have airtime to make short calls and not everyone can write or receive messages, there are information transfers for which mobile phones are clearly *not* used. As has become clear, people mostly call on a regular basis with the very same people they interact with face-to-face. So, whenever they have an emergency, 'an information' to share or something else they want to share that requires some time, they only call to convene a meeting. Face-to-face, they will not have the pressure of time ticking away, and they can discuss things in detail. Therefore, it is quite likely that a lot of information gets lost because of the phone.

4.5 Maintaining relationships over the phone

Mundane calls with one's intimate relations

There is a great disparity between the calling behaviour of the few people with a high social and economic status and the people lower on the hierarchy, as was also noted in chapter three. In practice, this means that most people in Sokodé receive calls more often than the other way around. For many of them, their phone ownership mainly serves as a way to be reached by others – and not to initiate a call themselves.

Though most mobile phone users in Togo are obliged to keep their calls short due to economic reasons, they call the people closest to them for the 'usual stuff' in their daily lives. It should not come as a surprise that we noted that a teacher called his wife for 45 seconds at 12.30 PM, announcing that he would not be home for lunch. The reason for writing down such a banality, is that it is so often thought that access to mobile phones will give people access to more or better information, which will automatically lead to their development. In our results from 100 persons[15], it appeared that two thirds of all their contact moments were indicated to be private – as opposed to business or both. Many short calls are made to greet beloved ones. Smith (2006: 506) speaks of a similar use in a Nigerian context: "The vast majority of ordinary customers use a good deal of their credit making calls that are the cellular telephone version of a friendly visit".

Some authors discuss the use of new ICTs for opinion making and information dissemination (Adeiza & Howard 2016; Akoh & Ahiabenu 2013; Ekine 2010; Mutsvairo 2016a; Goldstein & Rotich 2010). Obijiofor (2011) investigated how university students of several Sub-Saharan nations use the Internet for retrieval and exchange of information. At the same time, there are indications that while mobile phones are indeed used for accessing public information like online newspapers, they are mainly used for maintaining social networks (Sey 2011), in which communication with peers is given priority over work-related contact (Kibere 2016), which is also of major importance when assessing the use of mobile phones for civic engagement.

The empirical data from Sokodé also indicates that 'factual' information seeking behaviour does not seem to be the main activity of mobile phone users in Sokodé, whether it is to do with making calls, sending SMS messages or accessing internet through a smartphone. Only a minority mainly use their internet airtime for consulting news pages, entering Wikipedia and using Google to seek out facts or to get informed about job openings. Most people spend most of their time online on chatting and sharing jokes on platforms such as WhatsApp and IMO and scrolling through Facebook.

The people with whom I worked in Sokodé generally seemed to use their mobile phone to stay in touch with their closest relations. Though I refrain from universalising, this idea resonates with a four-year study among 300 households in Swiss, in which Broadbent and Bauwens (2008) found that the majority of their respondents' phone calls were made with the five most intimate persons in their life. They wrote messages to more than five people, but often, the people with whom they were most frequently in contact through the mobile phone did not exceed 20 persons of their inner circle. Of course, these results must be consid-

---

15 The mobile communication logs consist of 3324 entries over a week-long calls and messages in early 2016, showing among others duration, frequencies and moments when calls were made and received, relationships with interlocutors (see appendix 1 and 2 for the set of questions and some of the results in graphs).

ered with caution, as mobile communication changes quickly. To return to the case of Sokodé, by early 2018, nearly all smartphone users were part of numerous small and large WhatsApp groups. Nonetheless, what is interesting in the study in Swiss is the suggestion that mobile phones do not necessarily expand the inner circles of people's social networks.

This also touches upon another assumption that was noted before that deals with the de-socialising influence of the mobile phone. It appears that people most often contact people through the phone who they will meet face-to-face not long after their call, something which Ling and Yttri (2002: 139) call 'microcoordination'. For instance, a motorbike breaks down and the owner calls the repair man to come and fix it, or an uncle calls to inform the family that he will be in town. Currently, the mobile phone cannot and does not fully replace face-to-face encounters, but it is often used to strengthen relationships, something which was also noted by Kibere (2016). This is also corroborated by other ethnographic accounts, such as the study by Molony (2008, 2009) about the economic impact of new ICTs in Tanzania, where he found that the most successful businessmen were the ones who frequently sat down to share a drink with the people who were part of their network, and not the ones with the highest phone bills.

Maintaining one's social network: Urgencies and phone introductions

When analysing the reasons that were given for the calls in the mobile communication logs, it appeared that in 2015, a large portion of the calls were solely intended to be greetings, and there were calls with a specific practical aim, either to transmit information, to fix a meeting for transmitting goods or for 'relaxation'. In 2018, much of these greeting calls had changed into greeting messages – relatively young people with a specific social position would easily receive 30 to 40 greetings on checking their WhatsApp every morning. Felix, for instance, explained to me that he felt the pressure of this and tried to reply to the most urgent ones, using emoticons to get through the list quicker.

The phone can be used as an asset whenever it concerns an emergency. As the word repeatedly came up in my conversations, at one point I started to inquire about the range of subjects that can be designated under this term. It became clear that about anything can be or become an emergency, varying from "our brother is in the hospital, and we need 50,000 CFA for treatment" to "I badly needed to know you are in a good state". Messages to people who are more distant and (supposed to be) higher up in the hierarchy are sometimes overt, such as "I don't even have one penny at the moment, please help me". Such messages also exist in less direct and therefore less urgent forms, inquiring on the other's well-being while hinting with a joke or 'wink' at an unspecified moment in the future when the other can provide them something. I explain such 'greeting messages' as one of the many ways to maintain and strengthen one's social networks. Since most of the population cannot count on institutionalised help – such as a health insurance – in case of personal disasters or urgencies, they have to rely on their network.

Generally, not many details will be given unless the emergency is life threatening. Close friends or relatives simply say: "Please can we meet; I have an emergency to discuss with you". Firstly, the matter is usually not discussed on the phone, but the ones concerned convene upon a moment to discuss it 'in private'. This might be a way to show respect to a person's privacy: Though the mobile phone seemingly makes people more accessible, they cannot be approached by just about anyone at any given moment. This is especially important if there is a difference in hierarchy. Both voicing a request for help and turning down such a request, demand a certain diplomacy to avoid causing harm or even a break in the relationship. In some of these cases, the habit of having a mediator is widespread, such as a close family member or friend, which I describe in chapter three.

When looking at the information that is passed on through the phone, it is also important to look at cases in which the phone is *not* used as transmitter of information. Mobile phone use is especially avoided when it concerns shocking information, like a disease or death in the family. This is of course not always possible, as families are often dispersed. In this sense, one man explained the 'rules' for such calls: whenever possible, male family members should be called first, who then approach the other family members who live nearby to pass on the news. More people explained that passing on bad news through the phone can cause cardiac attacks; men often added that this was especially the case for women.

Like face-to-face interactions, interactions through the phone generally strengthen social networks with people who are close by or further away. Though only some phone calls are intentionally made only to greet others and thereby maintain one's network, such 'simple' calls nonetheless make up quite an important part of the calls. A particular way to strengthen one's network is introducing people to each other through the phone. Just like in the example of Johnny and Freddy in section 4.4, it was common for my acquaintances to call their most intimate relatives or friends and then pass over the phone to me, so that we could greet each other, especially people I had not (yet) met in person. Such 'phone introductions' seem to serve the strengthening of connections; one of the strategies to strengthen the ties with the persons physically present, with the interlocutor or both. It can also be perceived as sign of respect towards the person physically present, towards the interlocutor or both, depending on the situation.

Transnational and translocal relationships over the phone

In an interview with 24 year old Khadija about new technologies, she explained how she kept reminding an American acquaintance that she had to bring her a smartphone on her next visit to Togo. Sharing this wish during our interview at Dao's veranda in June 2016, this brought her to another story. One day her older brother who lives in the United States came for holidays and gave her a laptop. She refused the laptop, because she was longing for a mobile phone and did not know how she would use the laptop. The laptop was given to her younger brother. It was only after she saw him using it that she started to regret her refusal, and she still regretted it very much. This shows the expectations and dreams that Khadija has and her lack of information about technological devices at the time. It also gives an insight in the devices brought to Togo by the diaspora and proves that the gap in expectations that can be wide.

The city of Sokodé knows many 'brothers' who live outside of the city, country and continent. Most of them have 'projects' in their home region: building a house and shipping containers with second-hand fridges, phones, cars or other materials. Some run small development projects like constructing a school or orphanage or run a programme for a vulnerable group. For these projects, they need reliable people with whom they can communicate and to whom they can entrust the execution of their projects, at least partially. It is not uncommon for one's closest relatives to try to come up with bills with higher costs than the actual expenditures, and deals are not always respected; trust in these cases is precarious.

This relates to broader themes of migration, remittances and transnational relationships, as highlighted in section 2.3. When it concerns phone calls, some of my West-African acquaintances in the Netherlands told me that they only answer calls when they see it is their mother's number, or two or three people in whom they confide. Nyamnjoh (2005a) has given an excellent account of migrants in Europe who experience stress because of the flow of phone calls from their extended family and friends, who often inquire "have you forgotten about us?". Among them, many do not even bother to inquire about the migrants' well-being, but immediately present their problem of a hospitalisation or unpaid school fees. This can have the effect of migrants not answering their phone anymore or changing their number altogether.

Less intense interactions have people chatting or making video calls and learning about life 'on the other side'. Though for instance Stéphanie complained that her uncle "wants to chat for hours, as if we have nothing to do here!" (Interview with Stéphanie, 21 June 2017; the same is reflected in de Bruijn, Nyamnjoh and Angwafo 2010; Foster 2016), this can also be an enriching experience. As noted in chapter two, the possibility to connect with one's loved ones 'back home' can be comforting (Nyamnjoh 2014).

These experiences are widely shared among diaspora and to a lesser extent among passers-by who construct friendships and then leave again, like tourists, development workers, volunteers or researchers. Pelckmans (2009) has made a laudable effort to describe how relationships between researchers and informants have changed with the possibility of staying in touch without the restriction of time and place. I also noticed that a short call to one of my contacts in Sokodé can be perceived as invaluable confirmation of the connection. Recently, WhatsApp messages have come to have the same connotation. Freddy, whom I met in 2010, has been struggling to find a job as electrician-technician. Sometimes he expresses that he is touched by my encouragements, even though I experience my own role in relieving Freddy's hardship to be marginal and superficial. Nonetheless, this illustrates my assertion that the support of relatives and friends – even when it is through the phone and even when it does not materialise – can help people to get through a moment of hardship.

People take care to keep in touch with their network beyond the place in which they live, especially if it concerns close family members. Besides transnational relationships, translocal or urban-rural relationships are also maintained mainly mediated through mobile phones. An example is that of Désiré, whom I also got to know in 2010, who sold 'pure water' in rural areas during the dry season in 2015 and 2016. 'Pure water' is filtered water that is sold in small plastic bags, which can be bought for 25 CFA. Like other trucks or vehicles, Désiré and his colleagues also transported information. Other than transporting pure water into the rural areas around Sokodé, villagers would give them letters or small items to transport to relatives in town and vice versa. This was cheaper, quicker and usually more reliable than the post office. Since the senders and receivers always noted down the phone number of Désiré or his colleague in order to follow the transaction, they often sent their 'appreciation' in the form of 200 CFA or 450 CFA airtime.

In urban-rural relationships, just like in transnational relationships, it is expected that the person who has left, initiates the contact – after all, the chances of this person to have access to airtime are imagined to be higher than of the ones who stay behind.

4.6 What phones reflect: Desires, realities, identities

Displaying identities: Colours WhatsApp status and eating chicken

The things a person owns say a lot about them. This is especially the case when it concerns things that people take along with them into public spaces, such as clothes, shoes, bags, vehicles and phones. Hassan and Unwin (2017: 87) note that the cultural impact of mobile phone use on identity construction in 'poorer countries' as a focus of research has remained somewhat understudied, other than an edited volume they mention by Buskens and Webb (2014) for the African continent.

The brand, type and colour of the phone are the first to be visible. Depending on the type of phone, if one gets close one can see the wallpaper, and inside the phone the images, messages, contact list, applications and status updates: the image of a person's life. Phones are among people's most private objects, yet they are visible in public.

Carrying a snazzy or expensive phone can be one way to show that a person is in control and successful, and draw both admiration and jealousy as result. People who carry an original Samsung or Sony Ericsson will receive compliments and admiration, because the quality of these brands is believed to be high. Nonetheless, a new top brand is not within reach for most people, who emphasise that they just want a phone that works, no matter the colour and type. They are not in the financial position to choose the best phone, and when choosing between quality and one's favourite colour, quality prevails. Some people base their choice of a phone on the experience of others, but choices are mostly motivated by a limited budget. Whenever a batch of a certain colour of phones is sold with a promotion, for instance a pink phone in 2016, several adolescents are seen with this phone.

Wallpapers, profile photos and status updates are another area in which mobile phones play a role in identity construction. Partners and children often show up on people's wallpapers that I have seen, and I also took great interest in the images and written statuses of people's Whatsapp accounts. For instance, Mohamed's welcome screen of his phone often displays his car, since he is a driver and earns his money with his car. He often changes the image of his Whatsapp status, showing his car with or without him, or his wife and children. By contrast, the welcome screen of the phone of another driver called Pili-Pili (because he is "as hot as pepper") displays a woman in bikini on the beach (observations, 26 February 2015).

The way in which people present themselves, supported by their images on their phones, says a lot about their social position. Another example comes from

Didi, a girl who lived close to the house in Komah where I stayed in 2015 and 2016. I met her on the street in June 2016 and she invited me in, and I met her again some weeks later with schoolteacher Johnny who was part of the research team and who obviously knew her. In the years thereafter we met again in the group with whom Felix hung around in bars. Around June 2016, her Whatsapp status was: "*Bb jtem bcp bz (kiss) (kiss) (smiley)*". As image she often displayed either her small nephew, a niece, or herself dressed in something that drew the attention to her rich décolleté.

In an informal conversation, she explained to me that when she chats with certain male persons, she changes her image for a while. Her attitude is also reflected in the way she reacted to Johnny, when we were hanging out together, and he openly insinuated starting an affair with her. Didi was mostly giggling, not refusing, neither accepting. Playing with her phones and her messages might give her the opportunity to acquire another phone, other gifts and possibly even a wealthy marriage partner. Johnny assured me afterwards that he did not behave like this with any girl; they knew each other from previous encounters, about which he remained vague.

The phone can be used to shape and reinforce one's identity – for designing and displaying one's online identity as well as vis-à-vis the inner self. This last aspect became very clear to me during a workshop for the youth volunteers of the ICT4D development project I attended on 26 May 2016. In the lunch break, one of the participants kept his phone in the air with one hand and put a chicken leg in his mouth with his other hand. He tried to film himself eating chicken. When I asked him about the purpose of filming himself eating chicken, I got the sensation as if I 'caught' him in the act. I suggested that he might show it to others, to his friends who were not there, or to his mother. He replied to me that he did not make the film to show it to others. He made it for himself, so that later, in the evening, he could look at it again and enjoy the moment again.

He appeared to be a mathematics teacher who had come together with three male colleagues. They took many photos with their phones, first of themselves, then also with the others who were still present in the room. As I had shown my interest by starting a conversation, they invited me to join in their pictures. What followed was an extensive photo session, which others soon joined with their own phone cameras, posing with each other and eager to pose with me too. When one of the workshop organisers called us to return to the workshop session, he remarked "you, who are making photos of the things you love" while he obliquely looked up to me (see also figure 10). This is a picture of the phone as indispensable friend or as an extension of the self – at least of people's image of themselves.

Figure 10: Who is researching whom?

Matching one's phone with one's outfit: The case of Felix

Wealthy people in Sokodé often own more than one or two phones. They tend to have up to three, four, five or even six phones, and at least as many numbers. Among the wealthier people we interviewed in 2015 and 2016, most of them did not recall how many phones they had used since they got their first phone. They pass on many of their used phones to others, or they bought phones as gifts for their partners, lovers, relatives and friends. Depending on the function of their different phones and numbers, people do not take all their phones and SIM cards with them when they leave the house. This is mainly because disposing of different phone numbers is more closely connected to relating and relationships than to status, as discussed in section 5.3. The following description of Felix and his phones adds to the understanding of the significance of phones as identity marker.

In 2015, Dao introduced me to Felix, who was his close friend at the time. As mentioned in chapter one, their friendship became less close in the years thereafter. Felix was then 34 years old, father of a 15 year old son, and unmarried.

4.6 What phones reflect: Desires, realities, identities

Felix is employed by the state, which gives him a certain financial stability that many people envy. As he enjoys debating complex questions and quoting German philosophers and French writers, some friends call him the philosopher. He has several favourite bars, where he used to drink Awooyo or Guinness, frequently as his breakfast, until he checked his liver function in 2017 and switched to a lighter beer to diminish his alcohol intake. Often when I encountered him, he was accompanied by highly placed army officers or other male friends, but also by silent or giggling girls whom he offered a drink or two. At any time during a face-to-face conversation, he made and received many phone calls, to friends, uncles, colleagues and acquaintances.

Felix was one of the rare men in Sokodé who carried a small pouch with him. When we met in a bar for an interview on 5 March 2015, he took his mobile phones out of his pouch, one by one, telling their story. The first phone was an Illico-Togotelecom phone, which he bought three of during the time there was a promotional offer. He kept one for himself, gave the second to a close friend of his and the third to his son. The second phone was a blue Nokia, equipped with double SIM, carrying a Togocel and Moov number. The third one was HTC, for browsing the internet, and fourth, a Blackberry serving as a Wi-Fi network whenever he spent time with his friends or acquaintances who did not have an internet connection themselves but who had a device – laptop or phone – to connect with wireless internet. The fifth phone in his pouch was given to him by his brother who lived in the United States, and was a phone whose number nobody knew. The phone was dear to him, because he had contributed financially to his brother's journey, and it was the first present his brother could afford to send to him. The final piece was a digital camera he hardly used anymore, but he liked to carry it around with him. Felix explained me that he usually carried all his phones with him, although sometimes he forgot one phone at home.

Sipping from his drink, Felix explained that he bought many phones as presents for others, but he did not have the habit of passing on his used phones. According to him, his own phones are personal items, not to be given to others. Only if one of his closest friends would need another phone urgently, for instance if his phone would be lost, stolen or broken down, he could give or lend the friend one of the phones that he did not use a lot. Felix saw his phones as an extension of himself, saying something about who he is as a person. For instance, about ten years ago, when there was a promotional sale on Nokia, he looked for a blue one because blue and black are his favourite colours. Unfortunately, he could not find it, so he decided to choose a red one, because he had red elements in his clothes at the time. When he found a blue phone, he exchanged the red phone for the blue, so that he could match his phone with his shirt.

The joy of possessing technological gadgets is something that might be particular to Felix and other tech-savvy persons. For Felix and other relatively well-to-do people, phones can be considered as a status marker: both as a way to display their importance vis-à-vis the outside world and as a way to feel important vis-à-vis their inner self. Since smartphones are considered as a luxury object, it can be important to show others that one is among the lucky few to have access to this luxury. Some explained that in this sense, the phone has replaced the Mercedes or BMW, though the upper class obviously owns both smartphones and fancy cars. Whereas this could be the new signs of an emerging 'middle' class – people owning smartphones and tablets, not cars or villas – it could also be that these devices add to one's status as a wealthy person.

Showing people that one has a smartphone can be beneficial for one's social position, as argued by an adolescent girl in a heated discussion in one of the focus groups held by Silvia and me in July 2016. The girl was between 18 and 25 years and she sold rice as income generating activity. According to her, if she would hold a fancy smartphone, this would attract many boyfriends and other friends, who would gather around her in the hope of touching her phone. Their interest in her phone meant that she would hold power over them, and that she could send them out to do something for her. She added: "You see, it's the same, I am now providing rice to all of you and that is why you are gathered around me" (Focus group with PASEORSC youngsters, 12 July 2016). Felix, for that matter, never put it as straightforward as that, but the ways in which he displayed his technological gadgets clearly impressed the people he was habitually surrounded by in bars. In these cases, the phone can be seen as a vehicle to enhance one's status and power, potentially leading to new opportunities.

The theory of attainment and dreaming of an android

Besides the group of wealthier people, adolescent girls have also begun proudly displaying their smartphones, beginning from 2016. In the interview that Dao arranged with 24 year old high school student Khadija, she introduced us to the term 'filles Androïde', which apparently also comes back in popular songs, for girls who enter into a sexual relationship with a man in exchange for smartphones, clothes or other material things in return (Interview with Khadija, 26 June 2016). Having become a popular gift in exchange for sexual relationships, the smartphone is clearly a product of desire.

Khadija also explained that she befriended an American woman who resided in her neighbourhood for a while. Time and again she reminded the woman that upon her next visit, she had to bring her a 'luxury phone' from the States. Though it was several years later, and the woman had not returned, Khadija had not lost hope that one day she would come back and bring her a fancy smartphone. Khadija's hope serves as an illustration of people's longing for a smartphone.

This was confirmed in over sixty interviews by Dao, Johnny, Freddy and me in 2015, in which we asked people about the phone of their dreams. About half of them said that they just want a phone that works, a phone which enables them to make and receive calls and messages. The other half answered that they dreamt of an *Androïde* or a *portable de luxe*, often specified as 'the ones with a touchscreen'. In 2016, hardly anyone still referred to the smartphone as a luxury phone, and the fact that it had a touchscreen no longer needed to be specified.

Most mobile phone users in Togo would be extremely happy to own the latest Samsung, iPhone or another premium brand smartphone. The fact that such a phone is not a possibility for the biggest part of the population does not diminish this desire. People manage with phones that are within their reach, waiting for something better. As one broadcaster eloquently told Dao and me in an interview at his radio station: "There are some small things we can organise [*on règle*], everything else we manage [*on gère*]" (Interview with radio director, 9 June 2016). "We are managing" is a phrase that is common in Togo and in societies in the sub-region, holding the wish or hope that things will be better one day.

This resonates in some ways with the Theory of Attainment developed by Miller and Sinanan (2012), which gives a direction to an understanding of new media. Their theory is based on the premise that new media do not imply a dramatic change in the form of 'mediation' of previously unmediated communication. They argue that new media respond to wishes that have already been present in humanity, it was just that the technological means were not yet available to put that wish into practice – such as viewing the other physically, which has become possible through video chat such as Skype, IMO or WhatsApp.

The mobile phone has given people in Togo the possibility to stay where they are, to *not* go to the village when an important message needs to be transmitted such as severe sickness of a loved one. They would have done so in the past, would there have been a possibility to do so, to save money and time. The mobile phone enables people to maintain their social networks with much more ease than before. Once they own smartphones, people integrate new apps in their lives to connect with their existing networks in more diverse ways than before. However, for the moment, the 'attainment' is only partial, as the phones that are available to common people in Togo have technical problems often. People are aware that the world of possibilities presented by the smartphone is rarely fully within their reach.

The ways in which the attainment is visualized but often not materialized can be linked to Ferguson's *Global Shadows* (2006), in which Africans claim equal membership to a global world order in which they are often neglected. This does not mean that Africans have not been part of a global system since many centuries, on the contrary. Though their present realities are dominated by difficult financial conditions, an increasing number of people in Sokodé manage to buy a smartphone, claiming their space in the global world, showing their peers and others that they are modern world citizens.

4.7 Concluding remarks

This chapter began with an exploration of techno-social relations, considering the extent to which the mobile phone can be seen as an external body part, being almost continuously within an arm's length distance of the owner. Considered the ubiquity of the phone, it seems reasonable to approach it as integral part of a person's well-being. In this respect, technologies and technological innovation can be seen as part and parcel of what makes us human (Latour 2005; Stiegler 1994). Besides this 'human influence' of the individual, media in Sokodé is under the control of the repressive state, whereas 'techno influences' include the unstable state of networks and bad state of available phones.

Research and development projects in the field of ICT4D are often based on the optimistic assumption that mobile phones give people more access to information and enable them to form new connections, which would then result in economic and democratic development (Banks 2008; Bratton 2013; Jagun et al. 2008; Southwood 2009). This chapter shows that processes of mobile phone appropriation and their outcomes are much more ambiguous. A mere focus on 'access to information' therefore is inadequate for approaching the mobile phone as technological innovation.

Most people in Sokodé do not have full access to mobile communication. This material 'gap' is often overlooked in discussions (Brinkman and Alessi 2009; Mutsvairo 2016b). The purchase of mobile phones, airtime and internet airtime put pressure on people's daily expenditure. Mobile phone users in Sokodé spend an estimated ten percent of their budget on communication costs, which is high, compared to one or two percent in Western European countries, and also high compared to neighbouring countries. The latter is a well-known fact and the people in Sokodé interpret this as part of the maliciousness of a regime that does not only impose limitations on people's mobile communication, but also tries to fill its coffers through control of the telecommunications market.

This chapter has indicated the changes brought about by the introduction of the mobile phone into society. The phone primarily seems to be an economic tool with enormous appeal. As such, it has become fully integrated into society, clearly visible in the public domain, and offering numerous types of possibilities. The communication landscape has expanded, and the telephone has become integrated into it. Yet, this description of the integration of the mobile phone into the public domain and the communication landscape does not conceptualise the phone as a sharp political tool.

5 Sociality and the mobile phone as connector and liar

5.1 Introduction

Mobile phones and other new technologies emerge from and shape our human experience. They are an integral part of lives in the world today. This chapter explores the unique influence on people's communication and their relationships that the mobile phone in particular has. While the focus of the previous chapter has been on the material side of the phone, this chapter focuses on the social side. This chapter delves into the particular ways in which phones are employed and entangled in daily communication acts. As Horst and Miller (2006) elucidate, mobile phones are part of a specific 'communicative ecology', in which they are shaped and shape communication in new ways.

Along with the social and geographic analyses of mobile communication, from the most basic 'what, why and whom' questions to the extended questions regarding mobility, locality and reachability, this chapter investigates the morality of mobile phone use, dealing with the question of how people navigate their inner freedom with external social norms. Since communication through the phone is not face-to-face, people experience and trigger a particular form of insecurity about the trustworthiness of the information flow. In this way, the space between two (or more) interlocutors becomes a contested space; what can be considered the truth is revaluated and renegotiated in face-to-face and 'mediated' contact. Set against the broader context of social insecurity and mistrust, the role of the mobile phone with regard to the trustworthiness of information flows is ambivalent at best.

Nonetheless, it must be noted that encounters and exchanges between people have always been guided by a set of written or unspoken rules that serve as a 'buffer' or 'mediator' between the inner worlds of two or more actors. Therefore, even face-to-face communication cannot be assumed to be the most natural, balanced form of human communication and is not necessarily the antithesis of 'unnatural' mobile communication (Peterson 2008). Clearly, there is a lot of information that is concealed in the city of Sokodé, and there are many obstacles through which people address pieces of information. Metaphors provide a specific way to address facts, which is one of the reasons they figure in this chapter.

The metaphor gives a partial representation of something that is not and cannot be known. For instance, 'love is like a rose' represents only a part of love, because love is among the concepts that can never fully be grasped. Semiotics explains the usefulness of a metaphor as a strategic element, in which a difference should be made between the metaphors used in people's daily conversations in Sokodé, and scholarly metaphors that can be used when an exhaustive list of features of the 'thing' or concept is not available. In a context of concealing and not-knowing such as Sokodé, the characteristic indirectness of the metaphor is especially helpful in social connectivity.

5.2 Locality, mobility and phones in the public space

Mobility of the phone or '*camatche camale*': "Go and come back"

Locality is a determining factor for the form and content of mobile phone communication. One of the aspects that makes the mobile phone 'new media' is its mobility: people can instantly converse with others over great distances and either one or both can move while doing so. This also has another effect: one can never be sure of the context of the other. Is she in a private or public place, is there background noise, are there others who overhear the conversation or who can access the phone and read messages with or without consent? Even the most remote places have network coverage – something that was unthinkable a few decades ago. Contrary to the hypothesis that the mobile phone would render geographic locations obsolete, several authors contest that localising the other became even more important. They note that the question 'how are you' has been replaced by 'where are you' in many phone conversations (Arminen 2006: 320; de Lange 2010: 138; Laurier 2003; Licoppe 2004: 138; Plant 2001: 29, 61; Townsend 2000: 87; Wellman 2001: 239). As discussed later in this chapter, mobile phone users in Togo have quickly adapted their vocabulary to deal with these questions.

The mobile phone is not often used for the transmission of detailed information about a certain opportunity or a location. I have witnessed many instances when people were waiting to physically encounter persons who were passing through Sokodé on their way to the north. These encounters were sometimes intended for passing on a parcel, but also for transmitting specific information. One day, Stéphanie, introduced in section 4.4, walked to the roadside of the national highway to indicate to an acquaintance the exact location of an NGO in a certain neighbourhood in Kara. Taking this as an illustration, she explained to me that such information is usually not suitable for a phone conversation (Interview with Stéphanie, 22 June 2016). It is rare that both interlocutors have enough patience to either explain or listen carefully to such extended information, like Brice in section 4.4, who had his finger on the off button.

There is however consensus that information moves more rapidly than ever between people because of the phone, which is why one of the names of the mobile phone in the Kotokoli language is *'camatche camale'* [go and come back], as a customary chief told me. The information is sent out to one's interlocutor and the response comes back, without the people having to displace themselves. So even though information might move more rapidly between people, the phrase does not describe people as having become more mobile. A simple phone call can prevent people from moving to another place.

Whereas smartphones have arguably increased the distance between people who are in the same geographic location, they have arguably diminished the distance between people who are miles apart. Having a mobile phone at hand can console people, as it allows them to connect with their beloved ones. Khadija, the high school pupil introduced in section 4.5, can chat on WhatsApp for hours and look for images on Facebook, Instagram and IMO. She explained that her phone enabled here to spend the entire evening in her room, not feeling the need to go out. She finds comfort in her phone, which she emphasised with these emblematic words: "I don't have friends, but the phone is my friend" (Interview with Khadija, 26 June 2016).

Travelling without moving: Promise of unlimited possibilities

Like Khadija, whose mobile phone enables her to experience moments of sociality without physical interaction, mobile phone users in Sokodé generally indicate that the mobile phone is a positive change-maker, an accessible means for people to 'link-up', as Horst and Miller (2005) describe it. In verbal appraisals, the mobile phone is considered as a positive change that has rendered transfers of information, money and goods more efficient. Not unexpectedly, two broadcasters both speak in terms of the opening of new connections. Similar to many others, a positive aspect of the phone for them is their communication with people in faraway places like China or the UK; some of whom they do not and might never physically know. Their scope is broadened; they learn about life in other places and find this an enriching experience. This is similar to the experiences of youth in Mozambique who 'travel while sitting down' (Archambault 2012).

Désiré, whose examples have also figured in chapter three and four, offers 'couch surfing';[16] sharing his home with tourists who have a free place to

---

16 See http://ww.couchsurfing.com.

sleep. He is very happy with the possibilities offered by new ICTs, in his words to "travel to places without actually displacing myself" (Interview with Désiré, 1 March 2015). To be reachable for possible tourists, he needs to access the internet often, which is not an easy task in the available internet cafés that are affected by power cuts, instability in the internet connection and run-down infrastructure.

Some days before we left Sokodé in 2016, after a consultation with me, my partner gave one of his used smartphones to Désiré: an original Sony Ericsson (see figure 11). The experience of transporting used phones in my luggage and selecting a few 'lucky ones' to receive such a gift was both insightful and estranging. I had brought gifts to the people who were dear to me on other occasions, but this time I was very aware that I was an anthropologist doing research about mobile phones. Was this an ethical act? Like Piot (1999: 52–77), I tried to partake in the gift-giving system, and I certainly made many mistakes. It also enabled me to get a better view on what is at stake in this social environment.

Désiré was thrilled with the gift, as it greatly facilitated his keeping in touch with tourists who had already visited him as well as helping him contact potential visitors. On a Saturday evening in May 2016, he brought along a USB with photos of a journey with an Italian family into a Beninese national park, which we watched together. Earlier, he had explained to me that his 'mind travels' also result in physically taking him to places, because some tourists make use of his offer to come along their visits to national parks and other attractions. This allows him to learn more about his region and, more importantly, about the ways, morals and behaviours of *les blancs* [the white] (Interview with Désiré, 1 March 2015). When sharing dinner with Désiré and Brice after Désiré had told me about his interest to learn about *les blancs*, I notice that Désiré corrects Brice and taught him some 'white' customs. To my surprise, the normal gangster attitude of Brice fully disappeared as he watched Désiré carefully – which I interpreted as a sign of respect for Désiré's knowledge of 'how the white want it'.

In the months that followed our departure in August 2016, Désiré contacted me through WhatsApp daily. He also indicated that everyone kept asking him where he got his phone. On one hand this was one of his ways to voice his gratitude for the gift once more. On the other hand, on a more general note, this also shows that the gift could have an impact on his status, because of the reasoning that having access to an original smartphone might entail having access to other material or intangible benefits.

Access to people who are higher up than oneself in social or economic hierarchies is highly relevant in a context where opportunities are scarce. "Not having someone" is among the worst situations in which one can find herself, as explained in section 3.2. So, in the best case scenario, Désiré reaps double benefits

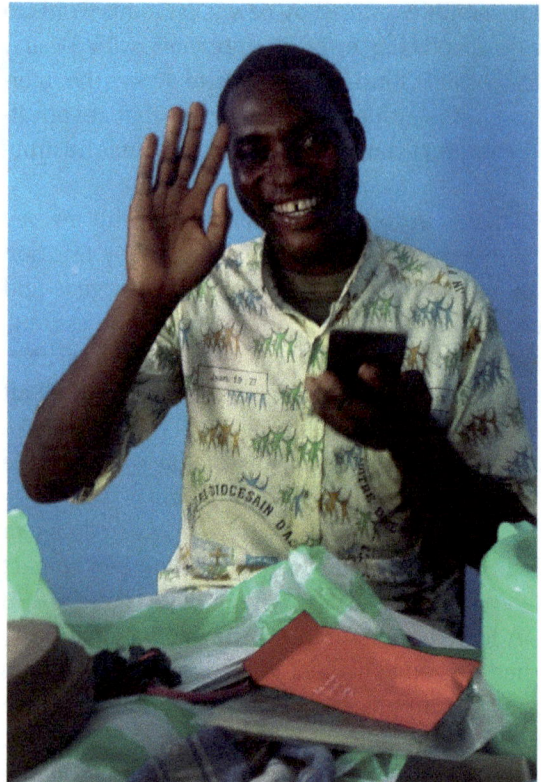

Figure 11: Désiré with his new phone.

from his smartphone: it improves his chances of prolonging and consolidating his access to the tourists who stay with him, and his improved status in the neighbourhood since he has access to this particular category of wealthy people who might at one stage also offer him new opportunities. At the same time, his position also leads to an increase in jealousy, which can result in negative inexplicable or 'mystic' events, and possibly a decrease in social support for him and his family.

The mobile phone as rope: Connectivity or tying up

Another consequence of unlimited connectivity of the mobile phone is exemplified by the canton chief of Sokodé, who agreed to be interviewed about the role of mobile phones in his society. In our exchange, the relatively young customary chief gave me a lesson in the history of the city before we delved into the subject of mobile phones, in which three other elders also partook. At one point, he used the image of the phone as a rope: a digital rope that connects people. Since these ropes are always exist between individuals and families, it is unthinkable for many people to turn off their phone willingly for many hours – it would be like cutting off this brand new rope. People want to be reachable in case of an emergency. Another reason for 'always' leaving one's phone on is the hope for an opportunity: An opportunity for a small job or some income, an opportunity to meet a friend or family member who is passing by, or an opportunity to learn something, get information one did not have before. As a matter of fact, most people do not have the luxury of not picking up the phone when it rings – one never knows (Interview with the canton chief, 13 June 2016).

Related to this belief in opportunity or 'sense of possibility' which I coined in section 4.2, is the list of phone numbers saved in one's phone. Since the contact list of phones can only contain a limited number of contacts, people do not save all numbers that call them. Some phones have a lot more storage capacity, so their owners do not have to dedicate time to select the contacts that should be saved, but nonetheless there is a limit. How do people deal with this, and on what basis do they differentiate between numbers? In the first years after the mobile phone was introduced, many people wrote down the most important numbers. Sweet Mama for instance, whose life history was introduced in section 2.5 and whose words resonate in chapter three, still uses a notebook with pages full of phone numbers, the names written in alphabetic order. Nowadays, the contacts that are saved on one's SIM can be retrieved in the Togocel office, which is a comforting thought to many.

The municipal officer with whom I had several exchanges at his office, about the ICT4D development project discussed in chapter seven, revealed the problem of differentiating between phone numbers. He used to go through his contact list and delete the numbers he had not contacted for an extended period. Remarkably, several times it so happened that he needed a number just a few days after he had deleted it, and he spent a significant amount of time and energy to get it, so from that moment onwards, he did not delete numbers anymore (Exchange with municipal officer, 27 July 2016). Others gave me similar examples. Again, this emphasises the idea that one can never know when someone in one's contact list can bring a new opportunity in one's life.

5.3 "The phone turns all of us into liars"

Always connected. But always available?

The mobile phone has opened different pathways of communicating with one's loved ones, acquaintances and possible new relationships, as mentioned before. Though most people in Sokodé consider it positive to be reachable through their phone on a 24/7 frequency, at least in theory, they have also developed mechanisms to deal with their reachability. The mobile phone has indeed made it easier to reach a person – if you go to their house and they are not there, you simply call them to ask where they are. As I hinted before, there are enough reasons for avoiding certain people at certain moments. The mobile phone has enabled people to develop both strategies to disconnect as well as strategies to connect to those who do not want to be reached.

The pressure to always be available is high, both for people who are higher up the social hierarchy and for others, though the underlying reasons for their connectivity differ. To be clear, I refer to their relationality here; though the hierarchies might be rather fixed, the identities of the people who occupy certain positions in society are of course fluid and dynamic. Though this list can never be exhaustive and positions often overlap, when I specify 'those higher up in social hierarchies', I mean public figures such as customary, religious, community or political leaders, high ranking security officers, opinion makers such as journalists or broadcasters, wealthy business people and directors of large NGOs. In the frame of availability, there are certain professions in which people are expected to always be available, like in the health sector.

Most reactions to my question whether people turn off their phone is one of dismay: 'Of course not, imagine that someone has had an accident in the middle of the night and needs your help'. The pastor, who was introduced in section 4.3, exclaimed: "A member of my church might be dying and needing my prayers" (Interview with a pastor, 25 February 2015). He is wary of the possible harm caused by radiation; his ear warms up during his usually long calls. In our interview under a tree at his royal courtyard in 2016, a customary chief also reports that his people should be able to contact him at any time of the day, as there can always be an unexpected problem in his neighbourhood (Interview with a customary chief, 10 June 2016). In this sense, both do not have the 'luxury' of being unavailable through their phone.

This is similar for the director of a radio station, who is always looking for business opportunities, and he is approached by people who want to share newsworthy information. In a lengthy interview with Dao and me at his radio station, an interview that he had postponed because of a treatment he was undergoing at the hospital, he explains:

> Only if it is for my health, I turn off my phone. It is the density of communication, the role that I have. I fight, and this fight interests 6 million people. You see, you are going to fall sick but the wealthy sleep sound. (Interview with radio director, 9 June 2016)

However, if he wants more privacy, he temporarily turns two of his three phones on silent and turns them upside down, so that he cannot see incoming calls and messages.

Even though the radio director is looking for opportunities, he has reached a certain status that others do not have, for example a young female student who studies in Lomé. She explains that she is immediately triggered when the director of her institute calls her. If she sees a missed call from him, she does everything possible to reply as soon as possible. Unhesitatingly, she adds that she experiences stress whenever she thinks about the fact that he can call her at a time that she is unable to pick up her phone (Interview with student, 5 July 2016). A second example is provided by Désiré, who during the time that he was selling 'pure water' sachets, also had to be available to his manager night and day. His manager would sometimes call him at 3 or 4 AM, when he needed Désiré's help to load or unload a truck full of bags that had just entered Sokodé. For people like Désiré and the student, their position or even their career depends on their superiors, so the consequences of their disconnection could possibly have a high impact.

However, even though most people would say that they are always available, there are numerous internal and external reasons that cause temporary unavailabilities. As demonstrated earlier, most people do not generally make or receive calls between 10 PM and 5 AM. People's availability should be regarded in this light; they express their desire to be available, which can be a source of stress at the same time, but when it comes down to it in practice, there are enough situations in which they do not immediately respond to a phone call or message.

Depending on the relationship and the context, there is a certain degree of accountability for the time that lapses between the beep and the moment of calling back. Not responding does not usually cause trouble right away, but if one is not responsive within a few hours, this can contribute to a feeling of distrust. Upon calling back, people often start with an explanatory phrase about their reason for not responding earlier, such as "I was in a meeting". Phones can especially create tension between partners if there is already a sense of distrust in the relationship, an aspect that is discussed again in section 5.4.

A lack of skills in manipulating the phone can also lead to people *not* using the phone for communication. For instance, a civil servant told me that he had gone to his friend's office in the morning, because he had been trying to contact his friend for several days without succeeding. Since he needed the friend for a service, but also because he was a bit worried, he decided to visit him in person. It appeared that the friend had unknowingly switched his phone to flight mode, and a colleague of his had just helped 'de-blocked' the phone. This is another illustration of the idea that phones can serve to enable communication as well as disable communication.

Using several phones to (dis)connect: Privacy and reachability

Most mobile phone users in Sokodé own SIM cards of both Togocel and Moov, in order to use every opportunity for network coverage around the clock and to benefit from the calling schemes at reduced tariffs. Similar tactics have also been described for other contexts, among others by Horst and Miller (2006). Switching networks and numbers can also be a business tactic to reach people who do not want to be reached. A third reason for network switching is the instability of the mobile phone networks, which is especially noticeable during peak phases like weekends and festive days.

I noticed that repair men, journalists and business people were among those who had at least three different numbers. This is not simply a status symbol, but it has everything to do with privacy and reachability. The use of a second mobile phone also mirrors the image of the second office (the infamous '*deuxième bureau*') as metaphor for extramarital affairs, explored later in this chapter.

A category of people call using their lesser known number whenever they want to reach someone who they know is reluctant to accept their call. Usually this concerns cases in which people still owe something to the caller – mostly money, but at times also information or something else. Repair man Mamah explained with a smile that such a number is only used on rare occasions, because if it would become known that this is actually one of their own numbers, the number becomes obsolete. He was not afraid that debtors would be suspicious; since they assume that such calls are made with a borrowed phone (Interview with Mamah, 13 March 2015).

The radio director who was cited in section 2.2, explains that he disposes of six numbers and three phones: one for a smartphone with WhatsApp, another one with a Togocel and a Moov number, and another with Togocel and Moov. He has many numbers, because the people he wants to call, know the reason why he is calling them. Cheeringly he says: "If they would know it is me, they would not pick up the phone" (Interview with radio director, 9 June 2016). He has one Moov number that nobody knows, which he plans to use only during a big emergency. Though he does not explain the type of emergency he means, it can be surmised that his critical attitude towards the regime could bring him into trouble at one stage.

Disposing of several phones and phone numbers can also serve to delineate and protect one's privacy, a concept that has been explored in chapter three. Many people with more than two numbers explained to me that there is an 'in-group' of intimate contacts who know all their numbers. One of the ways to create privacy is to temporarily turn off the phone with the numbers that are more widely known in silent mode. A businessman explained that he sometimes switches off his phone with his two 'public' numbers in order not to be disturbed by his clients or acquaintances for a while, like others who are frequently sought after. In the meantime, they remain reachable on the number that is known to only a handful of intimate contacts. However, it remained challenging to narrow down the frequency with which these 'popular' people 'disconnected' their more public phones. As I demonstrated above, because they are sought so often, it is difficult for them to disconnect.

This can be illustrated with the behaviour and words of a successful businessman whom I have known since 2010 and whom I will call Izak, as he made it quite clear that he discussed matters 'off the record' with me. In March 2015, Izak told me about three phones and four numbers that he had: Two of his phones and three of his numbers were publicly known, but the third phone with one number was only known by three persons besides him: his mother, his wife and his personal assistant (Interview with Izak, 11 March 2015). Derived from his overt interest in discussing 'intimate affairs' ever since I came to know him, there is a possibility that he has other phones or numbers that are known only to a handful of women.

"I'm in the fields!" The phone as *gnèridou* or liar

One morning in July 2016, during a somewhat contrived focus group in which I tried to gather common perceptions and uses of mobile phones from a mixed group of ten adolescents in Sokodé, one of the boys received a phone call. The person who was previously talking paused, and we could clearly hear a female voice, to which he responded: "I am in the fields", after which he quickly ended the call. This caused amusement in all the participants, and more laughter followed when someone joked "which field is this?" (Focus group with PASEORSC youngsters, 12 July 2016). This account reveals why the phone is also called '*gnèridou*' in Tem, meaning slanderer or saboteur, besides the more neutral term '*camatche camale*'. Both terms were mentioned by the canton chief and his elders, in what slowly turned into a group interview when I visited the chief under the trees at their royal courtyard in Komah in June 2016.

In my initial weeks in Sokodé in February 2015, I was awed by the versatility of the answers people gave about their whereabouts upon receiving a phone call. However, every time someone called me and I replied, "I am at home" and hastily added "… but I'm about to go out", I got to understand that it was socially much more accepted to say that one is on the road, in a meeting, in another city or working on the fields. When I asked the young man in the focus group why he brought up 'the field' as an answer and not said, for instance, 'in town', he explained that he did not want to meet the girl during the day. If he would have used 'town', she could get the idea that they could meet within a few hours, whereas he had no intention of meeting her before it was evening. By mentioning that he was in the field, she would immediately understand that she could not expect to see him during the day.

Obviously, there are all sorts of lies for different situations and relationships. In most cases, people know the reason their family member, friend or acquaintance is calling, and within a split second they decide the response they will give when they see the caller ID on their screen. As noted above, callers can circumvent this by using another number, but these type of lies in intimate relations are so common that most people do not mind being lied to.

When I first heard people using the term 'lying' for this practice, I was reluctant to apply the term myself and it still sounds odd, as there are many cases in which telling lies has an outspoken negative connotation. However, people did not seem to attach this connotation to this category of lies. Even the main imam of Togo, who is based in Sokodé, explained to me in an interview at his house that "the phone has turned all of us into liars, without exception" (Interview with main imam, 23 June 2016).

I am certainly not the first to point out the slippery notions of 'truth', 'lies' and the subtle but big difference between avoiding the truth and telling lies. For instance, Horst and Miller state that with regards to relationships in Jamaica that "one can reach a point where people see a lie as a kind of higher 'truth' because as an exposure of deceit it brings a person closer to reality, while a mere truth is seen as the continuation of what must really be deceit" (Horst & Miller 2006: 98–99). In March 2015, this was also explained to me by my research assistant Dao when I asked about his perception of the trustworthiness of my lengthy explanation about being half an hour late. He explained to me that he had not spend much thought on why I had been late, but once I started giving him reasons, his suspicion was immediately triggered. In his reasoning – and I noticed the same in other relationships – if I truly had good reasons, I would not have felt the need to share them with him. Whatever activity I was involved in before I met him, did not matter to him.

Just like Dao's advice to keep silent instead of explaining too much, the kind of 'lies' that I described above can be seen as a way of being discreet, and a way of respecting the other's privacy, as has been described in research on mobile phone use and intimacy in Tanzania (Kenny 2016) and Mozambique (Archambault 2009). Archambault (2009) states: "Respect and discreetness are often used interchangeably, and telling lies becomes somewhat acceptable when done to preserve respect. [...] Discreetness is all the more valued given the difficulty involved. In the peri-urban areas of Inhambane privacy is hard to come by." In this regard, the young man who told the girl that he was in the fields instead of in a focus group discussion in Komah, was being gentle: He both preserved his own private space and gave her respect by providing a reason for postponing their face-to-face meeting that was external to their relationship.

5.4 Freedom and control in intimate relations

Phones and intimate relations: Ignorance is bliss

When weighing the advantages and disadvantages of the mobile phone as a communication device, people in Sokodé perceive the mobile phone pre-eminently as a wonderful device that helps them connect with others with high speed and increases their opportunities. In most of the conversations in which this question comes up, as an entry to deeper appraisals of mobile communication, the narrative is given of a death in the family, for which people no longer have to travel to convey the news. Besides fear of negative health consequences caused by radiation, most negative connotations can be found in the field of intimate relations, in which 'lying' is most cited, as noted above. As telling lies and suspicions of being lied to are so closely related to trust and distrust – these concepts return in the examples given here.

The businessman I called Izak, cited in section 5.3, was immediately triggered by this subject when I asked whether the phone has changed anything in the relationship between a couple. He said:

> "Because of the phone, you can even go to the tribunal with your wife – girls use phones to menace men! Girls blackmail men; they will first wind the man around their little finger, but then they say 'I will transfer the messages to your wife'."

He continued on to say that the phone can contribute to divorce: "I know four couples that have divorced because of the mobile phone. A women calls her husband: 'Where are you?' 'At home' 'But I see you at the Hotel Central'. Because of the phone, you start lying" (Interview with Izak, 11 March 2015).

Among the dozens of people with whom I spoke about the social impact of the mobile phone in Sokodé, there is a consensus that 'the phone causes problems between couples' up to the point of divorce. Some add nuance to this statement, by adding that there might have been a divorce anyway between certain couples, but they emphasise that the phone speeds up the process, as cheating is uncovered more easily and quickly than before. Other informants strongly assert that the phone is the reason that couples break up. Pierre, a man who works for a local NGO, told me that he divorced his wife 'because of the phone'. Some weeks later, he explained to me: "In the past, an affair leading to divorce could be discovered only after ten years, but nowadays you see your wife with someone in a restaurant and you immediately call her and ask where she is. If she says 'I'm at home', you can immediately confront her" (Interview with Pierre, 12 March 2015). Another illustration of this is the story of a 45 year old traditional healer who complained that 'women call their boyfriends too much':

> Once on my way to town, I passed by the Komah market, as it was a Thursday like today and we sell there on market days. I made a stop to see one of my wives. It was my second wife, who had left her hangar and had gone out, but her comrades said she would not be long. After 15 minutes she had not returned yet, and as I was in a hurry and she did not arrive, I called her number. It did not work; her phone was switched off and I left.
>
> A week later, one of my acquaintances here in town crossed me and said he saw my wife with a man in the quarter of Tchalou. So next time when my friend saw my wife on a motor-taxi, he beeped me three times and I called him back. He said: 'I saw your wife on a motor-taxi and where is she going?' As it was a market day, she should be at her hangar. So I immediately called my wife and I asked, 'So are you going there?' Suddenly she told the Z-man to turn around without even hanging up the phone, as she was so worried. I kept listening until my airtime was finished, but anyway it was clear that we really had to talk. But now it is arranged, she is wise now. So the mobile phone is a blessing and a curse. (Freddy's interview with a traditional healer, 5 March 2015)

Clearly, the nature of phone communication, that is, the physical distance between the interlocutors, has made it both easier and more complicated to lie, which is also described by Meinen (2015). When trying to locate the other ('where are you'), one can never be sure whether the other speaks the truth or not, unless the other is in sight. Telling lies has become more complicated in the way that if one has doubts about the truthfulness of the other, it is relatively easy to find 'hard evidence' when scrolling through the other's phone (Archambault 2012). This 'evidence' is one of the reasons why people say that the phone has increased divorce.

Archambault (2009) states that blaming the phone for relationship troubles should not be seen as a form of technological determinism, but:

> When youth in Inhambane say that so-and-so broke up 'because of the phone', they are rather underscoring that the biggest harm comes from lack of discreetness and from the fact that the tangible proofs the phone provides are almost impossible to deny.

These are also the themes in the relationships in Sokodé with which this chapter engages. The story of the traditional healer and his second wife is an intriguing case in point, as it reveals both changes and continuities in intimate relations. There is an undercurrent about perceived changes in the possibilities of controlling one's wife, though his comment that 'she is wise now' indicates that he feels that he is back in control. The story also deals with the increased visibility of telling lies about one's whereabouts and the behaviour that such lies are suspected to be motivated by. Again, from his 'complaint', the problem seems to be not so much the fact that women might have boyfriends, but that this becomes known.

Trusting men, trusting women

Though men and women reproach each other that they cannot be trusted when it is to do with sexual fidelity, men are generally in a stronger position than women. This has several reasons, some which are deeply rooted in society. The likelihood that married women are often financially dependent on men rather than the other way around does not contribute to their bargaining power, nor does the prevailing idea that women should be protected against malevolent men – after all, the need to protect women would decrease if perceptions of men as being unable to control their urges would change. Regardless of my own feminist perspective, in Sokodé, infidelity of men has more acceptance and is probably more widespread than that of women. Of interest here is of course not their infidelity – which is not specific to people in Sokodé – but how the mobile phone plays a role in perceptions and behaviour concerning this theme in this context.

At least among each other, close male friends show solidarity concerning this theme; they cover up for each other to their respective wives or principal partners, whereas women are viewed as gossiping more than men, and sowing the seeds of doubt between couples. However, as with the opening incident in chapter one, in which David sent pictures of Felix and his girlfriend to a second girlfriend, male friends can also deceive each other with their access to hidden information. Another reason to share the secrecy of the relationship is given by one of the men that I often hung around with, who explained that he is obliged to reveal the identity of his girlfriends to his closest friends, because he does not want to be in a situation in which they drag one of his girlfriends in front of his eyes. Silvia and I had an interview with one of the 'drinking buddies' of Felix who was an overt womanizer. Sitting under the fan in his office, the young man gave an insight in how he handles difficult situations with his wife:

> When he comes home late and finds out she is still awake, he will immediately start talking in a joking, appeasing way: that she should not be so suspicious, that she knows him, that there is nothing to worry about. Once, when his wife had gone to her village for a family meeting, he had gone out to visit a girl in Kara. One day before he expected her back, she called him in the evening that she had arrived at the bus station. He rushed home and pretended he had been visiting a friend in the vicinity. He did this in an extra kind way, and caressed his wife, so that she would forget to be angry at him. (Interview with Laurent, 14 July 2016)

Several unmarried men in the age between 25 and 40 revealed to me that they did not necessarily seek trust in a relationship in the sense of sexual fidelity or in financial matters. According to them, the kind of loyalty that mattered most dealt with the agreement of keeping up morality towards the family and the outside world. In this context, the Achilles' heel for a man's honour is the behaviour of his wife. Therefore, the behaviour of a woman must be well studied, and the men who told me this, stated this as a main concern and reason for postponing their marriage.

Garage owner and private driver Mohamed meticulously studied his wife and her family background before convincing her to get married to him. During one of our many conversations in his car in July 2016, he shared with me the story about how he had managed to marry his wife. He told me that he chose 'polygamy' when signing the marriage contract with his wife, and he saw her tear up in response. That evening, his wife was more silent than usual, and he finally explained her that he had not wanted to draw his family's attention to their liaison – his father had to sign the marriage papers for his consent. He said that they would definitely have mocked him if he had chosen a monogamous marriage, making statements like "look how his wife controls him". Besides, Mohamed presented this to me as an extra motivation for his wife to keep up her impeccable behaviour, and he had begun his explanation to her with the phrase, "normally, you will remain my one and only wife". He mentioned that even when they remained childless for several years, and she suffered several miscarriages, and people urged him to take a second wife, he remained calm and told her to be patient. After five years of marriage, she finally gave birth to a girl.

I never asked Mohamed directly whether he was dating other women or not, because I knew he would not have shared this type of intimate information with me. On the contrary, several times, even though I did not hint at anything, he did his best to make me believe that he did not meet other women. I took this as part of his endeavours to present himself to me as a decent, trustworthy man. However, in a conversation with his wife in April 2017, she portrayed him differently, including regular visits to another woman. Sitting next to her on their couch, I asked her how she was so sure about this, and she pointed towards the top of their wardrobe, where she had found a box of condoms. Moreover, she said that she had found out "because of his phone".

'Trust does not exclude control': Scrolling through the phone of one's partner

"Trust does not exclude control" is a phrase that often reappeared during conversations. As explained above, it is often easy to find proof of a partner's infidelity by searching for messages and numbers in their phone. However, going through one's partner's phone is not considered wise or morally just. There is a significant gender difference in this regard. Men do not usually allow their partners to look through their phones, whereas they ask their wife to hand over her phone at any point. Of course, when one's partner leaves a phone unattended and takes a shower, it can be tempting for the other to quickly grab the phone and go through the phone, especially when notifications go off.

Something similar could have happened in the case of Mohamed and Rachida. In April 2017, some weeks after she had lost her unborn baby in the hospital after an eight month pregnancy, I had a lengthy conversation with her, during which she indicated the condoms. To say something positive, I commented that at least he protected himself, but this did not prevent her from being unhappy with the situation. She assured me that she no longer looked through her husband's phone, as this triggered too much emotional turbulence. However, over a year later, when she was halfway through another pregnancy, she sent me a WhatsApp text message asking for my advice: he had proposed to another woman that they could have a child together. Since I judged the matter to be delicate, I did not push her to explain what made her certain that this was the case. Possibly, she had not been able to 'control herself' and had looked through her husband's phone again. She seemed to prefer that he takes on the other woman as a second wife, instead of having to deal with his secrecy. Some weeks later, she sent me a text message that she had confronted him, and the issue had been settled, though I did not know what exactly this meant. Some months later, I received photos from him through WhatsApp of their second child, who was born in good health. Possibly, I might receive photos of his second marriage one day.

While both men and women generally refuse to allow their partner to look through their phone, there is a significant power difference. Not all women are in the position to refuse when their husband asks them to hand them over their phone. A 28 year old woman selling juice and *pure water* told Freddy that her husband gave her a phone at the time of their marriage. One day, in the evening, she received a phone call of a man she did not know, and it appeared that the man had dialled the wrong number. However, her husband was so suspicious that he called back the person and asked him who he was. He got so angry that he took away his wife's phone, and it was only three years later when he went on a business trip that he bought her a new phone (Freddy's interview with 28 year old woman, 14 March 2015). While this is an example of a comparatively extreme case of control, it is quite common for a man to scroll through his partner's phone, whereas a woman is not allowed to do so. However, some women are better placed to dictate access to their mobile phones than others, especially women who are economically independent. Moreover, the practice of scrolling through one's partner's phone could be changing, as people become more aware of the possible devastating effects of knowing too much.

Salim is Dao's friend, who Dao introduced to me in February 2015, and who eventually became one of the research team members. In the courtyard of a bar, Salim and I discussed his mobile phone history (Interview with Salim, 19 June 2016). He told me that his previous phone had some problems and that he had given the phone to his wife as a present. Further into the interview, he explained what had really happened: his wife had tried to unlock the phone in his absence, and she had pressed the wrong code three times and accidentally blocked the phone. This worked to his advantage; since it made her the one in the relationship who had to be ashamed of herself for not trusting him. But even if she would have managed to unlock the phone, he had already erased the secret messages she was looking for. The end of the story was that he gave his phone to her as a present – but not before he had erased all his contacts, messages, call logs, photos and other personal information. In a way, this phone became a gift and a warning, to not question the loyalty between partners – even if it is not about physical loyalty.

5.5 'Endangered' morality in social relations?

Degrees of control over dating behaviour of the younger generation

During the time I shared a compound with Brice and an old woman who I shall call Roukia, one evening, I heard Roukia talking on our courtyard in a very agitated way. I could not wait to hear from Brice what had happened. Later, he knocked on my door and came in to share the story. One of her nephews who was a student, had not been cautious, and the result was the unplanned pregnancy of a 15 year old girl. After she had given birth, her parents had told her to leave their house, and the family of the boy had to deal with the problem now. The boy had fled to Ghana. 60 year old Roukia had been selected by the family to take care of the baby and his mother for the first six months of his life, and she was clearly unhappy with the situation.

Clearly, such situations also occurred in the past, but the narrative is that it has become more challenging to protect the morality of adolescent girls because of the phone. It is commonly believed that the phone has increased infidelity, because dating has become easier and more widespread with the phone. On the road, any man can ask a girl for her number. 'Back in the days', men had to visit the house of the girls they dated and greet the family first. In this way, the caretakers of the girl could exercise some control, by studying the man and his family, and advising their daughter on how to deal with the situation. If the behaviour or family of the man was not judged as being proper, the man could be forbidden to enter the house. Nowadays, a girl can meet the man without her parents even knowing him. The reality is slightly different. In the past, most teenage girls were not constantly being watched, but the introduction of the mobile phone has given adolescent girls relatively more possibilities to dodge the control of their parents and caretakers. Men can simply beep or send a message, indicating they are waiting outside or at a pre-determined spot.

This 'free' and 'immoral' behaviour of girls is generally considered to be dangerous, because girls must be protected and maintain the 'right' morals. According to several of my Christian informants in Sokodé, this played an even larger role in Muslim families. Sexual intercourse outside of marriage is not generally approved of, and this is illustrated by stories of early pregnancies and diseases leading to an early death. A girl like this would bring disgrace to her family, and serious marriage partners and their families will disregard her. Especially when they are already married or part of a couple, people are expected to practice as much secrecy as possible, out of respect for their partner.

Men are less constrained when it comes to controlling their desires or guiding their behaviour. Though also not considered 'right', indulging in sexual intercourse with different women is socially more accepted when compared to women. However, there are several young women who date different men and who receive material benefits from engaging in these relationships. Archambault (2009) describes a similar shift in intimate relationships in Mozambique, in which women's phones serve to challenge existing power relations, as young men experience powerlessness because they must let go of their claim to exclusivity, "given that most do not dispose of the material base on which it rests." The many jokes that circulate in social media in Togo about women whose need for material goods cannot be satisfied, also points at the gap between men's economic capacities and women's desires. Some of these women will benefit from their increased freedom in this regard, though aspiring a lifestyle that includes a fancy original smartphone brings along other kinds of restrictions.

The narrative of smartphone use as a distraction for youth

The difference between smartphone and 'simple' phones lies mainly in the smartphone's ability to connect to the internet, which gives people the opportunity to access and appropriate all sorts of applications. Voice and video message applications like WhatsApp and IMO are immensely popular, and users share jokes and funny images that divert their attention away from the difficulties they face in life. The exchange of pornographic images is often mentioned as a nuisance – especially by women who indicate that they do not appreciate it when male 'friends' send them these images. Besides the fact that forwarding pornographic clips can be considered as digital expressions of sexual harassment, such messages can easily get women into trouble with their partners who regularly check the contents of their phones, as described in section 5.4.

Stéphanie, who studied Sociology with Dao in Kara, features in the mobile phone logs collected between February and April 2016. I knew her through the small local NGO in the compound where I stayed in 2015 and 2016. It is interesting to combine the information given in the logs with the interviews and interactions I had with her over the years, for which she gave me her explicit consent. In her 'reasons for calling' in the log, it is mentioned that one of her phones had a problem and she had it repaired by a repairman she had befriended (see figure 12). The last row is insightful, because a 10 seconds call from a friend is described as: 'for information about my absence on WhatsApp'. In our interview in June 2016, in the small NGO office where we are alone, Stéphanie explained that friends who disposed of a smartphone were used to give her a short call or send an SMS saying "connect yourself so that we can exchange" – again a strategy used to keep costs down (Interview with Stéphanie, 21 June 2016). Figure 12 displays more strategies: she often communicated through beeps (missed calls), and she mostly received calls, in this example.

Date	Time	Call/ SMS	Outgoing/ incoming	Duration (sec)	Relation	Reason for choosing this moment
7-3	18:29	Call	I	0	Friend	To come and see the mobile phone
7-3	18:37	Call	I	0	Friend	To repair phone
7-3	18:42	Call	I	20	Uncle	Just greetings according to availability
7-3	21:50	Call	I	325	Friend	Moment to exchange better after absence on WhatsApp
7-3	22:05	Call	I	63	Friend	Rediscovery (rétrouvaille) on WhatsApp after absence of several days
7-3	23:37	Call	O	0	Friend	Free moment to chat
8-3	06:17	Call	I	37	Friend	Network more fluent for exchanging
8-3	09:29	Call	I	32	Friend	For pleasure to greet me
8-3	11:29	Call	I	0	Phone repair friend	Information about phone repair
8-3	11:52	Call	O	0	Phone repair friend	Information about phone repair
8-3	11:55	Call	O	0	Phone repair friend	To make an appointment to see each other regarding the phone
8-3	13:38	Call	I	10	Friend	For information about my absence on WhatsApp
8-3	15:08	SMS	I	0	Younger brother	For airtime transfer
9-3	08:22	Call	O	60	Phone repair friend	Information about repaired phone

Figure 12: Stéphanie's reasons for calling.

The social and internal pressure to be online is high enough to keep oneself constantly connect, though it can be quite challenging to 'find the money' to buy internet airtime. Stéphanie remarked: "If I do 24 hours without Whatsapp, I am not at ease. When my phone got spoiled, all my friends called 'where are you' and I said, 'my android broke down ooooh'. In fact, they should all save up to buy me a new smartphone." Reflecting on her smartphone use, she later added: "It is only for us, the lazy ones, who have no job and who have ample time to chat and share jokes on social media" (Stéphanie, 21 June 2016). The increased social media use, especially by youth, is met with suspicion, similar to other parts of the world.

In Sokodé, the narrative is that youth use their phone 'in disorder', and many of them have not passed their final exams because of the distraction of their phone. This is a narrative that Stéphanie echoes. This complaint is mostly about smartphones. Overall, smartphones are perceived to distract students and prevent them from excelling in their education, which 'should' be their first and foremost aim. Instead of using the smartphone to 'do research' into the subjects they study at school, the belief is that they use their phone mainly to chat with their friends via WhatsApp, IMO, Skype and Facebook. In this regard, the smartphone is considered to contribute to immoral behaviour, because youth can see so many things they are not supposed to see, according to their parents and other adults. The exchange of pornographic images is often quoted as being the source of problems. Moreover, the phone is believed to entice girls to date all types of men, which also leads to 'immoralities'.

It was widely believed that the low graduation rate of the final exams in 2016 was due to the 'distractive' use of smartphones. Even though this narrative has a political edge, which is revisited in the next chapter, it was also prevalent among the youth themselves. These 'negative' evaluations of the smartphone were often punctuated with a sigh and the wish that the government forbid mobile phone ownership for children under 18 years. Besides, some people added that 'we Africans' do not possess the right knowledge to deal with the phone in a 'proper' way, unlike '*chez vous*' [at your place, in this case meaning in Europe], imagining that where I come from, people know how to regulate technology use. Their reasoning is that there are numerous technologies available in Europe, so the exposure began earlier and following this, people have the knowledge of balancing their use. This kind of reasoning aligns with the perceived foreignness of the mobile phone as an object among many 'things from abroad' that will profoundly change society, as argued by Hahn (2012: 185).

5.6 Concluding remarks

This chapter showed that the introduction of the mobile phone is an intriguing moment in the history of communication in Sokodé. Clearly, the phone has immense social impact, and changes people's lives in different ways. This change is not political, but involves social life. As social life is at the basis of political entanglements, the political impact of the mobile phone manifests far more subtly.

People attempt to protect themselves with a trustworthy circle of people around themselves, but it also involves a constant alertness, as 'elements' in their inner circle can become dangerous once they know too much. The case of Felix, who suspected his friend of having poisoned him, shows that issues of trust are complicated. This fundamental distrust also implies a level of acceptance of not-knowing, bringing along a type of freedom for individuals to share only certain information about themselves. At the same time, this influences the very conception of information in Sokodé, unveiling a part of its intimacy.

Can a parallel be drawn between society and the girl who steps out a circle of people in a bar upon receiving a phone call? With every step the girl takes away from the social circle, she endures comments from those in the circle. In a split second, she has had to weigh the consequences of accepting or rejecting the phone call, as well as the consequences of walking away to ensure her privacy or staying in the circle, where everyone can hear her part of the social interaction with her interlocutor. Answering the call has consequences either way. Such a situation could not have happened in the early 2000s, as many people did not have a mobile phone. With society embracing the mobile phone, new configurations of relationality have come about, and continue to do so.

In this analysis, the mobile phone can be considered a catalyst for increasing distrust in Sokodé and the instability of relationality in society. This might seem contradictory to my argument that the role of mobile phones for development should not be exaggerated, but in the next chapter I argue that development is not a 'project' that can be enforced; change simply happens, and most often cannot be controlled.

6 Civic (dis)engagement and protest

6.1 Introduction

On 24 May 2018, two persons lost their life in a tragic road accident on a bridge just north of Sokodé's city centre. While crossing the bridge, a motorbike tried to avoid another motorbike coming from the opposite direction and hit a truck, the impact of which threw both motorbikes on to the road. One of the bike riders and his pillion rider, a female school director died, the other was wounded. Out of fear of being lynched by the people on the bridge, the truck driver continued driving and was intercepted at the commissariat up the road.

There are several painful observations to make about this accident. It illustrates a political system in which only a select, privileged group of individuals have access to power and monetary wealth, which weighs heavily on individual actors on the micro-level. Firstly, regular road accidents are a clear manifestation of the country's 'unstable infrastructure', a term used by Atwood (2016) to describe the political and economic situation in Zimbabwe. Besides unfavourable road conditions, there are difficulties in sanitation and water, electricity, the health and education sector, and digital communication networks. There are no easy answers to these challenges.

Secondly, this bridge had been the location of the road protests in 2017, in which a truck filled with sugar had been set on fire, burning for days. On my return in March 2018, I often had to cross the bridge that is part of the national South-North highway, and one of the few tarred roads in Sokodé connecting the different neighbourhoods. It could not go unnoticed that the sticky remnants created dangerous situations, and I was certainly not the only one feeling uneasy whenever crossing the bridge.

Whose responsibility was it to clean the bridge? Does the accident underline the 'tragedy of the commons' (Hardin 1968), where the sticky bridge was 'everyone's' responsibility and therefore no one was inclined to be the first to act? Did the authorities remain inactive on purpose to remind the population that the protesters had been wrong, like what was whispered about the remnants of the burned motorbikes in front of the commissariat? I asked people where they could go in order to address the matter, like the town hall or the prefecture, even though I knew that they would respond with resignation. This question was asked not only to understand more about civic engagement, but also because I was sincerely concerned, though I must admit that I also did not address this particular matter on a higher level or organise a cleaning drive.

In some cases, the repair of a bridge or cleaning of a road is organised relatively quickly. This chapter explores the components of such organisation, looking into the role of the civic. It sheds light on the civic-ness of connectivity in this unstable context and takes the question of sharing public information a step further. After conceptualising the terms 'civil society' and 'civic engagement', these terms are matched to 'events of information' that carry a certain public element, such as the troubles in the second half of 2017, that have left their mark on sociality and civic-ness in Sokodé.

6.2 Civic-ness or civil society in Togo

Disentangling the concept of civil society

'Civil society' is one of the buzzwords among the circles of development actors and practitioners, especially in combination with 'good governance', 'democratisation' or 'decentralisation' programs. A strong civil society is imagined to be one of the most enduring solutions to democratisation, and ICTs are imagined to give a voice even to marginalised groups (Avgerou 2008; Bimber 2000; Hayes & Westrup 2013; Ochara & Mawela 2013). This image of the transformative power of ICTs for development is the foundation of dominant ICT4D thinking (Donner 2008, 2009; Donner & Toyama 2009; Walsham 2017), which is discussed further in chapter seven. The concept of civil society is connected to pressing issues in social studies, like questions of identity and belonging in a rapidly globalising world, the increased blurriness of boundaries of the nation-state, and power relations between different actors that constitute society. Before addressing the question of whether there is a civil society in Sokodé and the ways in which it is possible to speak of it, conceptual challenges related the term need to be discussed.

Though concepts of 'the civil' and 'civilisation' were debated in ancient Greece, a differentiation between the civil and the state only surfaced in the eighteenth century. From Enlightenment onwards, the concept of civil society has emerged in debates about state-society relations, public and private spheres and there are several links between these concepts. As much as it has emerged, as much its contents have been questioned, it has proven to be enormously difficult to pin down the exact meaning of the concept and what it relates to, and its variations in different historical and geographic settings, as several authors in the late 1990s have shown (Blaney & Pasha 1993; Hann & Dunn 1996; Krygier 1997). The image of the ideal civil society is not the same today as when it was first conceived of by Scottish enlightenment thinkers such as Ferguson

([1767] 1995), who described civil society as non-political organizations that precede and shape the state, or 'the political'. Defining what is 'the political' is as slippery an undertaking as defining the concept of civil society – especially in a highly politicised environment like the one under scrutiny.

Accounts of an ideal, or normative, civil society are often not congruent with the lived experiences and perceptions of the individuals involved. Following the same line of thinking, the forms that civil society can take in social formations that have been produced within a colonial context, as is the case in Togo, are necessarily different from civil society elsewhere (Bissell 1999; Mamdani 1996). Till today, the concept carries with it other ambiguous concepts such as 'citizenship', 'the state' and 'the public sphere'. The need to decolonise these concepts remains a priority; detaching it from a Eurocentric framework that often does not sufficiently consider the colonial context in which present-day social spheres and structures are rooted. Ground-breaking works like 'Citizen and Subject (Mamadani 1996) and 'On the postcolony' (Mbembe 2001) stimulated heated debate and are still of high relevance, considering for instance the more recent Rhodes Must Fall protest movement, that called for the decolonisation of academia (Bhambra, Gebrial & Nişancıoğlu 2018; Murris 2016).

The problematic distinction between public and private spheres

One of the main challenges that come with the dominant image of the ideal civil society is that the image often rests on a distinction between public and private spheres, which owes much to the thinking of Habermas (1991), who approached civil society as a social space in a bourgeois society, marked by civil liberties and voluntary arrangements. In this thinking, the 'public sphere' is a self-regulating sphere where civic action is wilfully pursued, separated from government and religion. In the same vein, Neubert (2011: 212) understands civil society as a sphere of voluntary organised collective action around shared interests, values and goals. Individuals, who are to a certain degree organised, act together to pursue a common goal, and civil society is to be found when private issues are converted into a public matter. However, the set of dichotomies that accompanies this approach have been criticised, especially the differentiation between public and private spheres (Weintraub 1997: 2) but also the voluntary aspect (Nyamnjoh 2005b: 30–33).

The distinction between public interests and private or intimate spheres is not so clear-cut and has probably never been compatible with African contexts (Comaroff & Comaroff 1999). It is also increasingly considered to be fading under the influence of new communication technologies (Broadbent 2016; Nippert-Eng

2010). For instance in Europe, there has been a clear spatial separation of the professional and the private from the time of industrialisation, the 'intrusion' by private messages into professional life, first on the office phone, then in one's E-mail inbox and some years later on one's mobile phone, has had a lasting impact on this separation. Broadbent (2016) is among the few who judge this as a predominantly positive development, arguing that a deep sense of connectedness with one's intimate contacts can add to one's feeling of comfort while being at work. This can also be linked to Licoppe's (2004) 'connected presence' as coined in chapter two, pointing at the continuous conversation that is established through the mobile phone. Several authors note that the mobile phone transgresses the private and the public (Goggin 2006: 4; Katz & Aakhus 2002; Wasserman 2011: 151).

In order to be able to contribute to existing debates, it remains useful to accept the existence of a public sphere, at least on a theoretical level, on the condition that its ambiguities are taken into account. In the late 1990s, the popularity of the concept of 'civil society' saw a revival. Several authors convincingly established that distinctions between public and private spheres, and between 'the state' and 'civil society', are not dichotomous but ambivalent and multi-faceted, if they exist at all (Comaroff & Comaroff 1999; Ferguson 2006: 89–112; Mamdani 1996; Weintraub & Kumar 1997). Lund asserts that civil society actors in fact have an ambiguous position between public and private spheres; they actually "operate in the twilight between state and society, between public and private" (Lund 2006: 678).

It is more useful to approach the public and private as two ends of a continuum beyond such dichotomies, as was also discussed in chapter three (Nippert-Eng 2010). Information sharing in Sokodé is largely a private act, evaluated through the lens of the relationship. In this regard, just like information, the 'public sphere' is always a relative sphere, theoretically on the sliding scale from entirely private to entirely public. This relative condition makes it easier to describe a public sphere in different ways, like Ferme's description of a Sierra Leonean public sphere: "based, in the local imagination, on a dialogics of compromise, of consensus forged through both overt and covert consultation, of communal and sectarian interest, of civility" (Ferme 1999: 185).

Ferme's approach of a dialogics of power can be related to Mbembe's (2001) approach of civil society, especially when he builds on Bakhtin's ritualised 'dialogism' between state and people. Mbembe approaches civil society as a process of relationalities, articulating relational differentiations among the rituals, signs and practices that often separate the ruling class from those they govern. In this way, civil society can be seen as a particular practice of constructing, legitimating and resolving disagreements in the public sphere. This resonates with

Nyamnjoh's focus on the articulation of interests and perspectives independent of or in conflict with the state (2005b: 31). The voluntary aspect is an interesting point in Nyamnjoh's understanding of where and how such interests may manifest themselves in complex, postcolonial, economically constrained African contexts. According to him, civil society does not necessarily have to be voluntary, as unelected ethnic elite associations have often been more successful than voluntary associations in striving for the concerns of ordinary citizens (Ibid.: 30). Another important point is that 'people may collaborate with the regime in varying degrees for various reasons of survival' (Ibid.: 32). In order to make sense of civil society in an African context, such configurations should also be taken into account.

Thus, civil society should be approached as a flexible concept that stands in relation to a highly dynamic notion of public and private that are interrelated but do not stand in opposition to each other. Taking this dynamic notion of the private-public continuum as a point of departure, and accepting the public as a highly ambiguous notion in need of contextualisation, it is possible to uncover specific initiatives or groups that pursue a shared goal in something that could be called the public sphere.

6.3 Towards a Togolese civil society?

'Civil society' actors and political entanglements

With the definition of civil society as a sphere of un-coerced organised collective action, I now turn to "organisational formations that are empirically identifiable" (Helliker 2013: 157). Helliker claims that these two different uses of the concept are often not spelled out, which obscures the debate. In the same vein, Lachenmann (2009: 14) criticises the particular use of civil society as 'container concept' that includes associations, NGOs and other forms of non-state approaches. To make Helliker's distinction clear, I distinguish between civil society and 'civil society' actors, putting civil society within inverted commas as I do not consider the actors to be equal to civil society. However, there are identifiable actors in Sokodé that call themselves civil society actors and are addressed by other actors as such, for instance in bilateral development programmes such as the one described in chapter seven. In this specific usage, 'civil society' can include all types of actors: besides the oft-included human rights organisations and associations for women, youth, farmers or other specific groups, other included actors are labour unions, NGOs and faith-based organisations.

The *Concertation Nationale de la Société Civile* (CNDS) with its head office in Lomé and the *Réseau des Organisations de Développement de la Région Centrale* (RESODERC) in Sokodé, both of which I visited for interviews, are examples of what Helliker (2013) calls 'empirically identifiable' organisations: 'civil society' actors that interact with political and development actors on local, national and international levels. Nonetheless, when considering the place of these actors vis-à-vis other actors, it is not so clear whether there is a significant difference between political and civil actors. Living under a repressive regime, it is extremely difficult for an organised interest group to carve out a niche and capture the attention of society and their leaders for a civic cause, without being discarded or becoming part of the establishment (see also Nyamnjoh 2005b: 31). This is also reflected in an audio message that was circulated on social media during the times of the troubles in October 2017 by a member of the Togolese diaspora:

> It must be recognized, however, that in Togo, there is no civil organization that can survive the terrible regime of RTP-UNIR. You are to be aware that any organization that is going to meet them is always infiltrated, and in most cases its infiltrations are as such that at the head of the organizations that claim to be against them, have as leaders those whom the internal regime has been infiltrated. In the end, when you put up a coup against them, they are informed and finally it is doomed to fail.[17]

Of course, this language clearly testifies to a certain political stance, and 'civil organisation' here is used in a rather functionalist way, denoting an opposition to the state that can be questioned (Förster & Koechlin 2011: 8). Considering the conceptual discussion of civil society above, it should be noted that not every 'civil organisation' strives for political change, but their interests can be seen as being different from the state. In this respect, Kaufmann (2016: 30–31) points out that framing civil society in opposition to the state neglects the mechanisms, dynamics, and transformation of social actors and their actions, as they are rooted in complex social networks. However, Lund (2006: 678) states that:

> [...] while the distinction between state and civil society has become a less than useful analytical tool, it has spilled over from academic to more popular political discourse with other effects. As it is 'no longer divorced from the agency of the groups of individuals it purports to describe' (Whitfield 2003: 380), it becomes part of a dynamic process of production of popular distinctions. As a consequence, we should not refrain from studying civil society. On the contrary, we should pay careful attention to how concepts and distinctions are produced, instrumentalized and contested.

---

[17] This is a translation of the first few sentences of an audio message that I received on 11 October 2017, forwarded via a WhatsApp group of one of the local development groups.

In this light, the audio fragment above can be seen as an illustration of the instrumentalisation of the concept of civil society, and I include it to underline that many matters are or can instantly become highly politicised in the Togolese context.

The political entanglements on the local level are clear in the everyday practices in Sokodé, where the municipality's leaders often call upon a range of directors and chairs of local NGOs and development associations to be a part of several committees. The crux is that these so-called 'representatives of civil society' are not only carefully selected by the town hall as spokespersons, but their participation is also effectively managed in these meetings: whenever their stance is too divergent, they are simply not given the floor. Since they are present, their participation is noted, regardless of the participatory value of their presence.

In the highly politicised environment of Sokodé, power differences play out on various levels, some visible, others less visible. Most of the time, they can only be found in a handshake, the wink of an eye, a sigh, or a sign of impatience when a person is speaking, to which I will return in section 7.3. These subtle power games in the borderzone between public and private can be linked to processes of legitimation and public authority (Dodworth 2014; Lund 2006: 678).

Competing actors in the public sphere

The question whether a civil society exists in Sokodé does not have a straightforward answer, as becomes clear from the above discussion. The environment is not conducive for engaged 'civic organisation' in many regards. This contributes to associations and movements coming up rather spontaneously or ad hoc, being reactive instead of proactive. This shows that whatever association or collective that could be seen as civil society actor, has difficulties in setting the agenda. If the analysis of the audio message in the previous section is taken into consideration, the belief that UNIR infiltrates all civil society organisations, the state is then always one step ahead. This could be seen as part of the cause of the weakness of these 'civil society' actors, but possibly is also the result of it. This aligns with Nyamnjoh's reflection of undemocratic infiltration as one of the complexities of civil society organisation in African contexts (2005b: 31–32). He argues that financial constraints, hidden donor agendas and lethargy of the targeted population contribute to the complexities of independent, democratic civil society.

Nyamnjoh's understanding of civil society does not only go beyond independent and identifiable organisations, but also can include social movements. This is consistent with other theories focused on democracy and media in Africa, such as the one by Ellis and van Kessel (2009). Social movement has become a popular yet differently focused alternative for 'civil society' and 'associational life', especially in combination with new ICTs (Ellis & van Kessel 2009; Engels & Brandes 2011). At times, social movements emerge that give people hope that their voices will be heard, but they do not remain in the centre of action for too long if their leaders are not part of the established actors in the public sphere. The paradox is that actors that become too well-established are no longer credible as actors that operate independently of the ruling party, regardless of their actions – the mistrust is simply too deep. This displays a gap between grassroots realities and more organised layers of society. These power dynamics and struggles are also fundamental to understanding civil society in Togo.

The organisations that strive to be considered civil society actors are often competing on different levels. Firstly, the size of the group which they claim to represent is often unclear, which makes it difficult to judge the extent to which they are striving for a public cause. Secondly, they are fishing in the same pond for funding by international donors, which also impacts their autonomy as noted by Harbeson (1994: 10, 286) and Makumbe (1998: 311). The management of these organisations is often more concerned with upward accountability or with 'keeping up appearances' towards their donors, than with the actual target group they claim to work for. A WhatsApp message of one of my informants who is employed in an international development programme hints at the impact of this:

> For me, on my side everything seems to be better. I felt an improvement in my health state after two weeks of vacation that I asked for at work. If I told you; the contract is finished again and I am waiting for the renewal, but the work continues. The nightmare continues as I told you, and worse. As you know most of the projects in Togo; the managers do not care about the impact of the actions, what matters to them is to justify the expenses. They say to themselves they know and do not even want to have the views of little ones like us, and this starts to act a lot on my conscience since I am always facing the communities for which we work. Ah! How will I do? For the moment this is what makes me satisfy my needs and take care of some people around me.[18]

This message is interesting because it shows the ambiguous position of local employees of groups that implement international development projects. Moreover, it also indicates power processes and the relative powerlessness of local employ-

---

18 Translation of a French WhatsApp text message sent to me on 12 January 2017.

ees and 'beneficiaries' vis-à-vis these large projects. Though there are ample 'public causes' delineated by international development donors that are supported by the population or that do not seem to harm the population, as noted above, civil society actors are coloured by the lack of public causes that emerge from internal forces in society (Harbeson 1994; Makumbe 1998). As shown above, besides this element of competition, the government interference in civil organisations also impedes civic organisation (see also Nyamnjoh 2005b).

Whereas development actors generally have a relatively more practical working definition of civil society and sometimes lump together different organisations under the denomination of 'civil society representatives', theoretically it is difficult to trace the contours of a civil society in Togo. There are some movements that struggle to position themselves as civil society. As described above, some actors or movements dominate the field at certain moments around certain pressing issues. However, their relative power vis-à-vis each other, the state and other actors do not provide a firm basis to answer the question of whether a Togolese civil society exists. Considering the complex conditions of civil society in this context, enables a deeper view into the meaning of these complexities for the development of the city of Sokodé, its institutions and society at large.

6.4 Public spheres and civic (dis)engagement in Sokodé

Civic engagement and social hierarchies in Relation

When considering civic engagement from the bottom up, it becomes evident quickly that social hierarchies are the core of understanding any type of organisation in this context. Though the concept of a social hierarchy implies a specific manner of categorising, social hierarchies are not necessarily vertical, nor static. In section 2.3, I have described the ways in which my approach is inspired by Glissant (1990), who, in his Poetics of Relation, presents a world view that transcends conqueror and conquered, perpetrator and victim, the opposition between the Self and the Other. Mbembe vividly accuses postcolonial theory of Glissant and others as having 'clouded the understanding of the relationship between sovereignty, homicide, fratricide and suicide' (Mbembe 2005: 14–15).

From Glissant's work, I take a perspective on the present and the future beyond time and space, a way out of the impasse that Mbembe does not seem to offer (see also Karlström 2003). Glissant's Relation is an appreciation of our 'unity-diversity', the understanding of the totality of the multiple differences in the world. In this view, much like Piot (1999) understands the world, centre and periphery are part of one and the same living organism, which is life itself, in all its facets. This is related to spirituality, and sociality in Sokodé cannot be understood without understanding the spiritual embeddedness of its fabrics.

The basic premise that people are an integral part of their relationality – that individuals are constituted of their connections with other human and non-human actors – places my use of the term social hierarchies in a different light than its more common meaning. Though an individual surely has her own personal interests vis-à-vis others – a mother asking her neighbour 5,000 CFA for medicines for her child, or a young man asking a director to loan him 100,000 CFA to start his business – are examples that indicate that people's relationships are carefully maintained and embedded in a system that is much more complex than banknotes can reveal. Following this, it can be understood that social hierarchies are not unidirectional but dynamic and ever-changing just like the status updates on people's WhatsApp profiles.

To get a better understanding of how people in Sokodé deal with certain problems that could be designated as 'civic issues', I often asked where they would go if they experienced 'a problem in their neighbourhood, for instance a broken bridge, but also other issues'. Of course, this is only a specific type of problem that does not sufficiently cover all the possible subjects that could possibly stimulate people's civic engagement. Moreover, I tend to place civil society in the context of community development, though I am aware that 'civil society' and 'community development' are not two interchangeable terms; the complexities and subtleties are many. However, in order to dialogue with ICT4D, I connect the ideal image of community development that is sustained from within and can be attained through civic engagement. The simplification inherent in the question 'where do you go if you perceive of a problem in the neighbourhood' reveals people's knowledge of and interest in the possibilities of addressing 'public' issues. Even though it remained a hypothetical question, in most cases people responded that they would take the problem to the chief's place, and never to the municipality or prefecture. Some also referred to low-level organised 'boys from the hood' who either organise themselves or are called upon by the neighbourhood development committees (CDQ) or chiefs to fix a certain road or to contribute to brickmaking for a community building like a school.

Fine and Harrington (2004) make the case for the importance of 'small groups' in framing civil society. For them, groups such as families, colleagues, friends and sports teams can be considered as "a cause, context, and consequence of civic engagement", and they emphasise the value of taking "local interaction contexts – the microfoundations of civic society" as unit of analysis (Fine & Harrington 2004: 343–344). This framing of civic engagement paves the way for understanding the commitment to one's community: the female committee cleaning the space around the neighbourhood mosque, the organisation of an annual traditional dance, setting up a new soccer team, the ability of the CDQs and chiefs to mobilise people to contribute to the new school building, the organisation of the 'month for the diaspora'.

One afternoon in March 2015, I decided to pay a visit to Eva, a young woman from the South who did an internship in a rarely frequented library next to the chief's royal palace in Komah. Every morning and every afternoon, the chief and his elders gather in the royal courtyard, sitting in a line, on chairs, chatting with each other or receiving people who come for a consultation. The chief consults with people regarding cases of family conflict, witchcraft accusations, land allocations and the like. On our departure from the library that afternoon, one of the elders called us to come and greet the chief. Timidly, we walked along the row of men on their chairs, making a small bow to each man, and mumbling some greetings in Kotokoli that Mohamed had taught me. The chief was friendly and asked me what I was doing in his neighbourhood, and he invited me to pass by another day to discuss my research.

When Eva and I walked away, I was not the only one who seemed relieved to have made it through the unfamiliar situation. I asked Eva whether she always greeted the chief and his elders in this way. She exclaimed that she had never been asked to present herself. However, she added, it was very normal that the chief would want to know the reason of my presence in Komah.

Clearly, there are conditions and circumstances under which people visit the royal courtyard. Later, Eva explained that in her case, 'going to the chief' meant that she would present her problem to a woman she would address as aunty, and plead with the woman to go to the chief on her behalf. It would not be appropriate for Eva to visit the chief herself, as she does not have the 'right' status, being a young, childless woman from a Southern group (9 March 2015). This shows that access to certain people and information is highly regulated. Not only the chiefs, but also other powerful people must be approached in the right manner, with the right kind of respect, or else they simply disregard the request. The person with the request, like the example of this young woman, is often represented by another person who acts as their spokesperson, and this individual is often a person of status. Some highly placed persons on the other side, also speak only to a confidential person who then communicates the message – even if the receiver of the message is present. It is a sign of respect to speak 'through someone', which is important in this society.

Sokodé as difficult environment for civic engagement

Similar to the Zimbabwean case that Atwood (2016) describes, in Sokodé, there are basic elements that are obstacles to civic engagement in an 'unstable infrastructure'. This ranges from sewage and water problems to weak mobile phone network coverage and instability in the socio-political and economic infrastructure. The power of telecommunication companies and their entanglements with the state are also part of this, as described in chapter two. To give an idea of the practical possibilities and obstacles for civic engagement, I present some examples that elucidate the complexities of striving for a public cause in the environment of Sokodé.

Unlike others, who approach civic engagement through the lens of an organisational format, such as 'civil society', 'associational life' (Simone 2001) or 'social movement' (Ellis & van Kessel 2009), this analysis starts from the individual perspective. Though I do not suggest that such organisational forms are non-existent or unimportant in Sokodé, my focus is different. I am interested in the micro-level of analysis, where the ephemeral nature of civic engagement surfaces. The experiences of a young man who I will call Jean here, underline the obstacles that are inherent in the gaping inequalities in existing social hierarchies. In the past, he has attempted to organise and realise several 'projects', which is a container term for future plans, that include carving out pathways in the mind and then try to realise them, in order to make something of one's life. Even though most of these projects cannot be described as 'civic', they reveal the societal and social mechanisms that make or break 'organisation'.

One day in March 2015, when Jean and I discussed civic organisation and development in its broadest form, Jean exclaimed that he had attempted so many things. As trainer of a neighbourhood soccer team, he was familiar with the pathways and obstacles in his rounds to find sponsors for the teams' shirts and equipment. When I accompanied his soccer team to a match, he pointed to a large house and said it was owned by a general, who had been interested in supporting his team. This was part of his strategy to invest in his connections with army officers, in whom he seemed to have some hope for support – a strategy I also noticed in other people's accounts.

After Jean had exclaimed that he had tried so many things, he did not take long to reveal the mechanisms that are, according to him, detrimental for the country's development. There was a time a meeting was organised at the prefecture to discuss the causes and solutions of the rampant youth employment. As he was present with some friends, the idea came to his mind of setting up a factory to produce mango jam. There are thousands of mango trees in the region, and a part of the mangos rot away during the harvest season. According to

Jean, this is partly because of a lack of infrastructure, and the lack of organisation that would be needed for transport, sale or processing. In the meeting at the prefecture, he presented his idea about a jam processing factory, which would tackle youth unemployment in the region. The leaders asked him and his comrades to design a detailed plan, which they did. They were even invited to present their plan at the concerned ministry in Lomé, but upon their presentation, the minister shook his head and said that their provisioned budget was too low; they should add another two million CFA. Jean had no doubt that half of that budget would go directly in the hands of the minister. He never heard anything about the proposal again, and he imagines that it might have been used to secure funding from international donors, so that the minister could reap the benefits.

In the same meeting, Jean presented many other ideas to the local authorities and customary chiefs, but he was disappointed when he made attempts through these official pathways that were filled with empty promises. When I shared a plate of spaghetti with him upon my return in March 2018, he grinned when he assured me that he had not remained inactive during the troubles in 2017. There was no way for me to verify the kind of actions that he had waged, and on which side of the conflicts that had erupted, but this surely did not indicate his textbook civic engagement of trying to get a sponsor for a soccer team.

Disengagement and lethargy: Follow the leader

There is a large gap between the management and the lower echelons, illustrated by the development worker, quoted in section 6.3, who lamented that "managers do not care about the impact of the actions, what matters to them is to justify the expenses". This gap is also apparent in the NGO sector, along with the question of whether the 'public cause' or the community development for which they apparently strive, is attained at all. The unstable infrastructures and the instability of the social environment have a deep effect on people's engagement in general. In the community development sector but also beyond, people leave whenever they get a chance to do so, for a higher position that is preferably outside of Togo. For instance, the director of a local development network in Sokodé was among the persons consulted regularly by the municipality's leaders. When I visited him, he did not only propagate his network, showing its value for the community of Sokodé, but he clearly manifested his personal ambitions (Interview with director of development network, 1 August 2016). Since his discourse was impressive, I was not surprised to find that he had secured a higher position elsewhere when I returned in 2017. Such key persons can have a large impact on local development, but in these conditions, it is obvious that their search for a position of financial stability prevails over their engagement.

It goes without saying that the disengagement of leaders influences the engagement of people in the 'lower echelons', which is true for all fields and levels of society. As described in chapter two, the general image persists that the higher levels only fend for themselves, and create obstacles for the lower levels to reach the same level. The story of a microfinance agent is exemplary: he presented an innovative plan to the management team and got a disinterested reaction, but in the months that followed, the management introduced a new system that was clearly based on his ideas, without crediting him.

Another case was presented to me by a colleague of Felix, with whom I was sharing a drink on a hot Sunday afternoon in March 2018. I had once again brought up the subject of the sticky bridge with Felix, who had to cross the bridge several times per day on his motorbike, as he lived in Kpangalam and worked not far from the prefecture. Every time we crossed the bridge together, he made fun of my fear that something would go wrong. This time, he seriously tried to find ways to help me understand why this issue could not be solved, and he invited his colleague to join our table to answer my persistent questions on the issue.

Felix introduced the subject to him, as follows: He, a stranger from the South, was asking his colleague, who was a local, to explain to me why the bridge at the entrance of Kpangalam, upon leaving Barrière, was not cleaned. The colleague immediately replied that even though he came from Tchamba, which is not even 40 kilometres east of Sokodé, he was still considered a stranger in some situations. Felix took over and shared that in the past, he had become close to Minister Folly Basil, and managed to bring quite a few changes to his direct environment. However, as he did not have his contract as civil servant yet, he feared that someone would depict him in a negative light and he would be dismissed at work, reasoning that a stranger should not have such a large say in the development of Sokodé. He distanced himself from the minister, something that he now regretted, because he could have helped more friends find good positions.

I gently brought the conversation back to the cleaning of the bridge, and his colleague continued with a story that could almost be seen as a metaphor for the current status quo of Togolese society. One day, in his office, he ran into a repair man who had been called to fix something. He kindly asked the man whether he could also look at a door, and it took just one nail to solve the problem. When his director found out about the nail, she was furious. How could the man have commissioned the repair man to fix the door, simply bypassing her? She punished him by deducting one nightshift on his salary. He explained that she had been cross with him, because she could not make another request and put a portion of the money for repairing the door in her own pocket. From that day onwards, he never addressed any issue again.

Having finished his story, he and Felix both looked at me, waiting for a new question. I told them that I had no more questions. The colleague asked permission to return to his beer, which had been unattended to during this conversation. I remained silent for a long time.

6.5 Civic (dis)engagement in Sokodé: Protest and voice

Protest and lack of voice

An essential characteristic of civic engagement and political participation is public opinion making or voice. Though it should be clear by now that the socio-political environment is not geared towards receiving the opinions of ordinary people, there is a need to emphasise this and sketch a few more details to complement the picture, because the impact of this on the social structure is hardly ever tackled in ICT4D programs. This contributes to the image of ICT4D as being based on illusionary foundations.

In the initial phase of the development project that aimed to enhance civic engagement in Sokodé that I describe in chapter seven, interactive radio shows were planned in order to create an overview of the concerns voiced by people who could call in. According to a young broadcaster I spoke to at the radio station, the shows were popular and many people called to voice their opinion. Among the priorities of the callers were the miserable conditions of the care provided at the regional hospital, the lack of transparency in the municipality's budget, the high taxes paid by the market vendors and the dilapidated state of the bus station. However, as Sokodé is a city where people easily know one another, the shows led to problems between certain individuals and the municipality's representatives. Even though not all people revealed their names, they did respond to the question "from where are you calling", and people's voices are often recognisable. When I commented on what I perceived as people's tendency to disengage, he sharply responded: "People have a lot to say about the authorities, but they are afraid to do so" (Interview with young broadcaster, 16 April 2017).

People from different sections of society have explained to me in many or few words that individuals who openly show too much ambition in the public space, are 'neutralised' sooner or later; any kind of civic organisation can easily be perceived by the higher echelons of power as going against their interests. As was briefly noted in section 2.2, it is said that individuals who become too powerful are either bribed or eliminated – silencing them by giving them a high position as director or suing and imprisoning them for alleged corruption. Finally, though it is extremely difficult to find tangible proof, on several occasions I have been told that it does not take much to stage a road accident, as it can easily be ascribed to bad road conditions. Even if there is no verifiable 'truth' in these whispered bits of information, they reflect a prevalent fear and play an important role in how individuals present and organise themselves in the public sphere.

Though fear is a major contributing factor for people's disengagement, there is more to it. In the Togolese context, the absence of positive, sustainable state interventions in the domains of healthcare, education and the provision of basic amenities, combined with the state's violent responses to demonstrations leads to a certain lethargy and a feeling of powerlessness. Another factor that feeds people's apparent disengagement is evident when despair is extended and becomes a simmering anger, as discussed in section 2.2. This was tangible on my return in March 2018, after the uneventful massive street protests and violent government reactions in the second half of 2017. Below, I return to descriptions of the period of unrest in 2017, about which my informants were unusually open and expressive.

Disengagement with the state?

The imagination of people in Sokodé about the role of the authorities in their lives is diametrically opposed to the ideal of the state that is dominant in political and development discourses, which also underlies ICT4D. This has been described in the introductory chapter. In an ideal world, there is a certain responsibility of the state towards its 'citizens'. In the area that is presently referred to as Togo, 'the state' is generally not regarded as having a positive influence in people's daily lives, and most people want to have as little as possible to do with it. The state has become much more of a debatable concept since Anderson's imagined communities ([1983] 1991) and Appadurai's imagined worlds (1996) in which globalisation has put into motion different *scapes*. It could be argued that the state should not be seen as the body opposite the society or the population but is a much more subtle concept; possibly the population is even the state in its relationality.

At this point, I confine myself to the Weberian view of regarding the state as the political structure that is in power in a country, responsible for the legal framework and striving to hold the monopoly on violence. The monopoly on violence is, at least theoretically, closely linked with the protection of the 'subjects' by those in power. However, not many in Sokodé would agree with the idea that the Togolese government protects her citizens. The influence of the state on the local level is mainly felt in the imposition of taxes – but not in public expenditure – the recruitment of youth for the armed forces, and the reinforced presence of armed forces in town. This 'deficient' relationship between the state and the people is one of the main reasons why, on an analytic level, common conceptualisations of the citizen do not seem to offer an appropriate explanatory frame. Isin's thinking on civic acts and the 'right to claim rights' (Isin 2008; Isin & Ruppert 2020) offers interesting possibilities in this regard.

The recurrent political disengagement of people in Sokodé should be obvious by now, and the clearest manifestation of this disengagement is a reluctance to express oneself about any issue that can be related to political issues, which is a recurrent theme in this work. I emphasise this, since 'voice' is a major theme when it concerns empowerment, civic engagement and citizen participation (Verba, Schlozman & Brady 1995). Though I had some exceptionally open exchanges about the regime, my attempts to discuss political issues were most often waved away with phrases such as "What do they do for us? Forget about them, I am just minding my own business".

However, even if people do not openly voice their criticism about issues concerning the civic sphere, there are myriad ways of expressing their disgruntlement. For instance, the word 'normally' (*normalement*) is often used in conversations about the public space, semi-public structures and utilities, in phrases such as: "Normally, this newly asphalted road will be rather broad" or "Normally, there will be network coverage even when it rains". Another, more political 'normally' would be that the state does not use tear gas and real bullets on her people when they are peacefully demonstrating. Though an extensive discourse analysis of the word 'normally' is too far-fetched, it can be regarded as an indication of people's unfulfilled expectations towards the state and semi-public structures. When applying this to the framework of 'normalisation of hardship' (de Bruijn & Bot 2018: 190 – 191), it indicates that there is some contestation, a certain level of hope that one day there will be a 'normally'.

Finally, as Breuer *et al.* (2017) also demonstrated, the lack of top-down accountability from Sokodé's local authorities also contributes to people's disengagement. Breuer and her team argue that the negative image of the local authorities is not helpful, and neither is the way in which the customary chiefdoms have been politicised and the low level of vigour of most CDQs. The fact that there have not been local elections for decades,[19] and the mayor who is officially called 'head of the special delegation' is not accountable to the citizens

---

[19] The last local elections took place in 1985. Due to the pressure of international actors to get out of the political impasse, local elections and a referendum about a constitutional change were finally held on 30 June 2019. As the opposition boycotted the elections, UNIR's display of 'political willingness' mostly resulted in the decrease of international attention, not in political reform.

but to the national leaders, does not contribute to the legitimacy of the municipal council. In this context, it is rather imaginary for people to believe that local authorities would be willing and able to consider the opinions of the citizens. This clearly has consequences for the imaginary of ICT4D.

The protests in late 2017, social media and the democratic imaginary

On 19 August 2017, thousands of people dressed in red took to the streets of the main cities in Togo, to express their disgruntlement. The opposition had called for manifestations to revive the law of 1992, calling for the limitation of the president's mandate to two terms, voting rights for the diaspora and a different voting system. The people on the streets simply requested "Faure must go". As tear gas is commonly used to disperse crowds, it was no surprise that this was used in several cities on that day, but in Sokodé, things quickly went awry: several public buildings were set on fire, people were beaten, one or more guns were stolen from soldiers, and a person was shot. Clearly, the authorities had been ill-prepared to manage the overwhelming crowds of people (see figure 13).

Figure 13: Protest in Sokodé on 19 August 2017.

The driving force behind this was opposition party PNP, led by Tikpi Atchadam, created in April 2014 and presented to the public in November 2016. Leading up to 19 August, Atchadam's discourses were widely circulated on WhatsApp, and DVDs with his speeches had been distributed even in the most remote regions of the country, as reported by journalists of *Jeune Afrique* (D'Almeida & Dougueli 2017). For the ones who had closely followed PNP's online and offline activities in the months leading to the troubles, the massive response to the call for mobilisation was probably not a surprise. Other opposition parties joined the PNP and more protests followed, and the government responded by 'turning off the internet' for five consecutive days from 5 September 2017 onwards, a measure that did not improve the situation, as reported by The Guardian (Koutonin 2017). As the political impasse was not broken, the coalition of fourteen opposition parties kept on calling for protests in September and October, not only in the form of massive street protests, but also general strikes, referred to as *'Togo mort'* or *'villes mortes'*. This mode of protest is often organised in contexts when authorities are renowned for their violent reactions (Harsch 1999, Roitman 2007).

The persons in Sokodé with whom I regularly communicated through WhatsApp – as far as the internet connection allowed – tried to continue their daily lives as much as possible. However, on the evening of 16 October, the electricity was temporarily cut, followed by the arrest of Imam Hassan, who had expressed his horror in his Friday sermon about the presence and the behaviour of the soldiers in Sokodé. He had also asked whether the Togolese citizens had become the enemy and he assured that the soldiers would pay for their acts if they would kill yet another civilian.[20] Though he emphasised a pacifist approach in

---

20 A French translation of his Friday sermon was sent to me by a broadcaster through WhatsApp on 18 October 2017. To cite a part of the translation: "I do not reject Faure but it is the act that he poses that I reject. The soldiers have been allowed to turn people into wild animals, that's why they are ashamed, but you have not seen anything yet, since you have set your sights on Sokodé, what you want you will find, your eyes will turn red in this city, not with weapons not with something else. [...] A child was brought to me here, I cried, they hit the child so hard until the nerves of the hand were broken, the child is 10 years old, he is a student. This child, even if he throws a pebble, cannot cause big damage. But what is this massacre, what did he do? [...] our struggle is peaceful, that's what President Atchadam keeps reminding us. They give us weapons, we say we do not want weapons, they want to transform us into soldiers, we say we are civilians. Do you see since we are peaceful, God himself is with us, but I assure you that if they kill another civilian, that day it is all Togo, this day 150 soldiers too are going to die, a civilian against 150 soldiers, until they reach 100 civilians they are already finished (laughing). What I say there is no way to cancel that, unless they come towards us and we will come to an understanding. If a civilian dies, they will no longer be themselves, not by weapon or anything else, we have prayed to God and he has already accepted".

his sermon, his words had been sharp. The Minister of Defence later claimed that the imam was arrested because he had called for violence. In the already tense atmosphere, this was the spark that fanned the flames and caused the town to erupt in violence after word of his arrest spread. Several buildings were set on fire and a number of persons were killed.

In the days following the arrest, more troops were sent to Sokodé, and people who dared to cross the streets were beaten. There were also rumours of militias, and some claimed that it had all been a set-up, with strangers brought to town from Lomé or elsewhere to incite the local youth to burn buildings and create chaos. Photos, texts, video and audio messages were overflowing in my WhatsApp account with descriptions, rumours and comments on the events. Inhabitants of some quarters fled to neighbouring villages, especially the youth, and several persons notified me that the soldiers went from door to door, searching for red clothes – the colour of protest and of the PNP – beating up young men and leaving houses in chaos. Most people locked themselves up in their rooms for three days, and the only sound that could be heard were the engines of military jeeps, which Sweet Mama referred to in the beginning of chapter three.

Several of my informants took care to emphasise that these were not the soldiers who were normally stationed in Sokodé and whom they had sometimes interacted with. Some of the people I knew who lived in the vicinity of the national highway in the northern part of town, commented that it had not been easy to deal with tear gas. One friend with six young children told me how he had picked up a tear gas grenade from his veranda and had thrown it as far away as possible, while the family was hiding in the house.

Like most of the young men in his neighbourhood, Désiré spent several weeks in another part of town. The area where he lived was heavily targeted because it was close to the commissariat that had been burned, and it was believed that some stolen guns of soldiers were hidden in this part of town. When I returned to Sokodé in March 2018, Désiré told me on several occasions about the day that soldiers had come to the neighbourhood in search of young men to seek vengeance. After the first clashes between the protesters and the security forces, Désiré had not been able to leave. When he heard a group of soldiers in the vicinity, he quickly lit a candle in front of the statue of mother Mary at the entrance of his fathers' room, and hid inside. He was saved from the beatings of the soldiers, who stopped and turned around when they saw the candle. In March 2018, Désiré also showed me the broken windows of the neighbours' house, who had fled and still had not returned.

On 24 October 2017, Dao confided to me on WhatsApp that "this time, I have seen a bit what war can look like". In the evening of the same day, he sent me

Figure 14: The burning sugar truck on the bridge.

another message: his grandmother had passed away after an illness. She lived along the part of the national highway where confrontations between security services and protesters had escalated. When I brought this up with Dao when we met each other about six months later, he mentioned that the 'troubles' had not contributed to her health situation. After these days in October 2017, filled with irregularities, the protests were smothered. This was mainly the result of the besiegement of Sokodé and other cities like Bafilo and Mango, that resulted in the call of the opposition parties for their supporters to stay at home, as their safety could not be assured.

Just like Désiré and his neighbours who were hiding from the security forces, a young man whom I knew quite well and who occupied a position in the local UNIR department, also had to flee his house and stay in a hotel for five nights. He was not hiding from the security forces, but from youngsters in his area who had been targeting him. As he was considered as being part of UNIR, he feared for his life, and not without reason. The remark earlier in this section about the population being the state in its relationality, gets a grim edge in this case.

The *troubles* as civic engagement or a fact of life in Sokodé

The situation caused major setbacks to the projects of many of the people I knew. For instance, the stock of tires with a value of 200,000 or 300,000 CFA that garage owner Mohamed had managed to purchase upon his visits to Lomé and that he had kept on his garage terrain, had been confiscated during the time of the troubles. He pointed at his tires when we were watching a soccer match in Komah in March 2018; they now functioned as demarcation of one of the military camps in town. Johnny, whom I also met again in March 2018, told me that he had been selected for a sub-regional training in Senegal. Just before the troubles began, he had versed his contribution of 150,000 CFA. He had seen his journey and his money evaporate, as the files had 'gone missing' in the chaotic times of the troubles.

Clearly, the street protests show that lethargy and disengagement are not the only side of civic-ness in Sokodé. They reveal that frustration and anger simmer just below the surface, and only need some sparks to set the city on fire. As Tikpi Atchadam is originally from Sokodé, his adversaries claimed that his followers are mainly Kotokoli and Muslim. On several occasions, Atchadam rejected this, saying he simply spoke the language of the people whenever he requested for Faure to leave. It was not only Atchadam, but also several of my more politically oriented informants who followed this line of argument: even though Sokodé has been an opposition stronghold since long, this does not mean that people in other corners of the country are satisfied with the way things are going. As the director of a radio station articulated, when I asked him about this 'special status' of Sokodé:

> Tchaoudjo is being bothered, because we do not vote. This is especially the case in Tchaoudjo. [I ask: "What about Mango?"] Yes also in Mango. But even the regime in place thinks that the regime in place has lasted for too long. The sad thing is that a baby who is born today, will experience the same desolation as we do. (Interview with radio director, 9 June 2016)

The street protests in Sokodé are not only an extreme example of civic engagement, but also underline the power of social media in protest movements, as was the case in Egypt (Tufekci & Wilson 2012) and in other African countries (Chiluwa 2015; Chiumbu 2012; Ekine 2010; Jacobs & Duarte 2010; Mutsvairo 2016a; Wasserman 2011).

Hirshkind (2011) described the run-up to the street protests in Egypt. From the early 2000s onwards, bloggers from two previously polarised 'camps' joined forces to criticize the Mubarak regime. This may well be called revolutionary, were it not for the fact that the more radical Muslim Brotherhood came to power and in the end, the everyday life of most people did not radically change. Whereas I share the view that revolution is not based on a sudden change, but rather is the outcome of a prolonged undercurrent of social discontent, this leads to contemplation about the conditions and prerequisites necessary for revolution. In their article on protests in Malawi and Hong Kong, Mutsvairo and Harris (2016) state that the mobile phone and social media alone do not lead to revolution. In the same vein, Valenzuela (2013) notes that social media do not necessarily create new forms of protest, but rather seem to reinforce existing techniques. Mutsvairo and Harris (2016) argue that: "an informed citizenry is far more powerful than any Internet tool for a genuine free and participatory democracy. But mobile media empowers them, even while we might still question whether digital convergence is a step forward in political participation debates" (Mutsvairo & Harris 2016: 227).

The potentially dangerous impact of the uncontrollable flow of unverified messages also became clear in Sokodé. For example, a provocative video of soldiers brutally beating civilians who had been hung on their tied hands widely circulated. The video actually emerged from Cameroon, but it fuelled already existing tensions. Phones became dangerous items: few people dared to film the soldiers, because the repercussions would not be mild, from people's phones being taken away to immediate beatings, imprisonment and possibly worse. Phones were also confiscated to find images and 'evidence' to imprison either the owner of the phone for owning too much harrowing material or served as evidence to arrest the people in the photos.

Though this is a rather unsettling example of civic engagement that reveals the high levels of frustration in society, for which there is no solution as yet, people carry on and try to make the most of their lives. This resonates with a conversation I had with two young men in February 2015:

> "We want change. At least that he [Faure] proposes good things." I ask the young men when they think he will resign and the first says: "In 2025". The other says: "No! It is in 2030 that it will finish." The first replies: "No, in 2025! You love Faure too much!" and one of them says, referring to the politicised South-North divide: "It is their insolence; the opponents want to take the power with vengeance. We, we are afraid." The first concludes: "it is better that it remains like this, than that it gets worse". (Conversation with two young men, 3 March 2015)

Obviously, sociality in Sokodé comes with a multiplicity of ambiguous interactions and relations in this context where peace is fragile and harmony is only an endeavour. During one of my visits in 2018, I met a young man who I had befriended. He had a position in the local UNIR department and had just returned from court. He explained that he had supported the case of the same youth who had been wanting to lynch him during the troubles (UNIR member, 19 March 2018). At the time and till the end of 2018, there were still about 20 persons in prison, who had been arrested during the troubles. The families of some of them had begged the young man to testify that their children had not been involved in the protests, which he had agreed to do. By helping the same persons who had wished him harm, he might have wanted to serve his community, or save himself and be assured of the support of certain important people.

It is also imaginable that this young man is as furious about the military siege of his city as the youth who had tried to lynch him, only that his position does not allow him to express his fury in the same way. Felix's frustration materialised in yet another way: He went straight to the bar on the military camp when he heard that another general strike was announced, drinking his beer to ease his mind, silently reflecting upon the situation.

6.6 Concluding remarks

In the exploration of civic engagement in Sokodé in this chapter, citizenship undoubtedly is a highly debatable concept in the context of an absent yet omnipresent state. Infrastructure that requires the attention of the state are highly unstable, as evident from the lamentable conditions of roads, electricity supply, water services, telecommunication networks, social services, education and health care. While the absence of state interference in these domains is all-encompassing, there is no doubt about the force and visibility of the state's security apparatus. Besides the interactions with soldiers, the population does not have a significant relationship with the state, which is why I argue that it does not make sense to conceive of people who live in Sokodé as citizens. They can instead be conceived as non-citizens, which, however, does not imply a lack of civicness.

There are very few signs that people in Sokodé have become more civically engaged through the arrival of new communication and information technologies. On the contrary, they have become more fearful and mistrusting considering the new possibilities of sharing various types of information with and about one another. In the complex social fabrics of this society, strategies to cope with political repression in Sokodé consist of multiple levels. In the company of people of a different age category, gender, or social position, people shy away from expressing their opinion about a variety of matters. At least on the surface, people are disengaged and disinterested when it is concerning politics. However, protest is never fully absent, as economic, societal and political constraints are persistent.

Social protests have been attempted, but are often immediately suppressed, as illustrated by the socio-political 'troubles' in late 2017. Between 2015 and 2020, the terrain of Sokodé has become that of a police state, in which people are being watched. Many people have internalised this sense of 'being watched' to such an extent that they think twice before they engage in any public act. Cleaning a slippery bridge that has been the site of social protest could easily be regarded as a provocative act. The risks involved in crossing the bridge might be judged to be milder than those of attempting a potentially political act. Besides, in their daily struggles to make ends meet, people have larger worries than cleaning the road. In the end, perhaps only the rain will wash the melted sugar off the bridge, little by little, till things will be alright.

7 The imaginary of ICT4D and civic (dis)engagement

7.1 Introduction

In this chapter, the limited possibilities for civic engagement that was apparent in chapter six is demonstrated in the case of the implementation of a multilateral development project in cooperation with local authorities, which among others aims to strengthen civic engagement. Analysing the implementation in terms of civil society and civic engagement brings forth ambiguities, as it does not offer a satisfactory framework for the empirical data. However, the framework is important because it allows for a dialogue with dominant development discourses such as ICT4D. The emergence and details of this lack of alignment provide a much-needed insight into the lack of coherence between fields in which terminology such as 'civil society' and '(digital) civic engagement' reign, and the everyday lived experiences of civic-ness of people in Sokodé.

In the context of a repressive regime, as is the case in Togo, it is important to take a closer look at the assumptions about democracy and citizenship underlying ICT4D projects. It has become clear that the perception of a basic level of democracy and statehood on which ICT4D is based, does not match everyday life in Togo. In this repressive political environment, transparency and accountability on behalf of political leaders are rather complicated issues, and so are acts or perceptions of citizenship. Legislative texts, opposition parties and presidential elections do not indicate democracy nor are they proof that people are heard and feel represented by their leaders. Against the backdrop of a type of 'escalating' civic engagement, the ICT4D project in Sokodé that was part of this study and its aim to strive for civic engagement was clearly ambitious. This chapter shows that in practice, the project evokes an almost forced form of civic engagement.

The second part of the chapter focuses on more 'voluntary' forms of digital civic engagement, through a discussion of a WhatsApp group aimed at local development. The group was launched by an informal group of local leaders striving for the development of the community. Exactly how informal the group and its administrators are remains a question to be unravelled. The chapter concludes with the biographies of two young people, Stéphanie and Salim, and shows how they deploy new ICT in their aspirations to contribute to the development of their community. Their biographies serve as a concrete reflection on ICT4D, and, also in their position of being the final empirical cases brought up in this study, they can be regarded as a new starting point to rethink the basis and rationale of ICT4D projects.

7.2 The ICT4D project in Sokodé

The rationale of the project: Democracy and good governance

The hypothesis prevalent in ICT4D projects such as the one in Sokodé, is that new technologies hold great potential for democratic development; they are believed to bring about increase in transparency, accountability and good governance. In this dominant development discourse, trust and social inclusion are imperative for a vibrant civil society that is the basis of a stable, functional democracy. Key to such processes is the strengthening of civic engagement, as stated in several studies (Bimber 2000; Hayes & Westrup 2013; Ochara & Mawela 2013). This reasoning expands with the idea that the 'digital era' provides people with the tools to overcome social exclusion and strengthen their social networks, a process that can be referred to as 'network bricolage' (Garud & Karnøe 2003). Social inclusion is seen as being imperative for building the social and institutional trust that are both necessary for and reinforcing e-participation, digital civic engagement and the like (Molony 2009; Ochara & Mawela 2013).

The rationale behind the specific ICT4D project under scrutiny here is to enhance citizen participation in an inclusive manner and to increase transparency and accountability on behalf of the local authorities. In the words of one of the stakeholders: "Participating municipalities see this approach as an opportunity to bring their work closer to the citizens and to enter into a constructive dialogue with young people and civil society" (Bott 2013). The point of departure of the project is not the situation of the people who are making a living in Sokodé, but an ideal that follows a linear logic.

The project serves as example to reveal larger societal mechanisms, processes and power relations. The analysis is not aimed to discredit this particular project but serves to give a more profound insight in top-down approaches in designing and executing ICT4D projects in a complex, poverty-ridden social and politically repressive environment.

The procedure and key actors of the project

The project is part of a larger bilateral development programme that was signed by the Togolese government and a consortium of international and local development actors in 2014, intended to support the decentralisation process as described in the country's constitution of 1992. Nyassogbo (1997) and Talla (1998) have discussed the decentralisation process in Togo in more detail, and

Breuer *et al.* (2017) and Breuer and Groshek (2016) can be consulted for a politico-sociological assessment of the same ICT4D project scrutinised here.

The ICT4D project is a system that manages SMS surveys or opinion polls for citizens about issues concerning their municipality. People with a Togocel SIM card with a minimum of credit can send an SMS free of charge to 2550 indicating the subject of the survey, and the system sends them the questions by SMS one by one. Only after they have responded to a message, do they get the next message. The procedure of the survey has been described from start to finish in a procedure manual (PAD 2016), from which the flow chart in figure 15 is taken.

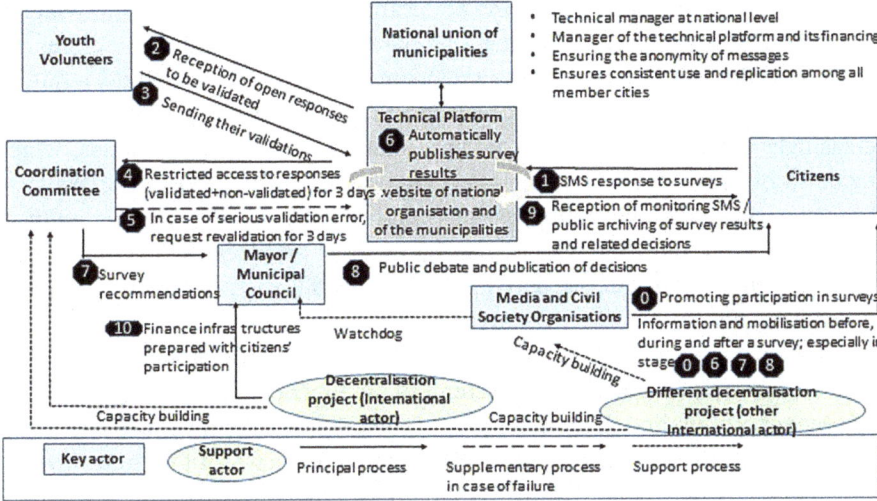

Figure 15: Flow chart of SMS citizen monitoring and evaluation system.

The figure puts a technical platform at centre stage of a highly complex web of actors and processes, differentiating between key actors and supporting actors. It would go beyond the scope of this monograph to discuss the development machinery and its powerful imaginations, but this figure fits perfectly in the dominant logics of development, in which complex development issues such as poverty are reduced to a technical problem from which individuals suffer (Escobar 2011; Ferguson 1990, 2006; Peet & Hardwick 2015; Scheper-Hughes & Sargent 1998). This frame, in which the ICT4D project can be placed, approaches people as 'citizens' or stakeholders encrypted with agency. Solutions for their individual suffering come with buzzwords such as good governance, civic engagement and participatory development, and support the idea of a thriving civil society as panacea for democracy. Development critics argue that this approach risks blurring the underlying inequalities inherent to global political and financial systems. In this view, development cooperation can be seen as a-political or even anti-political activity that obscures structural problems that cause poverty (Ferguson 1990).

Though I want to bring back the focus to the local level, it should be clear that the 'support actors' in figure 15 consist of complex and often internally competitive fabrics. As is often the case, technical support for the project is outsourced to international and local consultants who are not always concerned with or even aware of the local situation, whereas the financial donors seem to be more concerned with internal and external competition and accountability to higher management than with the applicability of their development model in a context like Sokodé, which impinges on the sustainability of their programs. *De facto*, sustainability is not a decisive factor, and actors hide behind terms as 'pilot project' and 'possibilities for upscaling'. For a further analysis of the increasingly managerial approach within dominant development circles, which tends to overlook power relations and cultural diversity, the work of Wallace, Bornstein and Chapman (2007) is important. Finally, in the complex political context of Togo, the independence of the national and local actors remains an issue, which is important considering the responsibility to ensure the anonymity of respondents.

The competition between and within different stakeholders on the macro-level cannot be overlooked in an account of the functioning of a multilateral development project, and their underlying assumptions and motivations need to be questioned. However, their 'target population' is the focus of the present work, which is why I delve into this ICT4D project at a micro-level, describing the individuals and groups involved in implementing the project in Sokodé. The information is derived from interviews with national and local consultants, municipal officers, committee members and other informed persons, mainly by Dao, Silvia and me, and my attendance at several meetings of the ICT4D project at the local, national and international level.

The procedure prescribes that survey subjects and related questions are to be developed by a committee that is representative of Sokodé's society in theory, headed by the mayor, and shall be revisited. At the heart of this committee is a technical committee of fifteen members that prepares the meetings, mainly consisting of municipal employees like the mayor, communication manager, director of markets, financial manager and the local consultant. Besides the committee, an important twofold role is reserved for youth volunteers: supporting the committee with the mobilisation of participants for the surveys and validating the answers of the citizens to the open questions in the surveys.[21] The youth volunteers have been recruited through neighbourhood development committees or CDQs, and through the networks of the committee members. As the CDQs often consist of teachers, there are many young teachers among the volunteers. Others are attached to associations, local NGOs, radio stations or handicapped organisations. In 2015, 70 youth had been accepted as volunteer based on their level of education and their age, and 45 of them were still active by July 2016. A WhatsApp group created by the municipality's communications manager in June 2016, still had 18 youth volunteer members in October 2018, who were asked by the communications manager to mobilise their peers for the rounds of survey.

During the days in which the 'line is open' for the public survey, the youth volunteers play a crucial role in the mobilisation of participants, guided by the local consultant. After the lines have been closed, the ICT specialist who hosts the technical platform, e-mails the results of the closed questions and an excel sheet with the open responses to the local consultant. Analysing the results is part of the task description of the committee. The procedure prescribes that the results of the survey are to be published online and shared with the public, ideally leading to a public discussion, among others in interactive radio shows. To finish the cycle, the committee is expected to formulate recommendations for the municipal council based on their analysis and the public discussion, leading to a set of actions taken by the municipality that are then again disseminated among the public.

7.3 Power relations in the ICT4D project

Selection of survey subjects: Along the lines of social hierarchies

The flow chart above does not show the manner in which the roles and decision making processes of the different stakeholders are specified at an individual level, which is of major importance for the level of analysis in this chapter. It is often argued that there can be no meaningful participation when the have-not-citizens have no 'voice' as noted above (Verba, Schlozman & Brady 1995), but also when existing power structures remain unchallenged (Arnstein 1969).

---

21 On a technical level this means that the answers to the closed questions (yes-no) of the survey are treated automatically by the server, and the answers to the open questions are sent in non-specific order to the phone numbers of the youth volunteers who then either validate or invalidate the message.

However, the communication between different layers in the ICT4D project under scrutiny here is rather hierarchical and top-down, leaving little space for participatory approach that cuts across lines (see also Breuer *et al.* 2017). Information is filtered at the higher levels before trickling down, and 'jumping' a layer is not a possibility, especially when it concerns communication that goes upward through hierarchies.

On paper, the centre of gravity is attributed to the committee, but during the first year it appeared that the expectations were too high to be realistic. Among others, its members lacked methodological knowledge and tools to design survey questions and interpret the results, and the posting of the results took much longer, as the analysis of the responses to the open questions was done manually – for instance, the survey in February 2017 had 2,500 responses. Furthermore, the website to publish the survey results was never created, and there were delays at the national level, which several insiders suggested were due to the government's reluctance to accommodate the project. To tackle some of the obstacles, an international consultant was flown in and stayed in Lomé for three months. She undertook several travels to the three target cities and developed a procedure manual.[22]

To give a better insight into the functioning of the committee, what happened in these meetings, and more importantly, what did not happen there, I discuss the choice of the themes for the four SMS surveys that have been held in Sokodé between 2014 and 2018. The choice of subjects for the first two surveys emerged from a two-day foundational workshop of the committee in February 2015. Even though there were interactive radio shows in which citizens readily shared their views on possible subjects, as discussed in section 6.5, it was already clear that sensitive themes for the municipality would not be chosen, for the simple reason that the mayor chaired the committee. The prestigious sanitation project that the municipality had undertaken and was considered a success was selected as the subject for the first test survey. This was a sensible choice from the municipality's point of view, as it shined a positive light on their efforts. It reinforced the image of the municipality as benefactor both to the actors higher up and to the committee members and the local population.

---

[22] To illustrate the tediousness of such procedures for all parties, the committees in the participating cities undertook validation sessions in which the 68-page document was discussed page by page, the comments and adjustments noted down meticulously. After these validation sessions, the manual was revised by the consultant in Lomé, and the final version was then approved by the Ministry of Territorial Administration, Decentralisation and Local Communities in the second half of 2016.

The 'poor' result of 43 participants pushed the committee to focus on the mobilisation of the citizens in the subsequent test survey.

The second survey, held in July 2016, dealt with the subject of straying animals, such as goats, sheep and dogs, creating dangerous situations on the road. The selection of the password 'mouton' was preceded by a long discussion about the most appropriate title for the survey. Some members of the committee preferred the word 'goat' whereas others found 'animals' better. The discussion started anew in the meeting held after the survey in April 2017, which I was able to attend, when the results were presented in a rush of success, until the mayor interfered. It can only be speculated whether some of the younger committee members made it a point merely because this was the only space given to them – a liminal space with no real influence, where they could disagree without endangering their position. Nonetheless, some youth volunteers also voiced their doubts about the choice for 'mouton', arguing it had led (potential) respondents to believe the problem was only about straying sheep and not about other animals.

The last two surveys that were organised up to date are of January and February 2017, both concerning the market. In this case, the internal organisation appeared especially hierarchical: the questions and timing of the surveys that were held did not emanate from the committee but were developed at the national level and driven by actors at an international level. The streamlining of the survey questions in the three cities was 'ordered from above', as an influential e-mail was sent from the international donor to the international consultancy group and the national consultants, with an urgent request to organise another survey before the sociological household survey that had been planned could take place. Clearly, neither the committee nor the mayor of Sokodé had been invited to set the agenda. In development jargon, these local actors had not been empowered.

This illustrates that power processes between the local, national and international actors play a large role to the extent in which meaningful participation can take place on the local level. Conditions that are imposed on the local actors by national and international actors have an impact on the possibilities available for meaningful participation. It also raises questions about the 'appropriation' of researchers by different stakeholders in research projects that accompany multilateral development programs. From this perspective, my own position can also be questioned, as highlighted in section 1.3. As this chapter clarifies, the internal power relations at play at the local level were not a major focus point of the international donor and the international consultancy group – these were considered the responsibility of local actors.

Mobilising people for surveys: Loyalty precedes over civic engagement

The number of people who participated in the different SMS surveys are results that can be measured and labelled as 'output'. However, in order to understand whether it was their civic engagement that drove people to send an SMS to 2550 and respond to the questions that were sent to them, the ways in which these results came into being are scrutinised here.

While the first test survey in Sokodé had a response rate of 43 participants and was considered a failure by the committee, the second and third survey were a success with almost 2,000 respondents.[23] All the committee members did not participate in the first survey, nor did they encourage their social networks to participate. For the second and third survey, a mobilisation strategy was employed. For instance, the communications manager took a group of motor-taxis and asked the Zeds to drive through town in caravan, holding a large banner. Though this was a visible way to share the news, many people did not understand what the banner was about. Also, the communications manager, local consultant and mayor spoke of the survey in several radio shows. They had to go back to a couple of radio channels because the information had altered in calls of some broadcasters, who had not fully understood the process. The message was also spread by imams after the Friday prayer and in church after mass. But the most successful part of the campaign was the personal approach of the local consultant, communication manager, youth volunteers and other members of the committee.

During the days in which the survey 'lines are open', the youth volunteers 'recruit' participants in their own neighbourhoods – their families, neighbours and friends. As noted above, a section of the youth volunteers work as underpaid teachers, others do unpaid work as 'interns', hanging around waiting for an opportunity, hoping that their association gets awarded a project and they will be lucky enough to get temporary employment. Like Mamah, whose story was fea-

---

23 Specific numbers are as follows: the survey on the straying domestic animals in July 2016 had an initial response rate of 1.868, of which about 1,200 completed surveys. After reminder messages, the number increased to 1,905, the only number communicated in the reports. The targeted survey for market vendors in January 2017 had 406 participants from the Komah market. I have not listed the participants from the Grand Marché. The total numbers of vendors according to the markets director are 2,355 at the Komah market and 1,794 at the Grand Marché. The city-wide survey about the rehabilitation of the markets in February 2017 reported a total of 2,005 participants. In one question in this survey, the sources through which people heard of the survey are mentioned. A total of 1,378 replied to this question, of whom 682 mentioned the radio, 358 word of mouth, 184 meeting, 61 tam-tam, 93 other.

tured in chapter three, these unemployed or underemployed graduates attend seminars and workshops, getting a sandwich or lunch, and a small per diem.

In a round of formal enquiries I asked Dao to conduct during the time of the surveys in January 2017, some of the participants told Dao that the same youth volunteer had come by several times before the participant was moved to take the survey. The local consultant of the project also reserved a morning at the *Grand Marché* and another at the Komah market, asking youth volunteers to gather at a specified spot at the market. Supported by the director of the markets, the youth volunteers passed by the market vendors one by one, helping vendors reply to the SMS questions. According to Dao, the market vendors perceived this help as not *only* considering their low literacy.

It was only in April 2017, two years after my fieldwork had begun, that I put myself in the position of being in the company of the director of the markets while strolling through the market – a situation he eagerly made use of, telling all the market women we passed that I was part of the people who would rehabilitate the market. Exactly this appropriation of me, the *blanche*, was the reason why I had waited so long before entering the market as a researcher. Imagining the youth volunteers at the market and the pressure of getting large numbers of respondents, I assessed how high his stakes were, and could imagine the situation of the director, keeping a close eye on his market women, who could hardly escape. The market women, and arguably also the youth volunteers who are often desperately looking for a job, faced a 'choiceless decision' (Aretxaga 1997; Coulter 2008).

The local consultant and the municipal officers held similar sessions at the courtyards of the chiefs' royal palaces, where people replied to the survey questions on the spot, as can be seen in figure 16. The photo was taken by Dao, who witnessed one of the sessions. The message was also widely circulated among the many local associations and NGOs in town – one NGO manager immediately showed me the paper that had been lying on her desk, when I introduced myself and told her that my research was related to the project. Even though the role of the radio should not be neglected, a large group of participants was found in the direct social surroundings of the municipality: the social networks of the CDQs and neighbourhood chiefs, and the many associations and NGOs active in the domain of local development. These intense mobilisation efforts bring into question the inclusiveness and sustainability of the project. Though it is a great achievement for the individuals involved in the project in Sokodé to get up to 2,000 survey respondents, this does not necessarily imply that there has been meaningful participation. It indicates the widespread and strong personal loyalties and relationships of dependency connected to the prominent committee members, as well as their engagement and embeddedness in the local political arena.

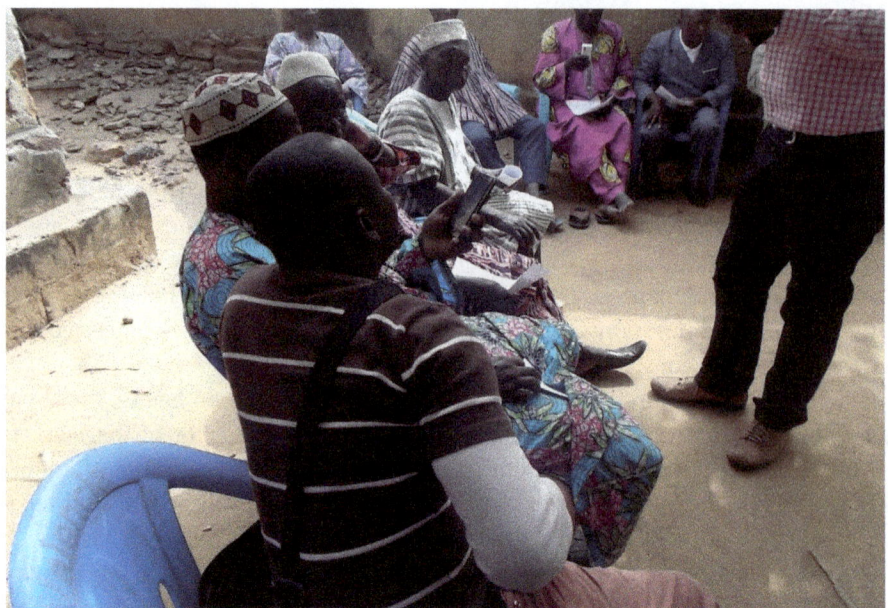

Figure 16: Mobilisation meeting for SMS survey.

In April 2017, I discussed the surveys over a beer with a group of young men several of whom were working in the field of community development, with some having been a part of the local research team. When I asked about the mobilisation campaign, the communications officer of a farmers' association exclaimed that the local consultant had also passed by his office. She had asked him to make sure that all employees replied to the survey. He blurted out that he had not replied to the survey himself, and quickly added "but please do not tell her!". He took care to emphasise that he had fulfilled his obligation by requesting all his colleagues to reply – "I really did" (Communications officer, 17 April 2017). What was interesting in his 'confession' was that his concern to maintain good relations with the local consultant seemed to outweigh his concern to reply to the survey call. It confirms once again the centrality of social hierarchies and maintaining good relations with the 'higher placed' people within people's social networks.

Expectations and power relations within the committee

To a greater or lesser extent, the committee reflects the town's leaders, a group of individuals representing larger or smaller parts of Sokodé's society. The committee comprises 30 members of a committee established earlier along with ten other members. It includes the main customary chiefs, religious leaders and representatives of the decentralised state services, local media and 'civil society actors'. The prefect, who is deemed to have more power in Sokodé than the mayor, is represented by a delegate of the decentralised state services. The ten other members consist of representatives of the three groups identified as being vulnerable: women, youth and handicapped people.[24] The committee is headed by the mayor who is officially called 'head of the special delegation', a delegation that has been put into place in 2001 by the regime that has been postponing local elections ever since 1987. The mayor's legitimacy is questioned by the population and within the committee itself, as shown here.

The meetings take place in the town hall, and the local consultant also holds office there. The municipality's agents are well represented in the committee and in the technical committee that organises its meetings. Besides being connected to power, this could be a pragmatic choice, as these individuals are on site and do not need further impetus to be present at meetings. Nonetheless, this gives the sense of partiality, especially the position of the mayor, who not only has the last word in the choice for survey themes, but also approves the committee's recommendations to his own municipal council, before finally deciding about the actions the municipality undertakes. It must be added that his own space for manoeuvring is limited, as his policies can be implemented only if they are in line with 'Lomé'.

At least on paper, participation in the committee is voluntary, though the members get refreshments during the breaks and a small per diem for their transport – which are important gifts in a poverty-ridden context. Evidently, people who want to remain on a good footing with the individuals representing the local authorities and pulling strings, have an interest in attending the meetings.

To get a better understanding of local social hierarchies, it is insightful to take a closer look at the mayor and other individuals' behaviour in certain committee meetings which I participated in, complemented with data from interviews with the local consultant and concerned municipal officers. The mayor chairs the meetings and allocates speaking time to the members. At times, the

---

24 In the programme proposal and in interviews with some of the key actors, people with HIV are also included in vulnerable groups.

local consultant or the municipality's communications manager takes over, with a PowerPoint presentation. The committee meetings can be lengthy: in a meeting after the survey about the market held in February 2017, 2,005 answers to the open questions had been read out loud to validate the messages. Within the committee, women are a minority. For instance, in the meeting I attended on 4 April 2017, six women were present, including the local consultant, and 24 men. The content of their input is often different from the input of their male counterparts – dealing with details and not with main responsibilities – and conceived differently.

In a meeting I attended on 19 July 2016, one or two men took the floor often, whereas others did not say much. At one point, the mayor sighed something like: "Oh, let a woman say something on this issue now, we have not heard a woman yet". Somewhat headmaster-like, he selected a woman, but while she was still speaking, he turned to the man next to him and started talking with him. This seemed to me quite bold, more so because I did not see him display this behaviour while others were speaking. Though it is difficult to pin down what underlies one's behaviour and I might be biased, my impression was that attendance by the women was more symbolic than substantive. However, this possibly counts for many of the members: I could not say whether the chiefs, religious leaders, civil society representatives and even the mayor himself, who were all male, were substantially engaged either. In essence, they had limited possibilities to circumvent their obligation to be present, since they were part of a committee that was stipulated in the terms and conditions of the development project.

In April 2017, one of the members of the committee told me informally that the leader of one of the women's associations had stopped going to the meetings, as a problem had occurred between her and a municipal officer. The same member confided me that the committee was not as stable as it appeared. It was reported that when a group of German students announced their arrival in early 2016, the leaders of the committee cancelled a meeting because they did not want the students to know that they had difficulties mobilising the committee members for the meeting (Conversation with CCL member, 16 April 2017).

These internal power differences are largely left untouched by the project's national and international consultants. The project's design is such that the responsibility for managing these differences for the population is relegated to the local actors. Addressing social hierarchies should be among the priorities for development actors, especially if they aim for civic engagement in a highly politicised environment. In its set-up, the project's lack of attention toward internal power relations between individuals who supposedly represent the town, their aspirations and attempts to protect their own interests, results in a type of civic participation that is controlled to such an extent that it is hardly meaningful.

In the current analysis of the project, the population seems to serve as empirical data in project reports in the form of numbers and percentages, whereas its impact on sustainable civic participation is questionable. As underlined by Arnstein (1969), sustainable participation benefits from closely collaborating with local leaders and 'target groups' in the design and implementation of a project. However, a section of people in Sokodé whom I interacted with viewed the project from another perspective: They interpreted the presence of international actors as a sign that they were not forgotten, giving rise to hope in a 'grey zone' (Mbembe 2003: 34). Finally, as previously stated with regard to competing actors in the public sphere, for some members of the committee, their very presence during the meetings might contribute to their emerging awareness about the potential transformative force of a civil society against all odds.

7.4 Phones and civic engagement from within the community

The civic-ness of connectivity: Crossing the sticky bridge

There are certain gaps to bridge between the daily workings of an ICT4D project and the use of ICT in various forms of everyday civic engagement, and it is these everyday practices that I describe, as they offer valuable insight about the framework of ICT4D. It might be worth considering the sticky bridge in Sokodé as metaphor for connectivity, using the metaphor of de Bruijn and van Dijk (2012: 2) who describe the massive bridge that connects the centre of the once mighty city centre of Saint Louis in northern Senegal with the outskirts. The image of people, cars, motor-taxis all crossing a busy bridge, brings about a powerful visual of connectivity: it reflects at once the use of different modes of transport, the differing speeds, the importance of infrastructure, and the aims, stories, dreams and expectations of the people who cross the bridge. The comparison might falter for people who know both bridges, as the size of the bridges and the breadth and depth of the water over which they are built, are incomparable. Nevertheless, the stickiness of the bridge might just be the metaphor needed to illustrate the constrained structural conditions, in which people reluctantly navigate, as their choices are limited. This brings the discussion back to the famous structure-agency dialectics in which Giddens' (1984) work has been influential.

The focus on people's agency, however limited their agency might be, has resulted in a conception that moves away from viewing people as victims of their circumstances, which was a change that was needed in the field of African studies (van Dijk *et al.* 2007). However, it is challenging to keep the tremendous obstacles faced by people in their everyday struggles, and their relative powerlessness vis-à-vis 'the system' in mind constantly. Empowerment and participation call for shifts in the power balance that are not evident. The context of Sokodé closely resembles the enduring experience of hardship in Chad as described by de Bruijn and Bot (2018), in which notions of 'chronic crisis' (Vigh 2008: 7–8) or 'everyday violence' (Scheper-Hughes 1993) do not fully encompass the experiences of people for whom extreme hardship has been a part of their inner worlds and of their family and village history; this is almost the normalisation of a longitudinal, layered hardship (de Bruijn & Bot 2018: 189). Even though ICTs offer people a new range of possibilities to uplift themselves from their hardship, the question remains whether they manage to do so (Ligtvoet 2018).

Balancing on the sticky bridge in the introduction of chapter six, I return again to the concept of connectivity, which is intrinsically linked to new communication technologies such as the phone. The concept of connectivity allows for a processual analysis in contrast to the more static 'network'. The sticky bridge is a powerful analogy for how I approach connectivity in Sokodé: the material conditions are just as important as its vital function of connecting places, linking Lomé with Bamako and Niamey, and connecting people, ideas and imaginations. The bridge is a place of confrontation between the 'forces of order' and 'civilians' who took their personal grievances to the street, into the public. The impuissance of hundreds of people to ensure their safety during their daily crossings across this bridge, is indicative of the difficult conditions of civic-ness in Sokodé. I approach civic-ness here in its broadest sense; a person facing her own environment and acting in it with an awareness of being in the world.

The civic-ness of connectivity in Sokodé cannot be captured in a linear flow, as it meanders through misty areas of mistrust, but also because of the instability of information itself as noted in chapter three. As shown in the introductory chapter, the level of mistrust resembles what Carey (2017) describes in a community in the Atlas Mountains in Morocco, where people live with the idea that other actors – from their most intimate relations to the largest institutions – are essentially unknowable and untrustworthy. Civic-ness, under these conditions, provides but a starting point to describe in a processual way the possibilities of individuals and groups to organise themselves around a specific cause. This cause affects their personal lives and is brought into the public sphere, along the lines of the ever-changing social webs of which they form an integral part. Above, I described this process as an emerging civil society. The civic-ness of connectivity, then, describes how civic information flows find their way through various media and ICTs, both influencing and being influenced by 'events' or 'moments' in time.

Early in my research, I noticed that the sociality that I had set out to describe, seemed to be sandy, and civic-ness as it could be described in the field was even more blurred. In this context, where disconnection and disengagement are prominent, the possibility for the type of civic engagement that the particular ICT4D project was aiming to improve remained minimal. The model of optimistic democratisation on which the logic of ICT4D are based seems to be illusionary, and an approach that considers people in Sokodé to be non-citizens sheds light on the civic-ness of connectivity in this environment.

The phone as semi-permeable membrane in the frame of citizen participation

In order to link the civic engagement of people – not citizens – in Sokodé to the assumptions on which ICT4D is based, a short discussion that centres participation might complement the framework I present to bridge the gap. Participation has two meanings: the first one indicating simply 'being there' or 'partaking', the second describes a process in which the participants are engaged in a certain event or process. When it concerns development or civic engagement, participation most often refers to the second meaning. In this sense, participation is about giving a voice to the voiceless and including their voice in decision-making processes (Friedmann 1992; Holland & Blackburn 1998; Rowlands 1997; Stiefel & Wolfe 1994).

Though participatory approaches are not without criticism,[25] they constitute a language in which both civic engagement and ICT4D assumptions can be approached (Cornwall 2008). Arnstein (1969) differentiates between levels of real or meaningful citizen participation and non-participation such as manipulation or tokenism. In his 'pathways to participation', Shier (2001) has included to the extent to which these levels are feasible in practice, asking at each level whether individuals and structures are ready to cede some of their power. This model shows that *willingness* does not equal *possibilities* for implementation, but that both are necessary. This means that meaningful participation does not only require the engagement of the participants – in the case above the 'citizens' of Sokodé – but also of the requesting party – a heterogeneous collaboration of the

---

25 See among others Cleaver (2001) and Cooke and Kothari (2001), who indicate that the antagonism between oppressors and oppressed easily obscures the heterogeneity of actors and individual interests, and Hildyard et al. (2004) who argue that participation can be 'the human software through which investments can be made with least local opposition'.

municipality of Sokodé and international and local development partners. Unequal power relations are a crucial point here, as participation requires a shift in power from the ones in power to the ones who are requested to participate (Arnstein 1969; Sinclair 2004). Already inherent in the term 'empowerment', a shift in power is often considered part of participation, as it concerns the deliberate inclusion of 'have-nots' who are – at least partially – excluded from political and economic processes (Arnstein 1969: 216). Considering the constraining power structures and the occurrence of 'choiceless decisions' (Aretxaga 1997; Coulter 2008) noted earlier in section 7.3, it is evident that the leeway for voice is narrow.

Undoubtedly, in the social and political structures that are not open to accommodate dissenting voices, it is difficult to create solid support, legitimacy and credibility from the population for projects envisaging municipal leaders to take into account their opinions in decision-making processes. Therefore, from a theoretical point of view, it is questionable if the ICT4D project discussed above reaches beyond Arnstein's levels of non-participation.

Till now, I have explained the constraints imposed by the experience of enduring hardship in Sokodé that is primary in people's motivations and interests to exercise anything resembling civic engagement. I have shown how the mobile phone serves as semi-permeable membrane; information can seep through from one side to the other, but this does not imply a horizontal exchange, as hierarchies largely stay in place. To illustrate this, even though someone may have one of the mayor's phone numbers, she cannot simply call or SMS the mayor, unless she has a personal relationship with him. An example taken from the opposite angle, is that the mobile phone is indeed used to access information that could be regarded as being on the public side of the scale. Dao demonstrated this to me when I asked him something about the town hall and he immediately grabbed his phone to call a municipal officer he had befriended. However, as I have emphasised before, I do not deny that new possibilities for civic engagement have been opened by the mobile phone, which could eventually lead to subtle changes in the existing social structures, with time.

Towards a new civic-ness? WhatsApp's transformative force

Though it might seem as if I have avoided a thorough exploration of new avenues for civic engagement that have opened because of the mobile phone, any expression of civic engagement should be understood in the framework of enduring hardship to which I continue to refer. I have centralised the experiences of hardship of the people, as these experiences inform their possibly 'civically engaged' actions, motivations and perceptions. Now as the bridge has been crossed, I address the theme of digital civic engagement in Sokodé. Although the mobile phone has several functions in its use as information and communication technology, smartphones are especially interesting in the sense that they give people access to the internet and social media platforms. Therefore, public social media platforms are the focus of study here, particularly WhatsApp, even though 'public' remains a blurry concept.

As noted in section 2.4 the mobile based messenger service WhatsApp is conceived of as social media platform in this book, as it fits common definitions of being a web-based user-generated service that allow people to connect and build community (McCay-Peet & Quan-Haase 2017: 17). Moreover, it is especially the widespread sharing in WhatsApp groups of the same visual, audio and video messages that has become important in the public debate. As I argued in section 6.5, WhatsApp largely contributed to the massive turnout at the street protests in late 2017. The enormous popularity of WhatsApp is bound to change private interactions, and this naturally has an impact on interaction in more public social structures.

In order to get a better understanding of the usage and role of the mobile phone for civic engagement, and particularly WhatsApp from mid-2016 onwards, I requested a few people to add me in some WhatsApp groups related to community development. I was not added to one of the groups, in which I had learned that there had been rather outspoken exchanges about a clash between two neighbourhoods. Possibly to prevent me from learning about exchanges that incited hatred, but also the administrators of the group might have thought it would be irrelevant to me, as they chat in one of the local languages. On 30 July 2016, my phone number was added to a community development group, and some of the exchanges in the group are discussed to provide certain insights into the discussion on digital civic engagement.

The WhatsApp group was aimed at the development of the Kotokoli and was created on 22 May 2016 by a member of the committee of the ICT4D project discussed above. Soon, the group had more than 150 members, and though its number has fluctuated ever since its creation, it had 160 members towards the end of 2018. Among those were 14 diaspora members, of whom five were based in Germany and five in neighbouring African countries. During the initial months, there were weekly or bi-weekly discussions around certain themes that were deemed important for development, such as education, the future of the youth, workers in the artisanal sector, and the ways in which the WhatsApp group could contribute to the development of the community. After these debates about the way forward for the community, the administrators of the group mainly shared employment opportunities, results of the national soccer competition, concerns about Sokodé's main soccer clubs Semassi and Unisport, death announcements of important people in the community, information on road accidents in which members of the Kotokoli community have been involved, communiqués of government assemblies and health advice. One of the three administrators also posts links to online news coverage on a website that also deals with the community's development.

Other than close monitoring to ensure that the rule that photos, videos, off-topic announcements, advertisements and jokes are not to be posted by anyone unless they have been allowed to do so by the administrators, they also balance the line between promoting the unity of the Kotokoli and rejecting racism, hate speech or political themes. In several cases when there was political trouble, the group's administrators requested members to maintain restraint, patience and unity. For example, their restraint channelled the rage in the WhatsApp group regarding the case of Kparió or Lama Tessi, a village in Tchaoudjo that is customarily ruled by the Kotokoli, where a Kabye chief was appointed under pressure from the regime (Cellulle de Réflexion de la Diaspora Tem en Allemagne 2017). During times of the protests and the besiegement of Sokodé and Bafilo in the second half of 2017, peaking in the last two weeks of October, a dozen of members left the group, which I connected to the refusal of the administrators to allow free discussion about the events.

Besides online activities, several in-person meetings were also planned in Sokodé in the second half of 2016 when the group was still relatively new, and a committee was formed. The creator and administrator of the WhatsApp group was elected head of the committee, with the online approval of other members. Besides the provision of information, some tangible actions emerged from the group: they contributed to a cleaning action in town in late 2016, collected money for the operation of an abscess on a boy's face between October and December 2017 and for a severe illness of a member by mid-2018, and some youth were able to acquire apprenticeships with the help of members who served as mediator. To understand the inescapable influence of social hierarchies, consider a case shared by a man on 27 August 2018, asking the family [the group members] what to do as two bags of blood had 'disappeared' in the regional hospital and the staff refused to repay him. He had purchased the blood bags for an operation of his wife that had turned out to be redundant, as she had given birth to a stillborn child. Upon their discharge, his request for the repayment of the sum was refused, though he went up to the department's director, and other patients had commented that this was a common occurrence. Several indignant reactions followed, coupled with wishes for a quick recovery for his wife. Some hours later, one of the group members introduced himself as a doctor, and the next day, the man reported that the case had been solved with the doctors' help.

The examples above show that this form of online self-organisation can be of decisive influence in offline situations, by assisting group members to find solutions in circumstances that are under the strict control of administrators. It might have been possible for the man to have his money returned for the unused bags of blood through other channels, but I am quite sure that his problem was solved much more rapidly, because the WhatsApp group gave him access to a person placed higher up in the hierarchy than was otherwise possible. Even though social hierarchies seem to persist even in these seemingly horizontal groups, this indicates that online platforms can provide a new range of opportunities for their members to connect and exchange, to further their own development and the development of their community.

7.5 Young people's quest for community development

Salim: "The community should be involved in their own development"

As member of a local royal clan, Salim was involved very early in community engagements, taking on the role as representative of his community. Together with Dao, he studied sociology in Kara. While Dao keeps his distance when it comes to political affairs, Salim is fully engaged. Salim's engagement is the reason that Dao took me to a primary school one morning in February 2015, where Salim was volunteering as a witness for the registration of voter cards. As Salim explained in the few minutes that he could step away, he is always eager to contribute to the development of his community, being a 'son of this place'. Salim speaks of himself as 'a communitarian, and politician, if you will'.

In 2015, Salim lived in his family house in Kpangalam with his wife and two daughters. During 2016, they moved to their own house a few streets uphill, where two sons were born to him. Since 2014, Salim has carried the emotional burden of witnessing his mother dying after a spleen operation, a death that he is convinced could have been prevented. He is bitter about the quality of care in Sokodé's regional hospital. His father, who could not bear the loss of his wife, passed away in 2015. This increased the responsibility on Salim's shoulders, as he had to take care of his younger siblings and the family of his older brother, who became depressed after losing his job in a factory in Lomé. On the insistence of Salim and others, he finally came to Sokodé with his wife and seven children. Salim was hoping to set up an agricultural business, which would also enable his older brother to have an income. In one of our conversations, Salim sighed: "How can you have seven children and not be able to take care of them!"

Apart from his family engagements, Salim was employed as adjunct secretary to one of the customary chiefs. He receives many phone calls every day, especially in the morning when 'the calls are too warm'. This is mostly because people are asking him to 'deliver a service'. He listed the services expected from him:

> Some are about fights. Another about the construction of a classroom, monitoring the work, come and see if no one is stealing. Whenever there is a problem with a sold or bought land. In short, the problems of the canton. For some, you give your number, if you call… This is for people who want to see the chief, they have to pass through me or the other secretary. (Interview with Salim, 19 June 2016)

The mobile phone has played a big role in Salim's professional success, as it has 'arranged' his life. In 2015, he explained that he spent up to 1,000 FCFA per day on credit, which is a large amount of money, but, in his words, 'it is the thing that yields me money so that is really nice'. He explains that he 'respects' the phone a lot, as it is thanks to the phone that he is in contact with people who bring him opportunities to generate income and solve community problems. In his wish to contribute to community development, he has started a neighbourhood WhatsApp group, which is a group of forty to fifty members who exchange ideas for the development of the canton. He explained his vision:

> That the community itself is involved in their own development. No one will do it in your place. Whether this is feasible depends on the community. [And for yourself?] I do not want to work in the public sector, I rather want to become the next mayor of Sokodé, to get myself elected for the community, so that they can see that I have accomplished this. (Interview with Salim, 23 February 2015)

In 2016, when we met in a bar for a follow-up interview, Salim wondered how people ever managed their lives without mobile phones. Similar to the image in section 4.2 of the phone as an extended body part, Salim reflected: 'If I do not have my phone with me, it is like it is my other half that has left, right?' (Interview with Salim, 19 June 2016).

Stéphanie: "WhatsApp is for us, the lazy who have nothing to do"

Stéphanie is a young woman who has studied sociology at the University of Kara. I met her at the compound within which I lived in 2015 and 2016, where a small local NGO was also located. Stéphanie started in the same year as Dao, but she had to redo the first year, which is where their roads diverged. However, as they both lived in Sokodé and were both engaged in community development, their paths often crossed, and they exchanged warm and cheerful greetings. Stéphanie has a boyfriend who was known to the family, and she lives in her parental house. Her parents are retired; her mother worked as a midwife before retirement.

Stéphanie frequently went to the office of the NGO, where she encountered the director and another colleague often. In the past, the NGO had acquired and executed an educational project, funded by a Swiss partner, for which Stéphanie had been hired. However, after the project had finished, the NGO did not manage to secure new projects. As Stéphanie also had not found another large project or job, she stuck around in the years thereafter. She explained that they sometimes wrote project proposals, but mostly she was simply present.

Unlike Salim, who is connected to a customary chiefdom and who considers himself first and foremost as community member and political agent, Stéphanie tries to find an occupation on the level of local NGOs, development associations and projects. Together with several dozens of young people who have a certain level of education, she joined activities organised by the municipality or a local NGO, mostly financed by international development partners. Every time the municipality or a development actor called for a group of youngsters, she asked her director for permission to partake in the activities. As he did not have much to offer her financially, he always granted her requests.

Among such activities were two-day workshops in the conference room of one of the hotels in town, awareness raising campaigns in which she was either informed or trained as volunteer to inform others, or she would be selected as a surveyor or interviewer for a short-term study. Some of these activities yielded some income, including 'per diems', allowances for travel, accommodation or food given to participants of workshops or seminars. The 'challenges' of the per diem are much debated in development circles – for example, some participants would be more interested in the per diem than in gaining knowledge, and the ones interested often could not even be reached (Samb, Essombe & Ridde 2020).

For Stéphanie and other young persons who have completed a certain level of education, such as having a Bachelor's degree in Sociology which she did, partaking in this system is a way to earn a little money from time to time, and also to network and show her availability in case a new project needed her services. In January 2016, one of these workshops in Lomé gave her the opportunity to save some money and buy a smartphone before returning to Sokodé.

There is a certain duality in Stéphanie's assessment of the mobile phone. On the one hand, she fiercely expressed her disapproval of the youth who are 'using their phones in disorder':

> The mobile phone is a very important tool, but it has been misunderstood, and people use it wrongly. People do anything with the mobile. They do not use it for development purposes. What can we do, we need to raise awareness. This tool is not built for such and such, explain its role: it is a development tool, to guarantee your future, there are job offers that can be found. Instead of looking for pornographic things and doing useless things, people have to ask themselves what good it will bring for them. (Interview with Stéphanie, 22 June 2016)

On the other hand, she explained that she easily could be on WhatsApp till midnight, joking with friends. She compared this with her boyfriend, who works from Monday to Friday and who 'does not have the time' to communicate on the phone. She sighed in a resigned manner: "WhatsApp is for us, the lazy, who have nothing to do". By sharing funny images and videos on WhatsApp, she and her friends try to forget their worries; the lived reality of limited job opportunities.

7.6 Concluding remarks

From the explorations in this chapter that are rooted in the processes discussed in chapter six, the fact emerges that tapping into the enormous possibilities of the phone to increase civic engagement is not straightforward in an environment in which there is a lack of opportunities, and mistrust prevails. The construct of the state and the role of information within the state leads to a docile form of citizenship, with little space for authentic voice. However, people are not simply lethargic and uninterested in civic development, and an ideal is indeed discernible. People are frustrated and angry about the political situation, but their anger remains very private, and its expression is by no means political.

In the ICT4D project described, aimed at boosting civic engagement, people are forced to participate and offer their opinion, though this does not lead to significant political expression. They mainly respond to the request of the people higher up in the social hierarchy compared to them. In this straitjacket of civic engagement, people do offer opinions and proposals, but most expressions are so general that they mainly contribute to the imaginary of civic engagement and ICT4D.

The community development WhatsApp group discussed in this chapter, entails a certain form of civic engagement, but whenever they voice their political concerns, they are actively being silenced by the administrators, who are part of the ruling political establishment in town. The administrators themselves are involved in a balancing act between silencing and being silenced by the state, as they secretly operate as opposition leaders at the same time.

The expressions of the population in the ICT4D project as well as in the development WhatsApp group do not have much meaning; they participate in the narrowest sense: they are present, but eventually, these projects remain a type of 'social civilisation' projects that are void of the political in what is an overly politicised domain. The underlying friction and the general scepticism with regard to whether local authorities bring or have the capacity to bring about positive change for the population remain untouched. Young people like Salim and Stéphanie cannot be assured that they will realise their potential, in an economic and socio-political landscape that does not reassure them in any way. It is important to note that in this context, if things are not going well, people prefer to remain silent in most cases. Therefore, political silence, should be especially understood for all that it is not revealing.

8 Conclusions: Political silence and new ICTs in a repressive state

8.1 Introduction

Over the years, in several of my research projects that were related to international development programs, an ancient Irish story would continuously pop up in my mind. It is about a stranger who asks for directions to the marketplace, and gets the reply: "I would not start from here". The starting point of international and multilateral development programs often seems to presuppose certain conditions that are not fulfilled. In the case of Sokodé, but not only in this city, the historical impact of the colonial period, lack of democratic institutions, powerlessness of the population vis-à-vis a strong military force, underlying causes of poverty and inequality, weak social services and the implications for people living under these circumstances of hardship all remain undisclosed.

This study has endeavoured to shed light on the links between mobile phones and civic engagement in the urban setting of Sokodé, Central Togo, in which people's everyday lives are marked by the enduring experience of political repression and economic deprivation. Duress has become a part of people's lives, to the extent that constraint is internalised. The central question which is a connecting thread through the different chapters is why society in Togo has not 'lapsed' into processes of civic engagement upon the introduction of new ICTs. This chapter unpacks this question in several layers. Firstly, the communication ecology of Sokodé is analysed, focusing on the changes that new ICT have brought about in the social fabric, and secondly the consequences of these changes with regard to civic engagement, which could also translate to civic protests. The third section discusses the scientific and societal contribution of this study, in which the limitations of the research and suggestions for further research are delineated.

Half a century of political repression in Togo have contributed to an atmosphere in which people's intentions often remain opaque. In this context of social, political and economic insecurity, elusiveness can save one from getting into trouble. Naturally, this has repercussions for the expression of civic engagement, in which the mobile phone offers new possibilities and reinforces existing structures. The following paragraphs link everyday usage and perceptions of mobile phones to the intimacy and instability of information and the (im)possibilities of employing mobile phones for civic acts and engagement in Sokodé.

The argument is built on the foundation of the description of politics on the interpersonal and household level, and the analysis of the links between mobile phones and civic engagement in the urban space of Sokodé. Political processes at the municipal and national level have been embedded within a deeper understanding of the cultural context in which these everyday meso-level politics are played out. In this sense, this study is consistent with a tradition in anthropology of studying 'small' politics, aiming to shed light on the dialectics between digital sociality, political subjectivities and social change in urban Togo. It is evident that the construct of the state, and the role that information plays in the communication ecology of Sokodé, lead to a docile form of citizenship, with little space for authentic voice.

8.2 Silence and civic (dis)engagement in a repressive state

The information ecology in Sokodé: Mistrust in digital sociality

By unveiling the stakes that are at play when people engage in processes of sharing information in Sokodé, it is indisputable that the mobile phone gives rise to new strategies to conceal and disclose personal information in Sokodé. It becomes apparent that the introduction of new ICTs in this context has contributed to an increased sense of mistrust in society. The main merit of Gleick's (2011) 'technique of information flow', in which he shows that information is multi-interpretable, and the approach of agency by Emirbayer and Mische (1998), is that they focus on the crucial point of interpretation. This means that the moment information is interpreted, people begin to act according to their interpretation. To underline how this plays out in everyday communication in Sokodé in which the mobile phone plays a major role, I return to the example of the message that David sent to Felix's girlfriend that had large impacts.

To frame this in a systemic approach of information as structured phenomenon, the 'source' is the subtitled photo of Felix and a girl, taken by David. This includes the material and economic aspects of David's phone use, which is important, as they form the medium through which the signal was transferred. The signal, a photo with a short subtitle, travels through the invisible lines of the telecommunication network that is dominated by a repressive state, and surfaces on the screen of Felix's girlfriend. A part of the 'information processing mechanisms' can be found in David's personal situation, motives and relation to Felix and his girlfriend, which, in this example, remain largely unknown. The mechanisms also comprise the internal processes in the girlfriend's mind, who interprets the piece of information presented to her in a certain way, and then acts upon her interpretation of it, which brings me back to the multi-interpretability of information. For Felix's mother, the same message could lead to a completely different reaction; she could well be worried about his excessive beer consumption or be frustrated that he had not sent her money via the mobile banking system Flooz.

The act of the girlfriend, based on the interpretation of this message and similar information, came some days later, and entailed the message for Felix that it was over between them. After a period of some weeks in which Felix insisted that she explain to him why she had suddenly broken up with him, she finally confessed that David had sent her images on WhatsApp. Felix's interpretation, in turn, had much larger consequences; this indicated a breach in trust by David, the final blow to their friendship. To frame this in Heitz Topka's (2013) terminology of mistrust and distrust, uncertainty was no longer suspended; distrust had become a fact. Regarding Felix and his girlfriend, depending on a complex combination of their shared history, envisioned future, their behaviour, character traits and available alternatives, a situation is conceivable in which they could, at one stage, continue their relationship. However, the fact that she had not checked with Felix to hear his side of the story upon receiving David's photos, most probably does not contribute to her credibility and loyalty from Felix's perspective.

Linking the interpretation of information to agency and trust as I do above, it can be noted that people's actions are based on a combination of the piece of information presented to them, their past experiences and their imagination of the future. In the outlined information 'structure', several elements of the process carry a high degree of untrustworthiness. However, leaving out these details entails the risk of decontextualizing the final breach of trust between Felix and David. This story serves to illustrate the complex social constellations in Sokodé, which are characterised by instability and unreliability. These social constellations are the basis of the forms that digital sociality can take, and the role that ICTs can play in this context. The distrust that exists in the communicative expressions analysed here is fundamental to the research problem, outlining the manner in which different sections of society are impacted by the introduction of new ICTs, and the ways in which this is expressed.

In this environment, people take great care to conceal their personal intentions, out of fear of the bad intensions of other people, including non-human influences. The links with Glissant's Relation (Glissant 1990) have be drawn to analyse the mobile phone in this complex network of meanings and uses. By approaching information as a structured phenomenon, the 'release mechanism' or interpretation is a key element (Karpatschof 2000). In Sokodé, every step in this structure – from source to signal to release mechanism to reaction – seems to be highly unstable, to the extent that it can be argued that information itself is unreliable and untrustworthy in this context. Mistrust is a basic feature of relationships in Sokodé, and many communicative acts are concealed in one way or the other, for instance by talking in metaphors. Communicative acts are not limited to verbal exchanges; paying a visit to someone or avoiding it conveys information too. A well-informed interlocutor may understand most of the information that is unsaid between the lines, but the intentions of the other are open for speculation in many information exchanges. As also evidenced from the case above, the people who are closest and who have most information about someone, can also cause the most harm.

The systemic approach to information brings depth to the analysis of misinformation and the value that people in Sokodé attach to the trustworthiness of information. From the empirical data, the conclusion can be drawn that mobile phones and social media feed and deepen the mistrust that already existed in society. The trustworthiness attached to information has become even more unstable, even though I contend that this has always been dependent upon the relationship between the sender and recipient of the information, and not so much on the factual correctness of certain information. In this sense, this adds an additional layer to existing debates on misinformation and fake news in relation to politics.

Political silence in view of the construct of the state

In Sokodé, most of the population live their daily lives, not trusting most information provided by national and local authorities. In the words of a broadcaster, only the death announcements are true. Instead, people tend to rely on Al Jazeera, France24, CNN on one hand, and their social networks on the other. The information ecology is constructed in such a way that news from national and local authorities is generally evaluated as untrustworthy. It is worrying that misinformation is spread rapidly through WhatsApp and has a real-life impact on social relationships, such as the emergence of lynch mobs in India. An example of misinformation in Sokodé was the video from Bamenda, Cameroon, where soldiers were beating up youngsters who were tied up, which was widely circulated in Sokodé in September and October 2017.

It is difficult to know exactly the extent to which a WhatsApp message or similar piece of information has fuelled the violence during these moments of overt conflict and oppression. This is exactly why it is imperative that social scientists embed the statements they make in empirical research and contextualise the data. This example of the street protests make it clear that the present government was completely taken by surprise by the massive turnout for the street protests on 21 August 2017, and the reason the turnout was so massive was because of the PNP messages that had circulated on WhatsApp and other more private social media channels.

As the main cities of protest were besieged rather rapidly, the status quo regarding the political regime hardly changed, and young people were pushed back again in their harsh everyday circumstances. The construct of the state as the structure that has a monopoly on violence, does not imply that this structure also protects its citizens, at least not in Togo. Relying on authors such as Mamdani (1996) and Mbembe (2003), people in Sokodé can be regarded as being among the 'denizens' in the 'grey zones' who must fend for themselves. NGOs and development associations step into the gap left by the state, trying to provide social security infrastructures, but largely failing to include everyone who live in this area, as everyone do not have the possibility nor are they eligible to be part of these organisations' 'target groups'.

For the moment, the current regime manages to stay in place, and the deep distrust of everything toward anything that emerges from the authorities is apparent. This is not so surprising considering the dilapidated state of social services and infrastructure, and the stark contrast between the dire poverty of the population and the exorbitant wealth of a minority who are close to or part of the leadership of the country. Moreover, there have been several moments in the recent and early history of the country, in which the regime has proven that it is not to be trusted, allowing soldiers to wield violence against the population. Even though people are tired after fifty years of rule by the same family, the regime still holds on to power, backed by the same circle of army generals. In order to remain in power, the regime has developed a multitude of strategies to silence political opposition, which includes offering opponents a high position in society to silence them or incarcerating them on the pretext of a scandal or subversive state activities. In response to this, the common people in Sokodé have also turned their back on the government, fending for themselves in their daily battles.

Digital sociality, social change and civic (dis)engagement of young people

The central question of why Togo has not organically engaged in any type of civic engaged processes upon the introduction of new information and communication technologies, can be answered by delving into the construct of the state. The state and information within the state in Togo leads to a docile form of citizenship with little space for authentic voice. The state can be considered as being the population in its relationality. In this context of deprivation, frustration and mistrust, the state appears to have few possibilities to blossom. People are resigned in this atmosphere; they are tired, they do not have the time to engage politically. Some of my informants even sighted that they live prison-like lives.

A WhatsApp conversation between Dao and me sheds a light on this theme:

Roos: Can Togolese society be considered, in certain ways, as a hostile place, in which every person must fend for themselves? This is not the entire story, as people cannot survive or live without the support and comfort of others. There is a strong interdependence, mixed with mistrust [...] (Text message by Roos, 1 April 2021)

Dao: At the level of Togolese society, there are no opportunities that reassure the hope of the individual, that reassure the hope of the youth. So that is why we lose hope. [...] There is no feature that the leaders put in place that will ensure that when someone evolves in Togo he says he is confident [...] that 'with this education I am doing, I will have the opportunity to find a job to earn a living'. That's really the observation, when discussing how things are going, people reply it goes *à la Togolaise*. Today, when the expression "ça va à la *Togolaise*" is used, this means 'I am fighting'. Of course, we need others in this fight. We fight, but who do we go to? It is the one who is closest to me, and at the same time does he have the means to be able to? In our interdependence, to realise my work, my ambitions, often it is [a relationship] between us who share the same skin. And you said it well, it is difficult to go to a higher level. [...] It is really this society that does not really have opportunities that reassure a person to feel comfortable to say 'Yes, I can realise my potential, I can cherish the hope to have a better life'. There is always suspense, the questioning of what tomorrow holds. (Voice message by Dao, 1 April 2021)

This uncertainty of what tomorrow holds can be linked to the lack of vision and accompanying implementation of a solid development of the country's health, education and economic sector by the state. Agenda setting by external donors does not only happen at the local level, but also at the national level. Concurrent with the image of 'grey zones' depicted by Mbembe (2003), the deprived parts of the population survive by the grace of local NGOs and religious organisations. The fact that the political regime does not shy away from political intimidation and the deployment of security forces to silence street protests, also means that existing relationships with international development partners are unstable.

As discussed in chapter two, the telecommunication networks are also to a large extent controlled by the state. It is common for oppressive regimes to shut down the telecommunications networks during times of political or social upheaval, such as during protests or during election days. The power of political regimes to prevent people from communicating over telecommunication networks also brings up questions about the enormous potential power of telecommunication companies, and large technology companies.

In some cases, like in Cameroon, it has already been noted that telecommunication companies send out broadcast messages requesting the population not to spread certain 'hate' messages, whereas it remains unclear which actor or algorithm has or should have the moral power to judge which messages contribute to disinformation and which messages do not. This is especially the case in countries where the political leaders themselves do not seem to take moral justice as a given. In these countries, like in Togo, digital publics are based on complex concealed information ecologies in which people navigate, and only attentive outsiders can locate well-organised voices and civic engagement. It must be emphasised, that in this tense political environment, every civic act can be interpreted as a political act. Especially in a city in which political opposition is regarded as being fierce, most acts of civic-ness can be interpreted as politically subversive acts. In such an environment, conceiving of and engaging in acts of civic engagement are only reserved for the rare people who are wealthy, extremely well-informed, protected by social networks of power, and who have the courage to do so.

8.3 Civic-ness and ICT4D

Social media expressions, civic-ness and ICT4D

Even though the massive mobilisation of participants for the street protests in August 2017 was successful mainly because mobilisation messages were widely spread through social media and WhatsApp in particular, the violent response by the government shows that political change takes more than a mobile phone. The high degree of political control can be illustrated by the director in section 2.2, who has accepted a position in a national institution that serves the regime, even though he used to be active for the opposition. There are many people like him who are faced with the dilemma of either being a target or having to be Janus faced with these extreme circumstances, circumstances that exemplify the term 'choiceless decisions' as discussed in chapter seven (Aretxaga 1997; Coulter 2008). Besides, this means that not only are people in lower positions reluctant to express their opinions, but that many people in higher positions also practice a form of self-censorship, bound by their position.

This study has shown that the mobile phone does not lead to profound changes in social hierarchies and power structures in this constrained environment, neither does it provide an escape from the experience of enduring hardship. However, the subtle changes that can be discerned are not without meaning. The mobile phone does offer people a sense of possibility (Musil 2017), and even though many dreams and imaginations never materialise, they are the fuel for changes on the long run, as part of the basis on which actions are built.

In the constrained context of Sokodé, social relations do not change suddenly, but are concealed in subtle changes. Within the space of the mobile phone contact list, or on a social media platform like Facebook, in which children can befriend their parents, people are obliged to find new ways to clarify hierarchical distinctions. The discontentment of parents and teachers in Sokodé about the 'disorderly' mobile phone use of pupils is indicative of this. For an individual in Sokodé, merely having the phone number of a highly placed person or being in a large WhatsApp group with highly placed persons, can be meaningful. While people might not immediately act upon such information, this 'latent stratification' of relations has become part of their reality. However, in a WhatsApp group with members who do not know each other personally, it is impossible to know who everyone is. Furthermore, this study shows that even if all members know each other, there is a considerable extent of not-knowing.

While this study considers civic-ness as not necessarily being related to the state, it has been framed in the context of state repression. Focusing on civic engagement from within, some communications that are either more or less public do offer hope. The WhatsApp group discussed in chapter seven, has achieved some small successes: participating in a cleaning action, collecting money for sick members, helping youth secure internships, and seeking justice at the regional hospital. This indicates that, at least for the individuals who have access to such platforms and groups, their adherence could gradually contribute to an improvement of their well-being, and possibly to a sense of community.

It remains to be seen whether such groups are inclusive enough to construct and boost an overarching sense of community, and exclusive enough that people feel connected to each other and connected to a common cause which might require personal action at some stage, or when the discussion moves to another platform. The most important aspect of the study remains the people who use technologies. The ways in which the administrators of the community development WhatsApp group in Sokodé employ new technologies to organise members of their community, might be a path leading to expressions and acts of civic-ness, contributing to the development of their community. This may also offer possibilities for future ICT4D projects.

The merits of a participatory approach for ICT4D

Toward the end of 2017, right after I had given a presentation in the European head office of the international development organisation, based on the ethnographic data that I had collected during several fieldwork periods in Sokodé, the sector economist in the room asked me: "Did you collect *data*, other than the two diagrams that we saw?" This question made me realise that he had either not understood the essence of my presentation about the instability of information, the reigning distrust and social inequalities in Sokodé, or that he had not been interested, or both. This remark contributed to my understanding of information, as it drew my attention to the fact that the relativity of the *value* attached to certain information defines the interpretation of information as much as the *trustworthiness* attached to it.

Furthermore, it captured two main challenges. Firstly, there remains a large gulf between the drawing board in the headquarters of some of the large international development actors and the everyday lived realities of their perceived 'target groups'. Secondly, it remains challenging to have ethnographic results be 'heard' within such organisations, whereas I strongly believe that their target groups would benefit if such results would be taken into account in the design of their programmes. As a form of engaged anthropology, I recommend that international development organisations invest in mechanisms of self-reflection about the imagined and real impacts of the strategies they have developed to support good governance and increase civic engagement. This would lead to engaged employees who propose changes in procedures and strategies, guided by local experts.

From my analysis of premises that ICT4D hold and the project described in chapter seven, it has become apparent that sustainable digital civic engagement in a context like Sokodé is difficult to achieve through the strategies already being used. Firstly, this is because the premises on which these projects are founded are often unfulfilled or unrealistic. Several theories about citizen participation indicate that a certain transfer of power is involved, if participation is to be meaningful and sustainable (Arnstein 1969; Shier 2001). This transfer of power is rather challenging when considering the local political conditions in Sokodé, which are considerably directed by Lomé. Local elections were postponed for decades, and therefore the municipal council was not considered capable of being held accountable towards its 'citizens'.

Another conclusion drawn from this analysis is that for ICT4D projects to be meaningful and sustainable, they should be based on the experiences of the people who use the technologies. The ICT4D project that has been described in this book, but also similar projects, would benefit from a shift of focus from the technologies to the users of these technologies, since they only become meaningful in the hands of people. In this study, key figures in the local domain of community development can be identified. As proposed by Arnstein (1969) and others, the meaningful and sustainable impact of a community project can be deepened by investing in participatory processes, from its inception and design to its implementation and evaluation. The inclusion of local development leaders is essential for sustainable development. However, it also depends on its execution.

Projects such as these call for a sensitivity towards existing social inequalities and hierarchies, and a need to engage with local processes of power. Striving for the inclusion of vulnerable groups remains shallow if it is confined to a project design that demands that several people representing such groups be part of a committee – even if the project's intentions are good. It requires an accompanying set of methods and techniques that enable these people to have their voices be heard.

8.4 Towards a political anthropology of communication

Researching digital sociality and communication ecology

Apart from following part of the WhatsApp messages in a local development WhatsApp group, this research has not consistently analysed social media expressions. The contents of the mobile phones of people other than myself were not scrutinised, even though there were many occasions when people showed me photos or videos in their phone, or a certain application, to underline the argument they were making. In this sense, it is not a digital ethnography in itself; it is a digital ethnography in its relationality.

Asking people permission to scroll through their mobile phones requires a transgression of certain unwritten social rules that I was unable and unwilling to do. Navigating unsteadily in a social atmosphere that was permeated with distrust, I did not want to jeopardise my position and be known as a spy. However, it would have been insightful to map the daily moments of mobile communication of some individuals, embedded in an ethnographic analysis of their family's everyday lives. A stronger focus on digital technologies as a research tool, common in the field of digital anthropology, could have yielded interesting results.

Nevertheless, the empirical grounding of this study makes a strong point for embedding messages and social media expressions in an empirical analysis of people's daily lives. This is the exact gap that can be discerned in the majority of existing research about digital lives, such as Twitter analyses that urgently need contextualisation. To what extent do we talk about young urban elites, and what does this say about the impact of new media in the countries we describe? How do we get insight into the effects of high profile Twitter feeds that are shared by a minor urban elite in their family WhatsApp groups with members dispersed over a country, and even internationally? In Sokodé, but also in many other places, there is a substantial influence of the diaspora in local debates and relationships. It would be very interesting to investigate the manner in which these links are cultivated, and how the value that is attached to the trustworthiness of the information they disperse relates to a talk with the neighbour.

Deeper insights into the impact of new ICTs and social media on political constellations and civic engagement can be received through contextualised research into communication ecologies and underlying information structures in society. How can we as researchers understand that a film from Cameroon can impact civic protest in Togo, while maintaining a certain sobriety like Désiré, who shrugged his shoulders and said: "Our soldiers are the same everywhere". Once an idea of acute crisis and violent confrontation is spread, through social media or theoretically even by a researcher, it quickly takes hold, and expressions that are part of a digital imagination become reality.

While political leaders show that they are impressed by the mobilising power of social media, in the form of shutting down telecommunication networks during times of elections or social conflict, there is little understanding of the enormous potential of a WhatsApp message. At the same time, this potential is also often overestimated because most people are preoccupied with the daily struggle to make ends meet.

8.5 Concluding remarks

As the research field regarding the impact of mobile phones in an anthropology of communication slowly takes shape, this study contributes to uncover parts of communication and information in an African context, parts that cannot be 'seen' but have to be detected from everyday practices and changes over time. There is a yawning gulf between the aspirations of people in Togo and their material realities, which this monograph underlines.

The story of Felix and David illustrates how the mobile phone has increased the possibilities for creating and feeding mistrust in Sokodé, in an environment that imposes constraints on people's agency. In this final section, I want to point to the mere fact that Felix was sure that someone had attempted to poison him. Regardless of whether this was 'true' or not, this is indicative of the mistrust in society, as Felix was not more paranoid than other people I met. To describe sociality in Sokodé in terms of paranoia is too extreme, but the term fear is appropriate to refer to the degree of insecurity that is engrained in social relations, even at the most intimate level.

Though the relationship between Felix and David did not continue, this was not the end of their stories. People always find ways to adapt to the new realities of life presented to them, however limited their real or perceived options may be.

Mobile phones have become part of the new social, political, economic, spiritual and cultural reality in Sokodé and in other places, and we are only beginning to understand what this means for the ways in which people relate to each other and to their environment. I set out to explore the question why Togo did not organically engage with civic engaged processes upon the introduction of new ICTs, and through this process gaining a deeper understanding of the level of intimacy of information has been important. The stories of Felix, Sweet Mama, Dao's grandmother and the many others that were revealed in this work bear witness to this and affirm their dignity and resilience. However, the source of their dignity and resilience resides in the stories that were concealed – in most cases by them and in some cases by me – and it is exactly those stories that have formed the core of this work.

In this unravelling of the social fabric and the material that facilitate connections, the trustworthiness of different social and political actors, aspects and constellations cannot be known. This is a determining factor for the inherent instability of information in Sokodé, even though mobile phones bring about subtle and prominent changes. The high degree of not-knowing and instability are taken for granted by the people in Sokodé, who are living their lives, hoping against all odds for some 'normalcy' to be part of their lives one day.

References

Adams, C.A., & Thompson, T.L., 2011, 'Interviewing objects: Including educational technologies as qualitative research participants', *International Journal of Qualitative Studies in Education* 24(6), 733–750.

Adeiza, M., 2014, 'New media, old politics: Digital media, elections and democracy consolidation in Nigeria'. CMDS Working Paper 2014(3).

Adeiza, M., & Howard, P.N., 2016, 'New social media practices: Potential for development, democracy and anti-democratic practices', in Hammett, D. & Grugel, J. (eds.), *Palgrave handbook of international development*, pp. 577–594. Palgrave, London.

Afreepress, 2015, 'L'Etat togolais conditionne le transfert de Moov-Togo à Maroc Telecom au respect du cahier des charges', Afreepress, viewed 13 October 2018, from http://www.icilome.com/nouvelles/news.asp?id=11&idnews=799416.

African Development Bank (AfDB), 2014, 'African Economic Outlook 2014', viewed 1 July 2014, from http://www.africaneconomicoutlook.org/fileadmin/uploads/aeo/2014/PDF/E-Book_African_Economic_Outlook_2014.pdf.

Aghu, 2009, 'MOOV-Togo: Les non-dits d'une rupture', viewed 13 October 2018, from http://koaci.com/moov-togo-dits-d%E2%80%99une-rupture-2702.html.

Akoh, B., & Ahiabenu, I. K., 2012, 'A Journey through 10 countries: Online Election Coverage in Africa', *Journalism Practice* 6(3), 349–365.

Alozie, N.O., Akpan-Obong, P., & Foster, W.A., 2011, 'Sizing up information and communication technologies as agents of political development in sub-Saharan Africa', *Telecommunications Policy* 35(8), 752–763.

Alpes, J., 2016, *Brokering High-Risk Migration and Illegality in West Africa: Abroad at any cost*, Routledge, London & New York.

Amit, V., 2000, *Constructing the Field: Ethnographic fieldwork in the Contemporary World*, Routledge, London & New York.

Amit, V. & Caputo, V., 2015, 'The Possibilities and Mobilizations of Connections', in Amit, V. (ed.), *Thinking through Sociality: An Anthropological Interrogation of Key Concepts*, pp. 156–180, Berghahn Books, Oxford.

Anderson, B., [1983] 1991, *Imagined communities: reflections on the origin and spread of nationalism*, Verso, London.

Appadurai, A., 1996, *Modernity at Large: Cultural Dimensions of Globalization*, University of Minnesota Press, Minneapolis.

Archambault, J.S., 2016, *Mobile Secrets: youth, intimacy, and the politics of pretense in Mozambique*, , University of Chicago Press, Chicago.

Archambault, J.S., 2012, "Travelling while sitting down': Mobile phones, mobility and the communication landscape in Inhambane, Mozambique', *Africa* 82, 393–41.

Archambault, J.S., 2009, 'Being cool or being good: researching mobile phones in Mozambique', *Anthropology matters* 11(2).

Aretxaga, B., 1997, *Shattering Silence: Women, Nationalism, and Political Subjectivity in Northern Ireland*, Princeton University Press, Princeton.

Arminen, I., 2006, 'Social functions of location in mobile telephony', *Personal and Ubiquitous Computing* 10(5), 319–323.

Arnstein, S.R., 1969, 'A Ladder of Citizen Participation', *Journal of the American Institute of Planners* 35(4), 216–224.

Atwood, A., 2016, 'Zimbabwe's unstable infrastructure', *Journal of Digital Cultures* 3, 1–18.
Avgerou, C., 2017, 'Theoretical framing of ICT4D research', in J. Choudrie & Islam, S. (eds.), *Information and communication technologies for development*, pp. 10–23, New York: Springer.
Barbier, J. C., & Klein, B., 1995, *Sokodé, ville multicentrée du Nord-Togo,* Orstom Éditions, IRD, Paris.
Banks, K., 2008, 'Africa's grassroots mobile revolution: A traveler's perspective', *Receiver (vodafone),* 20.
Bateson, G., [1972] 1987, *Steps to an Ecology of Mind*, Jason Aronson Inc, Northvale, New Jersey, London.
Baumann, R., & Briggs, C., 2003, *Voices of Modernity: Language Ideologies and the Politics of Inequality*, Cambridge University Press, Cambridge.
Bayart, J.-F., 1989, *L'État en Afrique: La Politique du Ventre*, Fayard, Paris.
Bell, J.A. & Kuipers, J.C., 2018, *Linguistic and Material Intimacies of Cell Phones*, Routledge, London.
Bell, J.A., Kobak, B., Kuipers, J. & Kemble, A., 2018, 'Unseen Connections: The Materiality of Cell Phones', *Anthropology Quarterly* 91(2), 465–484.
Best, M. L. & Meng, A., 2015, 'Twitter democracy: policy versus identity politics in three emerging African democracies', in *Proceedings of the Seventh International Conference on Information and Communication Technologies and Development* (ICTD2015), Singapore.
Bhambra, G.K., Gebrial,D. & Nişancıoğlu, K., 2018, *Decolonising the University*, Pluto Press, London.
Biehl, J., 2009, *Will to live: AIDS therapies and the politics of survival*, Princeton University Press, Princeton, Oxford.
Bimber, B., 2000, 'The Study of Information Technology and Civic Engagement', *Political communication* 17, 329–333.
Bissell, W., 1999, 'Colonial Constructions: Historicizing Debates on Civil Society in Africa' in Comaroff, J.L. & Comaroff, J. (eds.), *Civil Society and the Political Imagination in Africa: Critical Perspectives*, pp. 124–159, University of Chicago Press, Chicago.
Blaney, D.L. & Pasha, M.K., 1993, 'Civil society and democracy in the Third World: ambiguities and historical possibilities', *Studies in Comparative International Development* 28(1), 3–24.
Bledsoe, C.H., 1990, "No Success without Struggle': Social Mobility and Hardship for Foster Children in Sierra Leone', *Man* 25(1), 70–88.
Bonhomme, J., 2012, 'The dangers of anonymity: Witchcraft, rumor, and modernity in Africa', *Journal of Ethnographic Theory* 2(2), 205–233.
Bonhomme, J., 2011, 'Les numéros de téléphone portable qui tuent: Epidémiologie culturelle d'une rumeur transnationale', *Tracés* 21, 125–150.
Boswell, R. & Nyamnjoh, F.B., (eds.), 2016, *Postcolonial African anthropologies*, HSRC Press, Cape Town.
Bott, M., 2013, *More accountability through mobile citizen participation*, KfW Position Paper, KfW, Frankfurt am Main.
Bouman, A., 2003, 'Benefits of Belonging. Dynamics of Iklan Identity, Burkina Faso', PhD Thesis, Department of Cultural Anthropology University Utrecht and CERES, Utrecht.

Bratton, M., 2013, 'Briefing: Citizens and Cell Phones in Africa', *African Affairs* 112(447), 304–319.
Breuer, A., & Groshek, J., 2016, 'Assessing the Potential of ICTs for Participatory Development in Sub-Saharan Africa with Evidence from Urban Togo', *International Journal of Politics, Culture, and Society*.
Breuer, A., Blomenkemper, L, Kliesch, S., Salzer, F., Schädler, M., Schweinfurth, V. & Virchow, S., 2017, 'Decentralisation in Togo: The Contribution of ICT-Based Participatory Development Approaches to Strengthening Local Governance', German Development Institute Discussion Paper No. 6/2017, viewed 7 October 2018, from https://ssrn.com/abstract=2915509.
Brinkman, I. & Alessi, S., 2009, 'From 'lands at the end of the earth' to 'lands of progress'? Communication and mobility in South-Eastern Angola', in Fernández-Ardèvol, M., & A. Ros Híjar, A. (eds.), *Communication technologies in Latin America and Africa: A multidisciplinary perspective*, pp. 193–220, IN3, Barcelona.
Broadbent, S., 2016, *Intimacy at Work: How Digital Media Bring Private Life to the Workplace*, Routledge, Walnut Creek, CA.
Broadbent, S. & Bauwens, V., 2008, 'Understanding convergence', *Interactions: Toward a Model of Innovation* 15(1), 23–27.
Brown, J., & Duguid, P., 2000, 'Organizational learning and communities of practice: Toward a unified view of working, learning, and innovation', in Lesser, E., Fontaine, M.A., and J.A. Slusher (eds.), *Knowledge and Communities*, pp. 99 — 121, Butterworth-Heinemann, Boston.
Brown, T. M. & Dreby, J. (eds.), 2013, *Family and Work in Everyday Ethnography*, Temple University Press, Philadelphia.
Buchbinder, L., 2012, 'After Trafficking: Naming Violence against Children in West Africa', PhD dissertation, University of California, San Fransico.
Burell, J., 2010, 'Evaluating Shared Access: Social equality and the circulation of mobile phones in rural Uganda', *Journal of Computer-mediated Communication* 15, 230–250.
Buskens, I. & Webb, A. (eds.), 2014, *Women and ICTs in Africa and the Middle East: Changing selves, changing societies*, Zed Books, London.
Capurro, R. & Hjørland, B., 2003, 'The concept of information', *Annual review of information science and technology* 37(1), 343–411.
Carey, M., 2017, *Mistrust: An Ethnographic Theory*, HAU Books, Chicago.
Caribou Digital, 2015, *Digital Lives in Ghana, Kenya, and Uganda*, Caribou Digital Publishing, Farnham, Surrey, United Kingdom.
Castells, M. (ed.), 2004, *Network Society, a cross cultural perspective*, Edward Elgar, Cheltenham, Northhampton.
Cellulle de Réflexion de la Diaspora Tem en Allemagne, 2017, 'Togo, Problèmes fonciers à Tchaoudjo : Des terres injustement arrachées au canton de Kadambara'. 27avril.com, viewed 11 October 2018, from https://www.27avril.com/blog/opinion/togo-problemes-fonciers-a-tchaoudjo-terres-injustement-arrachees-canton-de-kadambara.
Chabal, P., 2009, *Africa: The Politics of Smiling and Suffering*, University of KwaZulu-Natal Press, Scottsville.
Chambers, R., Narayan, D., M.K. Shah & Petesch, P., 2000, *Voices of the poor: crying out for change*, Oxford University Press, New York.

Chiluwa, I., 2015, 'Text messaging in social protests', in Yan, Z. (ed.), *Encyclopedia of Mobile Phone Behavior*, pp. 1024–1031, IGI Global, Hershey.
Chiumbu, S., 2012, 'Exploring mobile phone practices in social movements in South Africa: The Western Cape Anti-Eviction Campaign', *African Identities* 10(2), pp. 193–206.
Clark, I. & Grant, A., 2015, 'Sexuality and Danger in the Field: Starting an Uncomfortable Conversation', *Journal of the Anthropological Society of Oxford* 7(1), 1–14.
Cleaver, F., 2001, 'Institutions, Agency and the Limitations of Participatory Approaches to Development', in Cooke, B. & Kothari, U., *Participation – the new tyranny?*, pp. 36–55, Zed Press, London, New York.
Clifford, J. & Marcus, G.E., 1986, *Writing culture*, University of California Press, Berkeley.
Coleman, E.G., 2010, 'Ethnographic Approaches to Digital Media', *Annual Review of Anthropology* 39, 487–505.
Coleman, J.S., 1990, *Foundations of social theory*, Harvard University Press, Cambridge.
Collyer, M., 2007, 'In-between places: Trans-saharan transit migrants in Morocco and the fragmented journey to Europe', *Antipode* 39(4), 668–90.
Comaroff, J. & Comaroff, J.L. (eds.), 1993, *Modernity and its malcontents: Ritual and power in postcolonial Africa*, University of Chicago Press, Chicago.
Comaroff, J.L. & Comaroff, J. (eds.), 1999, *Civil Society and the Political Imagination in Africa: Critical Perspectives*, University of Chicago Press, Chicago.
Comunello, F. & Anzera, G., 2012, 'Will the revolution be tweeted? A conceptual framework for understanding the social media and the Arab Spring', *Islam and Christian-Muslim Relations* 23(4), 453–470.
Cooke, B. & Kothari, U. (eds.), 2001, *Participation – the new tyranny?* Zed Press, London, New York.
Cooper, E. & Pratten, D., 2015, *Ethnographies of Uncertainty in Africa*, Palgrave MacMillan, New York.
Cornwall, A., 2008, 'Unpacking 'Participation': Models, Meanings and Practices', *Community Development Journal* 43(3), 269–283.
Coulter, C., 2008, 'Female Fighters in the Sierra Leone War: Challenging the Assumptions?' *Feminist Review* 88, 54–73.
Csordas, T., 1993, 'Somatic modes of Attention', *Cultural Anthropology* 8(2), 135–156.
D'Almeida, E. & Dougueli, G., 2017, 'Togo : Tikpi Atchadam, l'homme qui empêche le pouvoir de dormir', viewed on 8 April 2021, from https://www.jeuneafrique.com/mag/468648/politique/togo-tikpi-atchadam-lhomme-qui-empeche-le-pouvoir-de-dormir/.
DaSilva, I.S., 2015, 'Togo govt summons Etisalat, Maroc Telecom over Moov deal', viewed on 30 May 2017, from http://www.biztechafrica.com/article/togo-govt-summons-etisalat-maroc-telecom-over-moov/9483/.
de Bruijn, M.E. & Bot, J., 2018, 'Introduction: Understanding Experiences and Decisions in Situations of Enduring Hardship in Africa', *Conflict and Society: Advances in Research* 4, 186–198.
de Bruijn, M.E., Nyamnjoh, F. & Angwafo, T., 2010, 'Mobile interconnections: Reinterpreting distance, relating and difference in the Cameroonian Grassfields', *Journal of African Media Studies* 2(3), 267–285.
de Bruijn, M.E., Nyamnjoh, F. & Brinkman, I. (eds.), 2009, *Mobile Phones: The New Talking Drums of Everyday Africa*, Langaa Group, Bamenda.

de Bruijn, M. E. & Dijk, R. van, 2012, 'Introduction: Connectivity and the Postglobal Moment: (Dis)connections and Social Change in Africa', in de Bruijn, M. E. & Dijk, R. van (eds.), *The social life of connectivity in Africa*, pp. 1–20, Palgrave Macmillan, New York.

de Lanerolle,I., Walton, M. & Schoon, A., 2017, *Izolo: mobile diaries of the less connected*, Making All Voices Count Research Report, IDS, Brighton.

de Lanerolle, I., Schoon, A., & Walton, M., 2020, 'Researching Mobile Phones in the Everyday Life of the "Less Connected": The Development of a New Diary Method', *African Journalism Studies*, 1–16.

de Lange, M., 2010, *Moving circles: Mobile media and playful identities*, Erasmus University Rotterdam, Rotterdam.

DGSCN (Direction Général de la Statistique et de la Comptabilité National), 2011, *Questionnaire des Indicateurs de Base du Bien-être – QUIBB 2011*, République Togolaise, Lomé. Viewed 3 March 2017, from http://www.stat-togo.org/contenu/pdf/rapport-final-quibb-togo-dgscn-2013.pdf.

Dodworth, K., 2014, 'NGO legitimation as practice: working state capital in Tanzania', *Critical African Studies* 6(1), 22–39.

Donner, J., 2008, 'Shrinking Fourth World? Mobiles, Development, and Inclusion', in Katz, J.E. (ed.), *Handbook of Mobile Communication Studies*, pp. 29–42, MIT, Boston.

Donner, J., 2009, 'Blurring Livelihoods and Lives: The Social Uses of Mobile Phones and Socioeconomic Development', *Innovations* winter, 91–201.

Donner, J. & Toyama, K., 2009, 'Persistent themes in ICT4D Research: priorities for inter-methodological exchange', *57th Session of the International Statistics Institute, Durban, South Africa*, 17–21.

Dougnon, I., 2008, *Etude comparative des tendances migratoires des Sonraï et Dogon vers le Ghana*, Oxford: IMI.

Dretske, F.I., 1981, *Knowledge and the flow of information*, MIT Press, Cambridge.

Ekine, S. (ed.), 2010, *SMS uprising: Mobile activism in Africa*, Pambazuka Press, Oxford.

Ellis, S. & Kessel, I. van (eds.), 2009, *Movers and Shakers: Social Movements in Africa*. Brill, Leiden.

Emery, D., 2018, 'Death Calls: Killer Phone Numbers Warning Hoax', Netlore Archive, 9 April 2018, ThoughtCo, viewed on 6 September 2018 from www.thoughtco.com/death-calls-killer-phone-number-warnings-3299594.

Emirbayer, M. & Mische, A., 1998, 'What is agency?', *American Journal of Sociology* 103(4), 962–1023.

Engels, B. & Brandes, N. (eds.), 2011, 'Social Movements in Africa', Special issue, *Stichproben, Wiener Zeitschrift für kritische Afrikastudien* 11(20).

Escobar, A., 2011, *Encountering Development: The Making and Unmaking of the Third World*, Princeton University Press, Princeton.

Etzo, S. & Collender, G., 2010, 'The mobile phone 'revolution' in Africa: rhetoric or reality?' *African affairs* 109: 659–668.

Fanon, F., 1961, *The Wretched of the Earth*, translation by Constance Farrington, Grove Weidenfeld, New York.

Ferguson, A., [1767] 1995, *An Essay on the History of Civil Society*, F. Oz-Salzberger (ed.), Cambridge University Press, Cambridge.

Ferguson, J., 1990, *The Anti-Politics Machine: Development, Depoliticization and Bureaucratic Power in Lesotho*, University of Minnesota Press, Minneapolis.

Ferguson, J., 2006, *Global Shadows: Africa in the Neoliberal World Order*, Duke University Press, Durham.
Ferme, M., 1999, 'Staging *Politisi*: The Dialogics of Publicity and Secrecy in Sierra Leone', in Comaroff, J. L. & Comaroff, J. (eds.), *Civil Society and the Political Imagination in Africa: Critical Perspectives*, pp. 160–191, Chicago, University of Chicago Press.
Fine, G. A. & Harrington, B., 2004, 'Tiny publics: Small groups and civil society', *Sociological Theory* 22(3), 341–356.
Förster, T., 2014, 'Trust and Agency. An Analysis of Civil Relations during Civil War', in Feickert, S. Haut, A. & Sharaf, K. (eds.) *Faces of Communities Social Ties between Trust, Loyalty and Conflict*, pp. 43–60, V&R Unipress, Göttingen.
Förster, T., 2012, 'Shifting imageries: Memory, projectivity and the experience of violence in northern Côte d'Ivoire', in Korte B. (ed.), *Popular History Now and Then: International Perspectives*, pp. 231–62, Transcript, Bielefeld.
Förster, T. & Koechlin, L., 2011, 'The politics of governance: Power and agency in the formation of political order in Africa', *Basel Papers on Political Transformation* (1), University of Basel, Basel.
Fortier, A., 2000, *Migrant Belongings: Memory, Space and Identity*, New York University Press, New York.
Foster, R., 2016, 'Top Up: The Moral Economy of Prepaid Mobile Phone Subscriptions', *Unpublished paper*, Australian National University, Canberra.
Freire, P., 2001 [1998], *Pedagogy of Freedom: Ethics, Democracy, and Civic Courage*, Rowman and Littlefield Publishers, Lanham, Boulder.
Friedmann, J., 1992, *Empowerment: the politics of alternative development*, Blackwell, Oxford.
Froelich, J. C., Alexandre, P., & Cornevin, R., 1963, *Les populations du Nord-Togo*, Presses Universitaires de France, Paris.
Gambetta, D., 1988, 'Can we trust trust?' in Gambetta, D. (ed.), *Trust: Making and Breaking Cooperative Relations*, pp. 213–237, Blackwell, Oxford.
Gardini, M., 2012, 'Land transactions and chieftaincies in southwestern Togo', *Africa Spectrum* 47(1), 51–72.
Garud, R. & Karnøe, P., 2003, 'Bricolage versus breakthrough: Distributed and embedded agency in technology entrepreneurship', *Research Policy* 32(2), 277–300.
Gergen, K.J., 2002, 'The challenge of absent presence', in Katz, J.E. & Aakhus, M. (eds.), *Perpetual contact: Mobile communication, private talk, public performance*, pp. 223–227, Cambridge University Press, Cambridge.
Geschiere, P., 2013, *Witchcraft, intimacy, and trust: Africa in comparison*, University of Chicago Press, Chicago and London.
Geschiere, P., 1997, *The Modernity of Witchcraft: politics and the occult in postcolonial Africa*, University of Virginia Press, Charlottesville.
Geschiere, P., & Nyamnjoh, F. B., 2000, 'Capitalism and autochthony: the seesaw of mobility and belonging', *Public culture* 12(2), 423–452.
Geser, H., 2004, 'Towards a sociological theory of the mobile phone', viewed on 13 October 2018 from http://socio.ch/mobile/t_geser1.htm.
Gewald, J.-B., Luning, S. & Walraven, K. van (eds.), 2009, *The speed of change: motor vehicles and people in Africa, 1890–2000*, Brill, Leiden [etc.].
Giddens, A., 1984, *The Constitution of Society: An Outline of the Theory of Structuration*, Polity Press, Cambridge.

Gleick, J., 2011, *The Information: A History, a Theory, a Flood*, Knopf Doubleday Publishing Group, New York.
Glissant, E., 1990, *Poetics of Relation*, University of Michigan Press, Ann Arbor.
Glissant, E., Diawara, M. & Wings, C., 2011, 'One World in Relation: Édouard Glissant in Conversation with Manthia Diawara', *Nka: Journal of Contemporary African Art* 28, 4–19.
Goffman, E., 1971, *Relations in Public*, Basic Books, New York.
Gofman, A., 1998, 'A vague but suggestive concept: the 'total social fact'' in James, W. & Allen, N.J. (eds.), *Marcel Mauss: A Centenary Tribute*, pp. 63–70, Berghahn Books, Oxford.
Goggin, G., 2006, *Cellphone culture: mobile technology in everyday life*, Routledge, New York.
Goldstein, J. & Rotich, J., 2010, 'Digitally Networked Technology in Kenya's 2007–2008 Post-Election Crisis', in Ekine, S. (ed.), *SMS Uprising: Mobile Phone Activism in Africa*, pp. 124–137, Fahamu Press, London.
Habermas, J., 1991, *The Structural Transformation of the Public Sphere: An Inquiry into a Category of Bourgeois Society*, The MIT Press, Cambridge.
Hadlington, L., 2017, *Cybercognition: Brain, behaviour and the digital world*, Sage, London.
Hahn, H.P., 2008, 'Diffusionism, Aropriation and Globalization. Some Remarks on Current Debates in Anthropology', *Anthropos* 103, 191–202.
Hahn, H.P., 2011, 'Ethnologische Perspektiven aus Armut', *Zeitschrift der Arbeitsgemeinschaft Entwicklungsethnologie e.V.* 18(1/2), 113–127.
Hahn, H.P., 2012, 'Mobile phones and the transformation of society: talking about criminality and the ambivalent perception of new ICT in Burkina Faso', *African Identities* 10(2), 181–192.
Hahn, H.P. & Kastner, K. (eds.), 2012, *Urban Life-Worlds in Motion: African Perspectives*, Transcript, Bielefeld.
Hahn, H.P. & Kibora, L., 2008, 'The domestication of the mobile phone: Oral society and new ICT in Burkina Faso', *Journal of Modern African Studies* 46(1), 87–109.
Hamberger, K., 2013, *La parenté vodou: organisation sociale et logique symbolique en pays ouatchi (Togo)*, Éditions de la Maison des sciences de l'homme, Paris.
Hann, C. & Dunn, E., 1996, *Civil Society: Challenging Western Models*, Routledge, London.
Hannerz, U., 1998, *Transnational Connections: Culture, People and Places*, Routledge, New York.
Hannerz, U., 2003, 'Being there… and there… and there! Reflections on multi-site ethnography', *Ethnography* 4(2), 201–16.
Harbeson, J., 1994, 'Civil society and political renaissance in Africa', in Harbeson, J., Rothchild, D., and C. Naomi, C. (eds.), *Civil Society and the State in Africa*, pp. 1–29, Lynne Rienner Publishers, Boulder.
Hardin, G. 1968, The Tragedy of the Commons, *Science* 162, 1243–1248.
Harsch, E., 1999, 'Trop, ćest trop! Civil insurgence in Burkina Faso, 1998–99', *Review of African Political Economy* 26(81), 395–406.
Hassan, B. & Unwin, T., 2017, 'Mobile identity construction by male and female students in Pakistan: On, in, and through the phone', *Information Technologies & International Development* 13, 87–102.
Hayes, N. & Westrup, C., 2012, 'Context and the processes of ICT for development', *Information and Organization* 22(1), 23–36.

Heitz Topka, K., 2013, 'Trust and Distrust in Rebel-Held Côte d'Ivoire', Unpublished PhD Thesis, University of Basel, Basel.
Helliker, K., 2013, 'Civil society and state-centred struggles', *Journal of Contemporary African Studies* 30(1), 35–47.
Hildyard, N., Hegde, P., Wolvekamp, P. & Reddy, S., 2001, 'Pluralism, participation and power: Joint forest management in India', in Cooke, B. & Kothari, U. (eds.), *Participation: The New Tyranny?*, pp. 56–72, Zed Books, London/New York.
Hirschkind, C., 2011, 'From the Blogosphere to the Street: Social Media and Egyptian Revolution', *Oriente Moderno* 91(1), 61–74.
Höflich, J.R., 2005, 'A Certain Sense of Place: Mobile Communication and Local Orientation', in Nyíri, J.K. (ed.), *A Sense of Place: The Global and the Local in Mobile Communication*, pp. 159–168, Passagen Verlag, Vienna.
Holland J. & Blackburn, J. (eds.), 1998, *Whose Voice? Participatory research and Policy Change*, Intermediate Technology Publications, London.
Horst, H.A. & Miller, D., 2005, 'From kinship to link-up', *Current Anthropology* 46, 755–78.
Horst, H.A. & Miller, D., 2006, *The cell phone: An anthropology of communication*, Berg Publishers, Oxford and New York.
Howard, P.N., Argarwal, S.D. & Hussain, M.M., 2011, 'The Dictators' Digital Dilemma: When Do States Disconnect Their Digital Networks?', *Issues in Technology Innovation* 13, 1-11.
Isin, E.F., 2008, 'Theorising Acts of Citizenship', in Isin, E.F. and Nielsen, G.M. (eds.), *Acts of Citizenship*, pp. 15–43, Zed Books, London, New York.
Isin, E., & Ruppert, E., 2020, *Being Digital Citizens*, Rowman & Littlefield Publishers, London.
Jackson, M., and I. Karp, (eds.), 1990, *Personhood and Agency: the Experience of Self and Other in African Cultures*, Smithsonian Institution Press, Washington.
Jacobs, S., & Duarte, D., 2010, 'Protest in Mozambique: The power of SMS', viewed on 13 October 2018, from http://www.afronline.org/?p=8680.
Jagun, A., Heeks, R. & Whalley, J., 2008, 'The impact of mobile telephony on developing country micro-enterprise: a Nigerian case study', *Information technologies and international development* 4(4), 47–65.
Johansson, L., 2015, 'Dangerous liaisons: Risk, positionality and power in women's anthropological fieldwork', *Journal of the Anthropological Society of Oxford* 7(1), 55–63.
Johnson-Hanks, J., 2005, When the future decides: Uncertainty and intentional action in contemporary Cameroon, *Current Anthropology* 46(3), 363–85.
Kalfelis, M., 2015, 'Flexibel aus Armut. Die Lebeswelt von lokalen Entwicklungsakteuren in Burkina Faso vor dem Hintergrund entwicklungspolitischer Erwartungshaltungen', *Paideuma: Mitteilungen zur Kulturkunde* 61, 143–164.
Kareem, A.E.A., Olaewe, O.O. & Odeniyi, O.A., 2008, 'The Roles of ICT in Information Processing and National Development in Nigeria', *The Pacific Journal of Science and Technology* 9(1), 90–96.
Karpatschof, B., 2000, *Human activity. Contributions to the anthropological sciences from a perspective of activity theory*, Dansk Psykologisk Forlag, Copenhagen.
Kasuga, N., 2010, 'Total Social Fact: Structuring, Partially Connecting, and Reassembling', *La Revue du M.A.U.S.S.* 36(2), 101–110.
Katz, J.E., 2006, *Magic in the air: Mobile communication and the transformation of social life*, Transaction Publishers, New Brunswick and London.

Katz, J.E., 2007, 'Mobile media and communication: Some important questions', *Communication Monographs* 74(3), 389–394.
Katz, J.E. & Aakhus, M.A. (eds.), 2002, *Perpetual Contact: Mobile Communication, Private Talk, Public Performance*, Cambridge University Press, Cambridge.
Kaufmann, A., 2016, 'Spaces of Imagination: Associational Life and the State in Post-War, Urban Liberia', PhD thesis, University of Basel, Basel.
Keane, W., 2018, 'Cell phone antinomies: A commentary', in Bell, J.A. & Kuipers, J.C. (eds.), *Linguistic and Material Intimacies of Cell Phones: Material and Linguistic Intimacies*, Routledge, London.
Keita, F., 1984, *La culture traditionnelle et la littérature orale des Tem*, Steiner, Stuttgart.
Keja, R. & Knodel, K., 2019, 'Mistrust and Social Hierarchies As Blind Spots of ICT4D Projects: Lessons from Togo and Rwanda', *TATuP – Zeitschrift für Technikfolgenabschätzung in Theorie Und Praxis* 28 (2), 35–40.
Kenaw, S., 2012, 'Cultural translation of mobile telephones: mediation of strained communication among Ethiopian married couples', *The Journal of Modern African Studies* 50(1), 131–155.
Kenaw, S., 2016, *Technology-Culture Dialogue: Cultural and Sociotechnical Appropriation of Mobile Phones in Ethiopia*, Lit Verlag, Zürich.
Kenny, E., 2016, '"Phones mean lies": Secrets, sexuality, and the subjectivity of mobile phones in Tanzania', *Economic Anthropology*, 3(2), 254–265.
Keyewa, G.O., 1997, *Vie, énergie spirituelle et moralité en pays Kbye (Togo)*, L'Harmattan, Paris.
Kibere, F.N., 2016, 'The paradox of mobility in the Kenyan ICT ecosystem: an ethnographic case of how the youth in Kibera slum use and appropriate the mobile phone and the mobile internet', *Information Technology for Development* 22(1), 47–67.
Klute, G. & Hahn, H.P. (eds.), 2007, *Cultures of Migration: African Perspectives*, Berlin: Lit Verlag.
Kohnert, D., 2008, 'Togo: Thorny Transition and Misguided Aid at the Roots of Economic Misery', SSRN, viewed on 13 October 2018, from https://ssrn.com/abstract=1019974.
Kohnert, D., 2015, 'Donor's Double Talk Undermines African Agency: Comparative study of civic agency in aid dependent countries – The case of Burkina Faso and Togo', *Revised version of a conference paper for the APAD Conference 'The fabrication of public action in countries under an aid regime'*, Cotonou, 17–20 November 2015.
Komen, L., 2016, '"Here you can use it": Understanding mobile phone sharing and the concerns it elicits in rural Kenya', *for (e) dialogue*, 1(1), 52–65.
Kopytoff, I., 1986, 'The Cultural Biography of Things: Commoditization as Process', in Appadurai, A. (ed.), *The Social Life of Things: Commodities in Cultural Perspective*, pp. 64–94, University of Cambridge Press, Cambridge.
Koutonin, M., 2017, 'No business, no boozing, no casual sex: when Togo turned off the internet', The Guardian, 21 September 2017, viewed on 11 October 2018, from https://www.theguardian.com/global-development/2017/sep/21/no-business-no-boozing-no-casual-sex-when-togo-turned-off-the-internet.
Kreamer, C., 1995, 'Transformation and power in Moba (northern Togo) initiation rites', *Africa* 65(1), 58–78.
Krygier, M., 1997, 'Virtuous Circles: Antipodean Reflections on Power, Institutions, and Civil Society', *East European Politics and Societies* 11(1), 36–88.

Kulick, D., & Willson, M. (eds.), 1995, *Taboo: Sex, identity and erotic subjectivity in anthropological fieldwork*, Routledge, London.

Lachenmann, G., 2009, 'Renegotiating and overcoming frontiers and constituting crosscutting and overlapping social spaces and institutions: Conceptual and methodological issues in development', *Working Papers in Developmental Sociology and Social Anthropology* 360.

Lagerspetz, O., 1998, *Trust: The Tacit Demand*, Kluwer Academic Publishers, Dordrecht.

Lallemand, S., 1988, *La Mangeuse d'âmes. Sorcellerie et famille en Afrique*, L'Harmattan, Paris.

Latour, B., 1996, 'On actor-network theory: A few clarifications', *Soziale welt*, 369–381.

Latour, B., 2005, *Reassembling the social. An introduction to actor-network-theory*, Oxford University Press, Oxford.

Laurier, E., 2003, 'Why people say where they are during mobile-phone calls', *Vodafone Receiver 7*.

Levine, A., 2016, *South Korean civil movement organisations: Hope, crisis, and pragmatism in democratic transition*, Manchester University Press, Manchester.

LeVine, R.A., 2003, *Childhood Socialization: Comparative Studies of Parenting, Learning and Educational Change*, University of Hong Kong, Hong Kong.

Lewis, O., 1969, 'The culture of poverty', in D.P. Moynihan, D.P. (ed.), *On understanding poverty: perspectives from the social sciences*, pp. 187–220, Basic Books, New York.

Licoppe, C., 2004, "Connected' presence: the emergence of a new repertoire for managing social relationships in a changing communication technoscape', *Environment and Planning D: Society and Space* 22, 135–156.

Ligtvoet, I., 2018, 'Made in Nigeria: Understanding duress and upwardly mobile youth through the biography of a young entrepreneur in Enugu', *Conflict and Society: Advances in Research* 4, 275–287.

Ling, R. & Yttri, B., 2002, 'Hyper-coordination via mobile phones in Norway', in Katz, J.E. & Aakhus, M.A. (eds.), *Perpetual contact: Mobile communication, private talk, public performance*, pp. 139–169, Cambridge University Press, Cambridge.

Long, N. J., & Moore, H. L. (eds.), 2013, *Sociality: new directions*, Berghahn Books, Oxford.

Lowrance, S., 2016, 'Was the Revolution Tweeted? Social Media and the Jasmine Revolution in Tunisia', *Digest of Middle East Studies* 25(1), 155–176.

Luhmann, N., 1987, *Soziale Systeme*, Suhrkamp, Frankfurt am Main.

Luhmann, N., 2000, 'Familiarity, confidence, trust: Problems and alternatives', in Gambetta, D. (ed.), *Trust: Making and breaking cooperative relations*, electronic edition, pp. 94–107, University of Oxford, Oxford.

Lund, C., 2006, 'Twilight Institutions: An Introduction', *Development and Change* 37(4), 673–684.

Mairie de Sokodé, 2014, *Plan de Développement Communal de Sokodé 2015–2019*, Mairie de Sokodé, Sokodé.

Makumbe, J., 1998, 'Is there a civil society in Africa?' *International Affairs* 74(2), 305–317.

Mamdani, M., 1996, *Citizen and subject: contemporary Africa and the legacy of late colonialism*, Princeton University Press, Princeton.

Mamdani, M., 2005, 'Political Identity, Citizenship and Ethnicity in Post-Colonial Africa', Keynote Address at the Arusha Conference 'New Frontiers of Social Policy', December 12–15.

Marantz, D., 2001, *African Friends and Money Matters*, SIL Publishing, Dallas.
Maroon, B., 2006, 'Mobile sociality in urban Morocco', in Kavoori, A. & Arceneaux, N. (eds.), *The Cell Phone Reader: essays in social transformation*, pp. 189–204, Peter Lang, New York.
Maturana, H.R., & Varela, F.J., 1980, *Autopoiesis and Cognition*, Reidel, Dordrecht.
Mauss, M., 1990 [1925], *The Gift: The Form and Reason for Exchange in Archaic Societies*. (transl. W.D. Halls), Routledge, London.
Mbembe, A., 2001, *On the Postcolony*, University of California Press, Berkeley CA.
Mbembe, A., 2003, 'Necropolitics', *Public Culture* 15 (1): 11–40.
Mbembe, A., 2015, 'Decolonizing Knowledge and the Question of the Archive', basis for a series of public lectures, Wits Institute for Social and Economic Research (WISER), University of the Witwatersrand, Johannesburg.
Mcay-Peet, L. & Quan-Haase, A., 2017, 'What is Social Media and what Questions can Social Media Research help us answer?', in Sloan, L. & Quan-Haase, A. (eds.), *The SAGE Handbook of Social Media Research Methods*, pp. 13–26, Sage Publications, London.
Meijboom, F.L., 2008, 'Problems of trust: A question of trustworthiness: An ethical inquiry of trust and trustworthiness in the context of the agricultural and food sector', PhD thesis, Utrecht, Utrecht University.
Meinen, L., 2015, 'Tricky Trust: Distrust as a Starting Point and Trust as a Social Achievement in Uganda', in Pederson E., Liisberg S., Pedersen E. & Dalsgård, A. (eds.), *Anthropology and Philosophy: Dialogues on Trust and Hope*, pp. 118–133, Berghahn Books, Oxford.
Merleau-Ponty, M., 1962, *Phenomenology of Perception*, Routledge and Kegan Paul, London.
Miller, D. & Sinanan, J., 2012, 'Webcam and the Theory of Attainment', Working Paper for the EASA Media Anthropology Network's 41st e-Seminar 9–23 October 2012.
Miller, D., Costa, E., Haynes, N., McDonald, T., Nicolescu R., Sinanan J., Spyer J., Venkatraman S. & Wang, X., 2016, *How the world changed social media*, UCL Press, London.
Miraftab, F., 2012, 'Right to the City and the Quiet Appropriations of Local Space in the Heartland' in Smith, M.P. & McQuarry, M. (eds.), *Remaking Urban Citizenship: Organizations, Institutions, and the Right to the City*, pp. 191–202, Transaction Publishers, New Brunswick.
Molony, T., 2008, 'Non-developmental Uses of Mobile Communication in Tanzania', in Katz, J.E. (ed.), *Handbook of Mobile Communication Studies*, pp. 339–352, MIT, Boston.
Molony, T., 2009, 'Carving a niche: ICT, social capital, and trust in the shift from personal to impersonal trading in Tanzania', *Information technology for development* 15 (4), 283-301.
Moreno, E., 1995, 'Rape in the field: reflections from a survivor', in Kulick, D., & Willson, M. (ed.), *Taboo: Sex, identity and erotic subjectivity in anthropological fieldwork*, pp. 166–189, Routledge, London.
Morley, D., 2009, 'For a materialist, non-media-centric media studies', *Television and New Media* 10(1), 114–116.
Mosse, D., 2006, 'Anti-social anthropology? Objectivity, objection, and the ethnography of public policy and professional communities', *Journal of the Royal Anthropological Institute* (N.S.) 12, 935–995.
Mudhai, O.F., 2013, *Civic engagement, digital networks, and political reform in Africa*, Palgrave Macmillan, New York.

Mudhai, O., Tettey, W. & Banda, F. (eds.), 2009, *African media and the digital public sphere*, Palgrave Macmillan, New York.
Mullainathan, S., 2011, 'The psychology of poverty', *Focus* 28(1), 19–22.
Murris, K., 2016, '# Rhodes Must Fall: A posthumanist orientation to decolonising higher education institutions', *South African Journal of Higher Education* 30(3), 274–294.
Musil, R., 2017 [1930], *The Man without Qualities*, translated by Wilkins, S. and Pike, B., Picador, London.
Mutsvairo, B., ed. 2016a, *Digital Activism in the Social Media Era: Critical Reflections on Emerging Trends in Sub-Saharan Africa*, Palgrave Macmillan, New York.
Mutsvairo, B., 2016b, 'Recapturing citizen journalism: processes and patterns', in Mutsvairo, B. (ed.), *Digital Activism in the Social Media Era: Critical Reflections on Emerging Trends in Sub-Saharan Africa*, pp. 1–18, Palgrave Macmillan, New York.
Mutsvairo B. & Harris, S.T.G., 2016, 'Rethinking Mobile Media Tactics in Protests: A Comparative Case Study of Hong Kong and Malawi', in Wei, R. (ed.), *Mobile Media, Political Participation, and Civic Activism in Asia*, pp. 215–231, Springer, Dordrecht.
Neubert, D., 2011, 'Zivilgesellschaft in Afrika? Formen gesellschaftlicher Selbstorganisation im Spannungsfeld von Globalisierung und lokaler soziopolitischer Ordnung', in Axel, P. (ed.), *Globalisierung Süd*, pp. 210–232, VS Verlag für Sozialwissenschaften, Wiesbaden.
Nippert-Eng, C., 2010, *Islands of Privacy*, University of Chicago Press, Chicago/London.
Nkwi, W.G., 2015, 'Struggling for Survival: Youth and Cell Phone "Call Boxes" in Cameroon, 2000–2011', *Universitatii Bucuresti. Analele. Seria Stiinte Economice si Administrative 9*, 79–93.
Nyamnjoh, F.B., 2005a, 'Images of Nyongo amongst Bamenda Grassfielders in Whiteman Kontri', *Citizenship Studies* 9(3), 241–269.
Nyamnjoh, F.B., 2005b, *Africa's media, democracy and the politics of belonging*. Zed Books, London.
Nyamnjoh, F.B., 2011, 'De-Westernizing Media Theory to Make Room for African Experience', in Wasserman, H. (ed.), *Popular Media, Democracy and Development in Africa*, pp. 19–31, Routledge, London.
Nyamnjoh, H.M., 2010, *'We get nothing from fishing': Fishing for boat opportunities amongst Senegalese fisher migrants*, Langaa RPCIG, Bamenda.
Nyamnjoh, H.M., 2014, *Bridging Mobilities: ICTs appropriation by Cameroonians in South Africa and the Netherlands*, Langaa RPCIG/African Studies Centre Leiden, Bamenda/Leiden.
Nyassogbo, G., 1997, 'Développement Local, Villes Sécondaires et Décentralisation au Togo, in Betrand, M. & Dubresson, A., *Petites et Moyennes Villes d'Afrique Noir*, pp. 89–110, Karthala, Paris.
Obijiofor, L., 2011, 'New Technologies as Tools of Empowerment', in Wasserman, H. (ed.), *Popular Media, Democracy and Development in Africa*, pp. 207–219, Routledge, London.
Ochara, N.M. & Mawela, T., 2013, 'Enabling Social Sustainability of E-Participation through Mobile Technology', *Information technology for development*.
Orlove, B., 2005, 'Time, Society, and the Course of New Technologies', *Current Anthropology* 46(5), 699–700.
Orlove, B., & Caton, S.C., 2010, 'Water sustainability: Anthropological approaches and prospects', *Annual Review of Anthropology 39*, 401–415.
Orwell, G., [1949] 1977, *1984*, Houghton Mifflin Harcourt Publishing Company, New York.

PAD, 2016, Manuel de Procédures pour le 'Système de Suivi-Évaluation par les Citoyens' (SYSEC) dans les Communes Membres, Version 02, June 2016, Unpublished policy document.

Paragas, F., 2005, 'A Case Study on the Continuum of Landline and Mobile Phone Services in the Philippines', in Kim, S. (ed.), *When Mobile Came: The Cultural and Social Impact of Mobile Communication*, pp. 178–197, Communication Books, Seoul.

Patel, V., 1995, 'Explanatory models of mental illness in sub-Saharan Africa', *Social Science & Medicine* 40(9), 1291–1298.

Pederson, E.O. & Meinen, L., 2015, 'Dialogue tree: Intentional Trust in Uganda', in Liisberg, S., Pederson, E.O. & Dalsgard, A.L. (eds.), *Anthropology and Philosophy: Dialogues on Trust and Hope*, pp. 99–136, Berghahn Books, Oxford.

Peet, R. & Hardwick, E., 2015, *Theories of Development: Contentions, Arguments, Alternatives*, Guilford Press, New York.

Pelckmans, L., 2009, 'Phoning anthropologists: The mobile phone's (re-)shaping of anthropological research', in de Bruijn, M.E., Nyamnjoh, F.B. & Brinkman, I. (eds.), *Mobile Phones in Africa: the new talking drums in everyday life*, pp. 23–49, Langaa RCPIG/ASC, Bamenda/Leiden.

Peterson, M.A., 2008, *Anthropology and Mass Communication: Media and Myth in the New Millennium*, 1st ed., Berghahn Books, Oxford.

Piot, C., 1999, *Remotely global: Village modernity in West Africa*, University of Chicago Press, Chicago.

Piot, C., 2010, *Nostalgia for the future: West Africa after the Cold War*, University of Chicago Press, Chicago, London.

Plan, 2005, *La traite des enfants rédigé par les néo-alphabètes de la préfecture de Tchamba*, Unpublished document, Plan, Sokodé.

Plant, S., 2001, *On the Mobile: The Effects of Mobile Telephones on Social and Individual Life*, Motorola, Chicago.

Pollard, A., 2009, 'Field of screams: difficulty and ethnographic fieldwork', *Anthropology Matters* 11(2).

Pommerolle, M.-E. & Heungoup, H., 2017, 'The 'Anglophone crisis': A tale of the Cameroonian postcolony', *African Affairs* 116(464), 526–538.

Probyn, E., 1996, *Outside belongings*, Routledge, New York.

Przybylski, A.K., & Weinstein, N., 2013, 'Can you connect with me now? How the presence of mobile communication technology influences face-to-face conversation quality', *Journal of Social and Personal Relationships* 30(3), 237–246.

Putnam, R.D., 2000, *Bowling Alone*, Simon and Schuster, New York.

Pype, K., 2016, ''[Not] Talking Like a Motorola': Mobile Phone Practices and Politics of Masking and Unmasking in Postcolonial Kinshasa', *Journal of the Royal Anthropological Institute* 22, 633–652.

Reporters without Borders, 2016, 'Togo', viewed on 21 November 2016, from https://rsf.org/en/togo.

Rettie, R.M., 2005, 'Presence and Embodiment in Mobile Phone Communication', *PsychNology Journal* 3(1), 16–34.

Riesman, P., 1986, 'The person and the life cycle in African social life and thought', *African Studies Review* 29(2), 71–138.

Roitman, J., 2007, The right to tax: economic citizenship in the Chad Basin, *Citizenship Studies* 11(2), 187–209.
Rowlands, J., 1997, *Questioning empowerment: Working with Women in Honduras*', Oxfam, Oxford.
Salazar, N.B., 2011, 'The Power of Imagination in Transnational Mobilities', *Identities: Global Studies in Culture and Power* 18, 1–23.
Samb, O. M., Essombe, C., & Ridde, V., 2020, 'Meeting the challenges posed by per diem in development projects in southern countries: a scoping review', *Globalization and health* 16, 1–11.
Scheper-Hughes, N., 1993, *Death without Weeping: The Violence of Everyday Life in Brazil*, University of California Press, Berkeley.
Scheper-Hughes, N. & Sargent, C.F. (eds.), 1998, *Small Wars: The Cultural Politics of Childhood*, University of California Press, Berkeley.
Seli, D., 2013, 'Mobilité et moyens de communication au Guéra', in de Bruijn, M., Brinkman, I. & Nyamnjoh, F.B. (eds.), *Side@Ways: Mobile margins and the dynamics of communication in Africa*, pp. 17–35, Langaa/ASC, Bamenda/Leiden.
Serres, M., [1980] 1982, *The Parasite*, Johns Hopkins University Press, Baltimore, MD.
Sey, A., 2011, 'New Media Practices in Ghana', *International Journal of Communication* 5, 380–405.
Shier, H., 2001, 'Pathways to participation: openings, opportunities and obligations', *Children and Society* 15, 107–117.
Simone, A., 2001, 'Straddling the divides: Remaking associational life in the informal African city', *International Journal of Urban and Regional Research* 25(1), 102–17.
Sinclair, R., 2004, 'Participation in Practice: Making it Meaningful, Effective and Sustainable', *Children and Society* 18, 106–118.
Smith, D.J., 2006, 'Cell phones, social inequality, and contemporary culture in Nigeria', *Canadian Journal of African Studies* 40(3), 496–523.
Smyth, T.N. & Best, M.L., 2013, 'Tweet to trust: social media and elections in West Africa', in ICTD (ed.), *Proceedings of the Sixth International Conference on Information and Communication Technologies and Development: Full Papers-Volume 1*, pp. 133–141, ACM, Cape Town.
Southwood, R., 2008, *Less walk, more talk. How Celtel and the mobile phone changed Africa*, Wiley, London.
Spronck, V., 2017, 'Married with Wendel: Interview with Yvonne Dröge Wendel', *MacGuffin Magazine* 5, 122–127.
Srinivasan, S., Diepeveen, S. & Karekwaivanane, G., 2019, 'Rethinking publics in Africa in a digital age', *Journal of Eastern African Studies* 13(1), 2–17.
Steel, G., 2017, 'Navigating (im)mobility: female entrepreneurship and social media in Khartoum', *Africa* 87(2), 233–252.
Stephens, M., 1998, 'Which Communications Revolution is it, anyway?', *Journalism and Mass Communication Quarterly* 75(1), 9–13.
Stern, D.N., 2004, *The present moment in psychotherapy and everyday life*, WW Norton and Company, New York.
Stiefel M. & Wolfe, M., 1994, *A Voice for the Excluded: Popular participation in Development: Utopia or Necessity?*, Zed Books, London.
Stiegler, B., 1994, *La Technique et Le Temps 1. La Faute d'Epiméthée*, Editions Galilée, Paris.

Sztompka, P., 1999, *Trust: A Sociological Theory*, Cambridge University Press, Cambridge.
Talla, B.P., 1998, *Marchés nouveaux no 2, Togo cap sur l'an 2000*, GIDEE, Paris.
Tata, P.K., 2006, 'Approche sociologique des causes internes du sous-développement : La politique de l'" authenticité Africaine " et pauperisation – cas des céremonies funeraires traditionelles des Kabiye au Togo', PhD dissertation, Universität Trier, Trier.
Tazanu, P.M., 2012, *Being Available and Reachable: New Media and Cameroonian Transnational Sociality*, Langaa RPCIG, Bamenda.
Togosite.com, 2015, 'Togo : Opérateurs de téléphonie mobile au Togo: le partage du 'gâteau'', viewed on 30 May 2017 from http://www.togosite.com/index.php/societe/2241-togo-operateurs-de-telephonie-mobile-au-togo-le-partage-du-gateau.
Toulabor, C., 2003, 'Au Togo, le dinosaure et le syndrome ivoirien', *Le Monde Diplomatique* 588(3), 27–27.
Touré, I., 2017, 'Jeunesse, mobilisations sociales et citoyenneté en Afrique de l'Ouest: étude comparée des mouvements de contestation "Y'en a marre" au Sénégal et "Balai citoyen" au Burkina Faso', *Africa Development* 42(2), 57–82.
Townsend, A., 2000, 'Life in the Real-Time City: Mobile Telephones and Urban Metabolism', *Journal of Urban Technology* 7(2), 85–104.
Tufekci, Z. & Wilson, C., 2012, 'Social Media and the Decision to Participate in Political Protest: Observations from Tahrir Square', *Journal of Communication* 62, 363–379.
UAID (bureau d'étude Urbanisme, Architecture, Ingénierie, Design), 2001, *Etude de révision du schéma directeur de la ville de Sokodé – Analyse de l'état actuel*, UAID, Lomé.
Valenzuela, S., 2013, 'Unpacking the use of social media for protest behavior: The roles of information, opinion expression, and activism', *American Behavioral Scientist* 57(7), 920–942.
van Dijk, R., de Bruijn, M.E. & Gewald, J.-B., 2007, 'Social and Historical Trajectories of Agency in Africa: An Introduction, in Bruijn, M.E. de, R. van Dijk & Gewald, J.-B., *Strength beyond Structure: Social and Historical Trajectories of Agency in Africa*, pp. 1–15. Brill, Leiden.
Verba, S., Schlozman, K.L. & Brady, H.E., 1995, *Voice and equality: Civic voluntarism in American politics*, Harvard University Press, Cambridge.
Verbeek, P.P., 2000, *De daadkracht der dingen: over techniek, filosofie en vormgeving*, Boom Koninklijke Uitgevers, Amsterdam.
Verbeek, P.P., 2011, *Moralizing technology: Understanding and designing the morality of things*, University of Chicago Press, Chicago.
Verhoef, H. & Morelli, G., 2007, "A Child is a Child': Fostering Experiences in Northwestern Cameroon', *Ethos* 35(1), 33–64.
Vigh, H., [2003] 2006, *Navigating Terrains of War: Youth and Soldiering in Guinea-Bissau*, Berghahn Books, London.
Vigh, H., 2008, 'Crisis and Chronicity: Anthropological Perspectives on Continuous Conflict and Decline', *Ethnos* 73(1), 5–24.
Vigh, H., 2009, 'Motion squared. A second look at the concept of social navigation', *Anthropological Theory* 9, 419–38.
Vokes, R., & Pype, K., 2016, 'Chronotopes of Media in Sub-Saharan Africa', *Ethnos*.
Wa Thiong'O, N., 1986, *Decolonising the mind: The politics of language in African literature*, East African Educational Publishers, Nairobi, Kenya.

Wallace, T., Bornstein, L., & Chapman, J., 2007, *The Aid Chain: Coercion and Commitment in Development NGOs*, UK Intermediate Technology Publications, London.

Walsham, G., 2017, 'ICT4D research: Reflections on history and future agenda', *Information Technology for Development* 23(1), 18–41.

Wasserman, H., 2011, 'Mobile Phones, Popular Media, and Everyday African Democracy: Transmissions and Transgressions', *Popular Communication: The International Journal of Media and Culture* 9(2), 146–158.

Weintraub, J., 1997, 'The theory and politics of the public/private distinction', in Weintraub, J. & Kumar, *Public and Private in Thought and Practice: Perspectives on a Grand Dichotomy,* pp. 1–42, University of Chicago Press, Chicago/London.

Weintraub, J. & Kumar, 1997, *Public and Private in Thought and Practice: Perspectives on a Grand Dichotomy,* University of Chicago Press, Chicago/London.

Wellman, B., 2001, 'Physical Place and Cyber Place: The Rise of Personalized Networking', *International Journal of Urban and Regional Research* 25(2), 227–252.

Wendling, T., 2010, 'Us et abus de la notion de fait social total. Turbulences critiques', *Revue du MAUSS* 36(2), 87–99.

Willems, W., 2012, 'Interrogating public sphere and popular culture as theoretical concepts on their value in African studies', *Africa development* 37(1): 11–26.

Willems, W., & Mano, W. (Eds.), 2016, *Everyday media culture in Africa: Audiences and users*, London: Routledge.

Appendix 1: Graphs mobile communication logs

Dominant communication structures

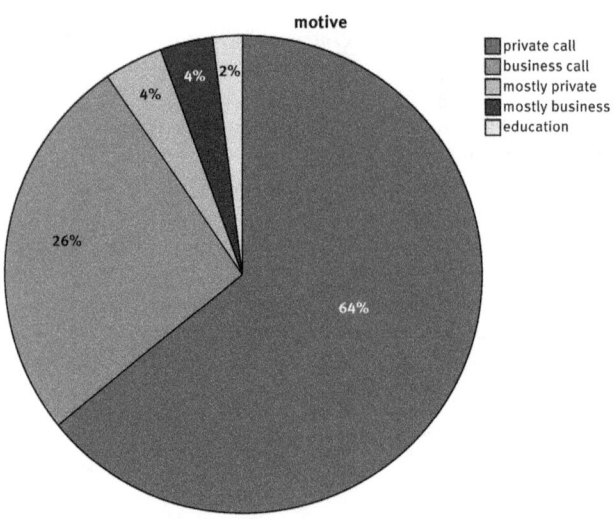

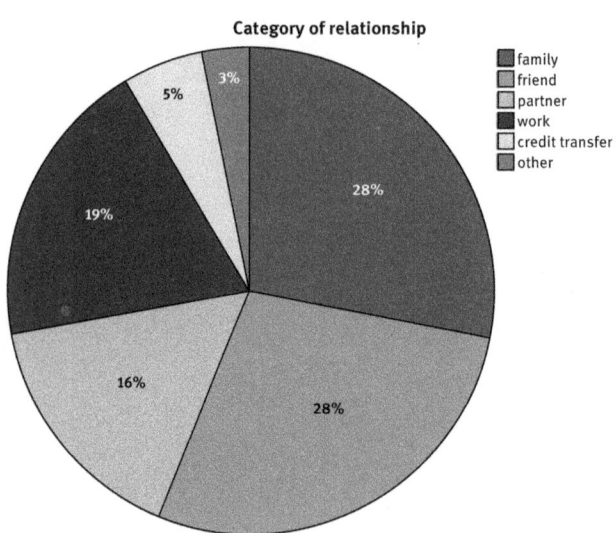

https://doi.org/10.1515/9783110675306-013

Appendix 2: Questionnaire mobile communication logs

First set of questions

- Respondent name (or first name, not obliged), respondent number (leave open)
- Gender (female=0, male=1)
- Age
- Level of education (*primary=1, secondary=2, higher=3, non-formal=4, None=5*)
- Principal religion (*Islam=1, Christian=2, Animist=3, Other=4*)
- Principal ethnicity (*Kotokoli=1, Kabye/Nawdba/Lamba=2, Diverse North=3, Sud=4, Foreigner=5*)
- Principal activities/profession
- Professional category (*Student/apprentice=1, Trader/craftsman=2 Managerial staff=3, NGO/organization=4, Teachers/nurses=5, Labourers=6, Others=namely....*)
- Number of simple phones (without internet option)
- Number of smartphones (with internet option)
- Number of second hand phones
- Number of new phones
- Number of active SIM cards
- Who has acquired your phone 1 (I=1, Family=2, Partner=3, Friend=4)
- Where is phone 1 acquired (*Sokodé=1 Lomé=2, Foreign country=3, Other=namely..*)
- According to you, where is phone 1 made (*West=1 China=2 Dubai=3 Other=namely...*)
- Who has acquired your phone 2 (I=1, Family=2, Partner=3, Friend=4)
- Where is phone 2 acquired (*Sokodé=1 Lomé=2, Foreign country=3, Other=namely..*)
- According to you, where is phone 2 made (*West=1 China=2 Dubai=3 Other=namely...*)
- Has your phone been lost/stolen? (*No=1, Lost=2, Stolen=3, Lost and I think stolen=4, Lost and not given back =5*)
- Has your phone been lost/stolen for a second time? (*No=1, Lost=2, Stolen=3, Lost and I think stolen=4, Lost and not given back =5*)

Second set of questions

Number of the respondent, and then for every call/missed call/SMS, during 7 days:
- Date
- Time of call or SMS (for example 8: 52)
- Missed call (=0) or SMS (=1)
- Effectuated (=0) or Received (=1)
- Duration (in seconds)
- Motive for calling (*Private=1, Business=2, Mostly private, somewhat business=3, Mostly business, somewhat private=4, Studies/school=5*)
- Relation (open question)
- Category of relation (*Family=1, Friend=2, Partner=3, Work=4, Airtime=5, Other=6*)
- Reason for choosing the moment (open question)

Index

airtime   45, 47f., 52, 70, 72, 130, 137
– airtime sales point   37, 48
ancestors   32–35, 40
android   44, 114, 137
appropriation   5,, 86, 89, 90, 91, 116, 171, 172,
Archambault, Julie   5 6, 7, 12, 43, 64, 79, 82, 88, 120, 129, 131, 136
army general   3, 23–25, 54, 151, 192
army officer   23, 113, 151
Arnstein, Sherry   169, 177, 179.,180, 196
Atchadam, Tikpi   158, 161
attainment
– theory of, 114, 115

Barrière   49, 153
Bateson, Gregory   57
beeping   44, 73
beer   1, 82, 83, 113, 154, 163, 174, 190
– tchouck   38, 82.
Benin   44, 121
Breuer, Anita   8, 156, 167, 170
Broadbent, Stefana   70, 105, 142
Bruijn, Mirjam de   4, 5, 9, 11, 22, 68, 90, 109, 156, 177, 178
Burkina Faso   4, 30, 40, 90

Cameroon   162, 191, 193, 198
Canada   20, 29., 30, 91
Carey, Matthew   9–11, 14, 58, 178
Castells, Manuel   11
CDQ   9, 59, 149, 150, 156, 169, 173
China   30, 53, 92, 120
choiceless decision   9, 16, 194
Christian   25, 43, 135
church   22, 34, 39, 58, 124, 172
citizenship   7–9 21 142, 163, 165, 186, 189, 192
co-construction of knowledge   16
colonial   3, 13, 21, 40, 142, 188
Comaroff, John and Comaroff, Jean   7, 73, 142, 143

communication landscape   17, 18, 24, 26, 55, 64, 84, 117
conflict
– family   150
– land   24, 40
consultant
– international   4, 6, 12
– national   7, 12
control
– by scrolling through partner's phone   75, 130, 133f.
– of telecommunication, state   51–53, 117, 193
– over dating behaviour   135
Côte d'Ivoire   24
creativity   9
cultural biography of things   15
customary
– chiefdom   21, 24, 156
– law   21

death call   73
decentralisation   8, 12, 141, 166
decolonisation   7, 12, 21, 35, 142
democratisation   3, 5, 8, 141, 179
despair   26f., 31, 54, 155
development programme   144, 147, 166
diaspora   41, 68, 108, 109, 145, 150, 157, 181, 197
Didawré   39f.
digital publics   6f., 194
dignity   9, 27, 199
disinformation   191, 194
divorce   13, 63, 130f.
domestication   5, 89f.
Donner, Jonathan   141
Dubai   30, 91, 92

Egypt   3, 53, 161f.
elections   198
– local   11, 156, 196
– presidential   3, 23, 44, 53, 165
Emirbayer, Mustafa   9, 57, 189

Facebook 3, 5, 14, 45, 103, 105, 120, 138, 195
fake news *See* disinformation
Ferguson, James 30, 116, 143, 167
first phone 68, 93, 95, 112, 113
Förster, Till 10, 88, 145

German 12, 39, 40, 99, 113, 176
Germany 17, 30, 74, 181
Geschiere, Peter 11, 31, 33, 40, 73
Ghana 30, 104, 135
Giddens, Anthony 9, 178
gift-giving 87, 96, 97, 102, 121
Gleick, James 57, 189
Glissant, Édouard 35, 148, 190
Gnassingbé, Eyadéma 3, 23, 25
grey zone 22, 177, 192 f.

Habermas, Jürgen 7, 66, 142
Hahn, Hans Peter 5, 11, 27, 30, 59, 68 f., 82, 89, 90, 91, 138
Heitz Topka, Kathrin 9–11, 68, 190
Horst, Heather 5, 85, 89, 90, 118, 120, 126, 128
hospital, regional 154, 182, 183, 195
Hotel Central 20, 33, 130

ICT4D
– imaginary of 157, 165, 186
imagination 13, 88, 143, 155, 165, 178, 190, 194, 198
IMO 105, 115, 120, 136, 138
in-depth interviews 16
infidelity 56, 75, 129–133, 135
information
– concealing 6, 17, 65 f., 79 f., 82, 119
– instability of 59, 60, 178, 188, 196, 199
– intimacy of 57, 76, 199
– systemic approach to 18, 57 f., 66, 189, 191
Ivorité 24

Karpatschof, Benny 57, 190
Kpangalam 40, 72, 99, 153, 183

lethargy 27, 146, 152, 155, 161
Liberia 5

Libya 3, 27
Licoppe, Christian 42, 119, 143
loyalty 29, 132, 134, 172 f., 190
Luhmann, Niklas 10, 57 f.

Mali 40
Mamdani, Mahmood 21, 142 f., 192
marketplace 12, 36, 188
marriage 63, 132–135
Mbembe, Achille 22, 24, 35, 142 f., 148, 177, 192 f.
meaningful participation 8, 169, 171, 173, 179
mediation 59, 67, 115
mediator 35, 62, 79, 98, 106, 182
metaphor 18, 24, 84, 86, 118, 119, 126, 153, 177, 191
migration 31, 100, 108
military camp 161, 163
Miller, Daniel 5, 41, 85, 89, 90, 115, 118, 120, 126, 128
Mische, Ann 9, 57, 189
misinformation 58, 191
mobile communication logs 15 f., 98, 102, 105, 106
mobile money 48
mobile phone
– and identity 85, 110 f.
– as total social fact 87 f.
– biographies 15, 94
morality 6, 118, 132, 135
mosque 36, 39, 58, 150
motor-taxi 50, 70, 130
municipal officer 123
Muslim 25
Mutsvairo, Bruce 3, 5, 105, 116, 162

narrative 3, 44, 71, 73, 129, 135 f., 138
national highway 36 f., 49, 59, 61, 119, 140, 159 f.
neighbourhood development committee *See* CDQ
Niger 40
Nigeria 5, 30, 73 f., 75, 92, 105
Nippert-Eng, Christena 13, 38, 66 f., 142 f.
normally 156, 199

Olympio, Sylvanus 3, 25

participant observation 10
participatory approach 170, 179, 195
PDV *See* airtime sales point
phone cabin 45, 94
PNP 1, 25, 54, 158 f., 192
poisoning 1 f., 16 f., 32
political participation 1, 4, 154, 162
political silence 3 f., 18, 187, 191
political subjectivities 7, 189
pornographic 88, 136, 138, 186
postcolonial 13, 21, 33, 144, 148
pregnancy 13, 48, 133, 135
prison 29, 155, 162 f., 193
public-private continuum 18, 66
Pype, Kathrin 5 f., 35

radiation 124, 129
revolution 3, 25, 162
royal courtyard 124, 128, 150

scamming 73
second-hand 31, 46, 51, 91, 95, 108
secrecy 18, 65, 132 f., 135
security forces 2–4, 23, 28, 159 f., 193
security officer 30, 124
self-censorship 12, 44, 194
Senegal 4, 30, 161, 177
Skype 115, 138
SMS survey 167, 170, 172, 174

soccer 39, 150–152, 161, 181, 182
social change 2, 6, 21 f., 57, 90, 189, 192
social inequalities 21, 29, 196 f.
social navigation 9, 18, 64 f., 90
solidarity 17, 28, 131
spirits 32–34, 39, 65
stillborn child 18
strike 45, 59, 158, 163
subsidiarity 28 f., 31

Tchaoudjo 161, 182
Tem 40, 128, 182
Togolité 24
town hall 36, 38, 60, 140, 146, 175, 180
transnational relationships 6, 73, 108 f,
Twitter 5, 197

UNIR 25 f., 51, 145 f., 156, 160, 163
United States 30, 91, 95, 96, 108, 113
unstable infrastructure 140, 151

Vigh, Henrik 9, 65, 178

WhatsApp
– as social media 44 f.
– profile 110, 149
WhatsApp group
– for community development 22 f., 195
– for local development 45, 197
Willems, Wendy 7
witchcraft 33, 73, 150

www.ingramcontent.com/pod-product-compliance
Lightning Source LLC
Chambersburg PA
CBHW050523170426
43201CB00013B/2066